There is a crisis in American film, claims David Thomson in this provocative, insightful book. Thomson turns Hollywood inside out as he examines directors (Coppola, De Palma, Kubrick, Rafelson, Schrader, Lucas, Spielberg), producers, screenwriters, stars and the movies they are making today to uncover the origins of the crisis.

For decades film audiences have continued to decline as has the number of films actually released. At the same time the cost of making a film has skyrocketed. To reduce the risks involved, worried studio executives are trying a variety of techniques that David Thomson believes may hasten the destruction of American film.

So desperate are the studios for moneymaking films that once they find one, they will make it again and again. Thus, argues Thomson, one seminal and stylistically original film —Alfred Hitchcock's *Psycho*—has given rise to an entire new genre of look-alike horror/suspense pictures.

But this is not just a book of film criticism. It has a special feeling for such diverse but related topics as the community of Los Angeles, the playground lobbies of movie theaters, the turbulent personalities of Pauline Kael and Jerry Lewis, the dangerous originality of young director James Toback, and the chilling implications of *The Shining*. *Overexposures* is a portrait of the furious mixture of seriousness and fantasy, achievement and hype, at work in American film.

David Thomson writes with the passion of a man in love with the movies. His observations are penetrating and disquieting, and his book will arouse and disturb film lovers everywhere.

Other books by David Thomson

AMERICA IN THE DARK
A BIOGRAPHICAL DICTIONARY OF FILM

OVEREXPOSURES

The Crisis in American Filmmaking

DAVID THOMSON

WILLIAM MORROW AND COMPANY, INC.

New York   1981

Copyright © 1981 by David Thomson

Library of Congress Cataloging in Publication Data

Thomson, David, 1941–
    Overexposures: the crisis in American filmmaking.

    Bibliography: p.
    Includes index.
    1. Moving-picture industry—United States.
I. Title.
PN1993.5.U6T47   1981   791.43'0973   81-944
ISBN 0-688-00400-8   AACR2
ISBN 0-688-00489-X (pbk.)

Printed in the United States of America

First Edition

1 2 3 4 5 6 7 8 9 10

BOOK DESIGN BY MICHAEL MAUCERI

for Pat McGilligan

Acknowledgments

A few chapters in this book appeared originally elsewhere, often in a different form: "Calling the Strikes" was published in *American Film*; "Alfred Hitchcock and the Prison of Mastery" and "James Toback: Odds Against Success" appeared first in *Film Comment*; "The Discreet Charm of the Godfather" was published in *Sight & Sound*; and "The Runner," "Angel Face," and "The Godmother" appeared in *The Real Paper*. I am grateful to the editors of those publications for permission to reprint the articles here.

"Directors, Producers, and Studios" and "To Write a Movie" will be appearing in *Anatomy of the Movies* to be published by Macmillan Publishing Company, and I am grateful to the editor and publisher of that book for permission to include the articles here.

Contents

1

Lost on The Tonight Show

A cold Monday night on the Carson show. No Johnny, no Ed. It is more disheartening that McMahon is absent, I think. He is the program's core of kindness and civility: the dull, decent bourgeois beside whom Johnny looks an insatiable marauder. Ed has managed to make his support of Johnny seem like the generosity of a friend rather than the braying of a paid stooge. He is bogus old-fashioned, while Carson is fake modern. They are a version of Jekyll and Hyde in which Jekyll is half-asleep but can always be woken by his own booming laughter, and Hyde is the parched malice of dried-out insecurity.

Neither of them is there tonight, but the machine is still running—as if when Johnny eventually follows his practiced golf swing to another network, it may be sufficient to bring up the studio lights, have the band—as long-suffering as the musicians in the *Titanic's* sloping ballroom—producer Freddie de Cordova, the messages, plug-in guests, and the audience. The time slot has been established: It need only be kept open, like a test card or a parking place. After all, what the show says is tonight is Tonight. Our midnight and our milieu have been subsumed in the medium. It's an affirmation—this is this—an identifying signal. We use our television like a clock-scenario: It gives us the time and a code for feeling out the day. The role of the mass media is to keep the mass from panic, to provide something that we all can witness. It is a piece of furniture on fire so that everyone may honor the idea of warmth and community. But it burns endlessly without ever wasting away, mocking our energy crisis.

To protest that you are not warmed by it is to volunteer for the grim role of outcast. Your mind may not be strong enough for that yet. But critical alarm with one night of TV can warn you of a deeper discontent that will require extensive cultural diagnosis if it is not to leave you uselessly sour and misanthropic. Of course, Carson has always provided a tame irony that treats nothing seriously but pretends to be aloof and unsuckered. He has never been brave enough to urge any attitude upon us. His message is "take no messages": He stands up, poker-faced and sly, the personification of McLuhan's principle that the medium has set in. He is his own depressant, bristling with timidity. He is hurt more that a monologue go dead than that the language, humane instincts, or the hope of tolerant freedoms might be endangered. If you wanted to argue that, you'd get five minutes at the end of the program.

There is no need for this or any other program to catch fire. TV personalities should merely be there. To burn, to shine, to glow is wasteful and distracting. Bob Newhart is guest host tonight. He looks dragged off the street, and so mangles his comic monologue on the disasters of the hardware trade that he does a cutoff sign and closes his eyes in despair. The band comes in with a coda like a groan. His eyes open, and he is appalled that the thing is still going on. TV has a palpable flicker: The watcher feels he might pass out or collapse in every blink. With all those lines, segments, and dots, there is a constant danger of falling through. We hang on to the scattered form, like night watchmen determined not to doze. But we know as we watch that Newhart was willing to slip through the sieve there and then, to fade into the electronic maelstrom.

Newhart turns to his first guest: Shelley Winters—a tent dress, chain-link pearls, a tumbledown knickerbocker-glory hairdo, and a sprawling manner that leaves you wondering whether she's drunk, concussed, or dangerously disenchanted. She describes a TV mini-series she's made recently and tries to tell its cluttered story. "I don't know," she begins to give up. She has the concentration of the overweight. An ill-drawn hand jerks up in pained blessing or to wave away worry. "I *think* that's what happens." The movie's narrative escapes her, but she implies that this mishap is like life, her life, and therefore authentic. It is not madness or creeping self-pity, but a bloodcurdling disclaimer of responsibility. Shelley Winters doesn't do scripts anymore; she does herself, and it is self-inflicted devastation.

Why is she on? We could look at the chairs, the desk, and that altar-cloth blowup of Los Angeles. Sometimes the set on *The Tonight Show* seems as convivial as a living room, albeit one exposed—front and back—by the black-comedy slicing which L.A. anticipates from earthquakes. At other times, it resembles a stage waiting room, ice rinks between the chairs, every individual in a cavity of space, chilled by solitude. We could study this sketch of a room and wonder if murder had occurred there. We don't need much between the commercials. We never complain because we know Nielsen can only record our acquiescence. We know the story's not as necessary as being *on*. Shelley Winters is a token celebrity, just as she has become a facsimile character actress. She is so much less potent or controlled than the disdainful, magically unsoiled Johnny who is announced as the star of the show whether he's there or not. That's the intriguing thing in Johnny, his longing for control; he's like a colonial dressing for dinner in the jungle. Control is the last gesture of caring, and it whispers to us about our readiness for less diffident controllers in our larger world.

Shelley is talking about a book due out months beyond: This is pre-plug, or the frantic search for some way of reassuring us about her dismaying presence. The need to sell something will be the sluggish pretext for her segment: The actual commercials come as a relief because their marketing is so pert and confident. She says that her stage name was taken from the poet Shelley's after she had been named Shirley by her parents. Shirley Schrift. She dictated 1,200 pages for her book, but they cut half, scrapping two husbands and three lovers. We need a viable product, Shelley. We have to get the extent right. It will be about her life, she claims, with the good-natured bewilderment of a B-picture whore regarding her body: dull home to her and, can you believe, a haven for others? *

Newhart seemed dead that night, or emptied of self. You wondered what grief or tax demand had overtaken him. Is there a spinal tap that will do it, leaving the person numb? But Shelley Winters was simply the discount version of aimless, incoherent vitality, a blurred, disconsolate life-force. Not even vitality. Only the battered persistence of a marketability that has lost track of dignity or integrity. The feeble creed of being yourself, doing your own thing, easily disguises the abandoning of difficult identity. Show people have been so exposed, so much presented, posed, and seen, that the light shines through them. They could be ghosts, celluloid packets or dummies made of garments, skin, and Leichner greasepaint, script lines and problems, waiting to be occupied. A star is sexy, hot, strong—whatever you want to call it—when he or she feels the millions of eyes and appetites scrabbling to get into the packet. We so much want to be there, and the stars smile because they know there is nowhere to be occupied. They are the people who have inhabited Gertrude Stein's Oakland, about which the lady allegedly said that the trouble with it was that, once you got there, there was no there there.

What we are talking about is an industry that manufactures phantoms. Of course, the product is sometimes passed

* Shelley's book, of course, proved to be a national number one best seller.

off as art or entertainment. But that is the intrusive force of respectability or wholesomeness speaking. This is really a factory system that makes projections, illusions, ghosts—all are adequate descriptions. The thing purchased is immaterial and unreal. The cans of film, the primary product, are only a cumbersome means to the desired end, which is excitement when the contrived images of times past are run at the proper pace on a white wall—a wall possessed. The audience absorbs light and mood, things it cannot hold or stop. It's like buying a can of Colorado mountain air, cautiously opening it and peering into the empty place. You know you've been conned; you can accept the joke; or you can breathe beyond reason and feel refreshed. So, with moving images, motion pictures, there are fraud and absurdity to be negotiated as well as the uncertain pleasures of being moved, delighted, or terrified by the ghost. It would seem to be a mechanism for legitimizing unreason, yet it may be the best time some of us have had.

And I teach "film studies," which often feels very close to selling patent medicines and canned elixirs. Nor is it so unlike serving as pimp to the various intangible and (let us hope) uncontagious whoring actions of the movies. It is often my quandary to face young people and their placid and not very energetic hope to make movies. Is it the energy or the hope they believe I may be able to furnish? I have several recommendations for them:

1. That the would-be filmmaker can see only the talent or genius of filmmaking.
2. Whereas that talent is nearly negligible compared with the stamina, charm, deceit, ruthlessness, and luck that get the filmmaker into the position of working.
3. That it is an error of strategy to say you want just to make pictures.

4. More people may trust you enough to mistrust you with the resources and means it takes if you say you want to make money-making pictures, if you let it be known that you simply wish to be in the business.
5. And, inasmuch as that commercial force is strongest, movies are the version of art, the example of man's creative appeal to his fellows, that first identified the imperative of America—to be successful.
6. And in the American situation, success is measured in the numbers and attributes of money.
7. But in the nature of the original American ideal, success was also pledged to the pursuit of happiness.
8. And because many Americans have grown up in material and imaginative hardship, so happiness is often thought to be tainted by the deviousness or brutality that acquires money.
9. So that the hardest task of those who get into movies is to reconcile money and happiness.

There may be no better way of understanding the Monday night disarray of Shelley Winters than to recognize the strain she has faced in achieving number 9. It is so much less strenuous to the imagination to be:

(a) poor
(b) unhappy
(c) poor and happy
(d) rich and unhappy

To be both rich and happy, that is a prize worth playing for. It is so elusive and ambiguous that the quest may become wretched or angry with its own riddle. Only the finest and the most supple can negotiate all its passages; and it is a rare fineness that can countenance such wriggling. No one prepared to embrace Hollywood's conditions will ever make a film as good as we all need. But no one anxious to make films for all of us can avoid the place and its trials. Traveling to L.A. is one step along the way—though L.A. exists in Manhattan apartments and sometimes it lounges on Riviera beaches—but the true journey is as mythical and demanding as the world of dungeons, dragons, ghosts, potions, knights, ladies, magicians, young men on the way to market with prize cows, monsters a little more volatile than those that guard the La Brea tar pits, and the occasional fairy.

Movies are put together like machines. They are assembled from different directions, no matter that they need an intense arena of conjunction, like theater or life. It is even possible that on the first morning of shooting, an actress will have to kiss a man she has never met and sigh, "If only I had known, my darling. All this could have been avoided." "You're telling me," her bored darling replies, knowing the proper sound will be looped again later, breathing staleness back in her primed face—only the dark back of his head is in the shot. He is still only the thing this beauty trembles over, the front row of the audience, if you like, staring in at her. The director discusses alterations in her reading with her. Something a little more carnal in the expression? I should be hot for him—physically? I think so. Okay. She jams the gum behind her teeth and tries again for art's sake. For this moment will come after 123 others that the crew and the cast must put on film over the next three months.

It happened to the actress before that similar closeup revelations vanished from a finished picture. Sometimes she plucked up nerve and talcum powder to let a towel slide from one breast—casually, dear, can it be casual? grease the towel, maybe?—and that bold moment was clipped away. She wonders where those slivers of film go; it occurs to her that sometimes such situations are put in a script but are never seriously intended for a finished picture. Perhaps the towel and her breast were exported to Japan to be cut into some film on American air hostesses overnighting in Tokyo.

Once she was paid for several weeks' work on a film but did not appear in the version released. Sometimes people in the film said things spoken to her in the shooting but which were now directed at another character in a story no one had thought of while the film was being shot. Once she saw her shadow, but it spoke with a Latin accent about the scent of roses. It's enough to make you believe in reincarnation.

Film is a medium of moments, but it is an assembly, too. The "ending" to a picture may be its proper resolution, but it may be merely the point after which there is nothing else. On *Apocalypse Now* Francis Ford Coppola's perplexity began to multiply endings, none of which ever satisfied him or persuaded him the film was complete. But many of them were tried and argued over. In any event, the 70 mm. version ended with Willard leaving the temple where he had killed Kurtz and making his way back down the river. But the 35 mm. general-release version ended with credits—provided in a program for the 70 mm. audience—superimposed on infrared footage of the bombing of the temple. Only someone weary of his own film, or daunted by its higher ambitions, could say as Coppola did that he didn't see much difference between the two.

That kind of indecision, and the nightmare of a million feet of film being the maze in which a 140-minute movie is hiding, suggests how the processes of film began to undermine sequence and coherence in this century. The order in films does not have a secure basis in the script or some real event. Literary texts may emerge from terrible doubts about what to omit and keep, what arrangement to give the parts. But texts confirm their own order: They are bound together so that narrative suspense is embodied in the turning of pages and the eye's adventure along every line. One thing happens after another, and the order is morally significant and decisive.

The texts of films once released are nearly as emphatic. But their order is a force in its own right; it is motorized according to the way the projector is powered. We do not need to turn the pages, or even attend to the text, for its sequence to be enacted. Books are latent experiences: They are tunes we play only when we take them up into our heads. Films are explosions, happenings, which do not actually need an audience. This means that the spectators they do attract feel relatively powerless and insignificant. We are less aware of an order that our imaginations can perceive. Instead, films have the characteristics of flow—elemental, heedless, and unconscious. We do not worry so much whether the order is coherent because the flow does not wait for us to puzzle it out. The nature of the film makes us more resigned to the headlong abandon of going with the current. We may be less determined to live our lives once we have seen this allegory of life pouring through us.

But this is a fearsome abandon, and one that American films have religiously avoided. To look away from the primitive momentum of duration, they have set themselves a regime of beginnings, middles, and ends that amounts to more than the orthodoxy of plot. It diminishes the possibilities of the world, the limits of the imagination, and the unexpected force of experience. American movies have been capitalist: They accumulate incidents and turn them into narrative. The industrial method of making films fell meekly into the cultural consequences of their own process. The way of making films never acknowledged or learned from the way of watching them—the delirium of dream, the headlong passage of time and image, the siren that is lyrical but not consequential. That refusal to heed the nature of the experience has restricted nearly every American film. It has led the media of moving imagery—film and TV—away from extraordinary chances for enriching consciousness toward the means for establishing a pattern of anxiety. Film might have brought us closer to psychic awareness of existence, yet it has made for a state of embittered but cool alienation in America: the spirit of Carson.

I have sought something similar to the rush of film in this book. There is an order, provided by print and bindery technology, but the book can be traveled in in other ways—as one might read a newspaper, a magazine, or a collection of essays. Working outward from any randomly chosen point, one might feel the current of one of the parts and the wash of mood—as if one wearied of Shelley Winters and turned over to *Columbo* or the late movie only to discover the nerveless continuity of TV. The essays overlap, they even contradict one another. A weak lob in one is decisively put away by a volley a hundred pages later—oh no, that dunce on the line called it out.

This is not a book with a case that could be coded, capsuled, or put into practice; it may instill feelings of disquiet, like trying to sleep on an L.A. afternoon but being kept awake by the traffic noise one must hear if the room is not to be stifling. It is an attempt to convey an industrial/creative climate and the ways it has influenced all of us. But it is more a travel book than a treatise. The analogy with weather is also useful, and it will keep coming back like the crushing afternoon haze in the Valley on days when the sea seems so much farther away than we know it is.

The focus of the book is the years 1970–1980. But it is not a thorough portrait of the new Hollywood, because it reaches out to the mentality of anyone who ever strove and succumbed in the business, to anyone who might take it on in the future, and to anyone now waiting in an L.A. room for the phone to ring. They put Bibles and telephone directories in all those rooms, and TV sets and shower cubicles. But the pilgrim has need of something else, a game to play, like Dungeons and Dragons, that could turn into the real thing in the scenic twilight when sunset bleeds into the limelight.

2

The Crisis in American Film

There must always be a crisis in Los Angeles if the city's ease is to mean anything. The metropolis was gathered originally to mask alarm that America's last edge had been reached, and structure is a feeble disguise of the uncertain ground. The community likes to think of itself as reflected in the gloss of calm because of that inner quake; a stammerer is just as anxious to be fluent. In the Hollywood film, a happy ending wraps up all the suspenseful moments; we are not meant to learn the habit of steady peril. Drastic conservatism presides over dissolution in California; Ma Kettle ignoring a running tap. Metaphor ravishes fact and gratification cheats difficulty. Like the Constitution, the city and its stories seek a plateau of happiness (the stasis to end all politics, and the hope that keeps Ronald Reagan young).

L.A. is a place for gamblers, spiritualists, and sunbathers, poets and druggies, stars and therapists, messiahs and people at the movies. They are all escaping the waste of "ordinary" life by believing in moments of transforming decision. The wheel's base is secure, even fixed; but the ball palpitates on its rims and pockets, inspiring us with the chance of change. Gamblers know the fineness of every moment from photo finishes. And they are grateful for the rapidity with which time and the brain are alleged, in *Reader's Digest,* to alter. Better to move on than stagnate in pain and problem. The highest purpose of American movies has been to dispel boredom and dismay, to move on beyond that last edge. The ocean along the western edge of L.A. is the ultimate screen.

Pictures slip through projectors like the thought of journeys or the draft of movement.

"What'll it be?" the barman asks Jack Torrance in *The Shining*: Mix your life like a drink. Every genius and scoundrel, whore and virgin, waking to the oven-fresh day, hopes that it can be so. But the streamlined, sanitary city nurses the tremor of danger in change. What fulfillment to be living on a fault in the land, for it keeps alive the prospect of transience and a sudden chasm between one's feet. Disaster films are a kind of reassurance in L.A. The lovely cars glide past outside, immaculate and vulnerable, but on the screen vehicles can collide and crumple in unrestrained outbursts of anger and will. *The Blues Brothers* costs so much, and trashes so many cars, to redeem the pain and repression of our insurance premiums.

No one in the community fails to mention the crisis four or five times a day. It is always *the* crisis, yet the conscientious listener (Joan Didion perhaps) could compile Yellow Pages of dilemma. They would be only as weighty as the moment, that critical node in L.A.—was the quiche the smart selection, the cerise serape suitable at a Little League barbecue; will Kareem have it today or must Magic work; do you like it like that, darling; and was he best in the fifth take or the eighth?

Gambling and unease must be resourceful in a kingdom where the sun shines so regularly and the players of the game patrol a board so devoid of hardship, so stunned by neutral chaotic good. Doesn't everyone have kidney pools where wafer diving boards flutter while the water makes a Perrier froth from your daughter's perfect-ten dive? The pool is a gift of stoned aplomb, the confidence that can let any member of the household cry out "I'm ruined" in the Christmas game of Monopoly.

Hey, fellow . . . you did say a crisis, and let me have a martin with it, very dry with a twist. You have any more cashews? I'm stopping smoking.

It is a kind of crisis if the edgy communicants worry about the wrong things. Pointing that out marks the writer as the inhabitant of a bygone age. After all, he is writing still, about a civilization that honors the telephone. No one in Hollywood would concede that the phone is a slacker form of communication than letters, novels, or moral essays. They believe in it as William Gass cherishes words: People confide in you their huge phone bills in the way Gass blows off a curled phrase. The phone is for being, not messages: You have the intimacy of the other person breathing in the silences; it is amassed in the present tense; Touch-Tone dialing lets us all think we could be songwriters; and phones can now be designed to key in with home decor.

One day soon, radio phones—no cables—so that everyone may drift and murmur like characters in a Robert Altman film. *Nashville* was L.A. No wonder Tennessee was pained by the picture. Its jelly light, the slippery sexual mingling of interior and exterior, the affection for presence, the promiscuousness of the film's attention, the dazed tolerance for oddity, the wish to see without prejudice, and the throng of extras—these are the conditions of Los Angeles.

But I promised you a crisis. Very well, movies are nearly at an end.

Oh shit, that one again. Like a lissome starlet, Hollywood rolls over to sun the other side. There are diets to wrestle with, the readings of astrological charts to divine, and the first weekend's gross on *The Empire Strikes Back* to wait for. And this guy wants to give us the end of the world. . . .

The climactic crisis of American film is that the movies were unworthy of a culture dependent on imagination. I suspect that they have never been worthy, but that they have come close enough, often enough, to tempt anyone interested in a communication that might touch everyone.

There was never an art before film with that opportunity. Still, Hollywood proved the difficult of keeping faith with that opportunity. Films can move the mass of the people and grant them a shared sense of experience. What other consolation matches a world of unmitigated problem? Film coincides with that stage in human history at which reality became so unmanageable that all of a people might seek fiction as relief. The merchandising of unreality has only occasionally led escapees back to what director Nicholas Ray called a heightened sense of being. All too easily the process and the trade blind us to life if films are not made with an integrity, care, and vision that have been afflictions for the filmmaker as grave as running over Louis B. Mayer's dog.

But the trade of films in America has been comfort. Movie illusion subtly shifted existence and identity from actuality and into the photograph. We live in movies now, permitting the most limited depiction of ourselves—as victims of terror, delusion, and appetite. Film asserts that people are appearances, frantic visible exteriors for whom the labor of reflection is impossible. The photograph allows us to be our own ghost, in a trance cut off from our minds or our fellows. The filmmaker or the photographer must try to employ the fiction of his medium to make us more conscious of ourselves. But time and again their work substantiates the dream, and so the society addicted to imagery becomes one of sleepwalkers who use one another as mirrors and shrink into the lonely fear of being surrounded by hard, cold, shining screens.

I am attempting to maintain that the movies are more than a business. (Put the paper napkin down, diamond-wise to the drinker, and set the martini neatly on it—I need a good tip.) Incidentally, I think they are also beyond art, their texture is so reckless, so fantastic, and so averse to fixed meaning or responsibility. But they have a force that can only be entrusted to those appreciative of power; and that appreciation cannot be rational or sensible. It is a commitment of superstition, just like the audience's willingness to recognize super reality, or truth, in a film. No one has more faith in movies than audiences. They have always been the chief artists or auteurs in the dark. The making of films is so practical and stultifying. The filmmaker can never find the solitude that attracts most artists. He must talk with a hundred others, explaining as he goes, bargaining with inescapable budgets, obedient to money that is not his, the clumsy servant of machines he does not comprehend. It is a craft that breeds a meticulousness which could make a free spirit depressed. That is what Stanley Kubrick has always known and suffered from, and it may be what made Orson Welles weary of movies once he had finished *Citizen Kane*.

Film has always encouraged its own tendency toward the industrial: the total audience, mass production, mechanical manufacture—Walt Disney was the epitome of that pressure. And Disneyland is the ultimate American movie experience. But there is a contrary urging toward the private, the secret, the underground: Film is a voyeuristic medium, it reaches the lonely in the pit of their seclusion, and it has always offered the prospect of making forbidden things visible.

The crisis evident in the summer of 1980 is only the latest clash of those two forces. It may be less than a crisis if you believe that long ago the culture of movies altered the way we looked at reality, simply because it presented a model for seeing that extracted it from the immediacy of being. So now we look at one another as if we were all on film, all enclosed in the cold, glowing screens. In which case, it is only tactful of films themselves to retreat. When everyone is a ghost there is no longer room for distinctions of life and death, world and screen. Yet in the summer of 1980, the movie theater business twitched in alarm. As the new films which would dominate the summer season opened, *Variety* noted that business for the month of May was down 5½ percent from 1979, down 14 percent if one adjusted the dollar for inflation. Those May figures involved about 80.5 million admissions at an average ticket price of $2.72; whereas in May, 1979, there had been 93 million admissions.

In both cases that was predicated on a five-week month, giving a weekly rate of admissions of 18.6 million for 1979 and 16 million for 1980.

Variety was disturbed for immediate reasons. Even assuming a strong summer box office—built around *The Empire Strikes Back, The Shining, The Blues Brothers*—it seemed unlikely that 1980 could equal the previous year's box office gross of $2.821 billion. And merely equaling it, of course, would be doing less well because of inflation: about 8½ percent on the year, as far as ticket prices were concerned. The business seemed likely to shrink unless a dramatic coup could be made by an admitted sequel, a horror film that had many people laughing in derision, and a comedy that was receiving agonized reviews. That responsibility is not exaggerated. In May, 1980, for instance, 19 percent of the entire box office was secured by just *The Empire Strikes Back* and *Friday the 13th*.

Let us step back from immediate reasons a little. The seventies had been a decade of encouragement for the movie business, with legends of a new kind of stability becoming second nature after twenty years of decline. By the seventies all the business concentration was on distribution: The major companies participated in the making of films only to sell them, and they generally did no more than provide financing and studio facilities. That is still a good deal, but it is essentially cold-blooded. Nearly every film was an independent venture, conceived outside the studios and brought into them for manufacture. The studios that were still household names retained their involvement as merchants and packagers. The people who controlled those companies were not filmmakers. They were ex-agents, ex-lawyers, ex-accountants, ex-businessmen who owed allegiance to parent companies. For nearly all the studios were small parts of conglomerates.

Legend had it that this situation was more businesslike. In an age when the audience was more choosy, when production costs were higher, it was good business to make fewer films, to concentrate on "blockbusters," and to promote them as diligently as anyone might make them—so diligently, indeed, that the making of the film might strive to imitate its subsequent promotion. In other words, movies came to be influenced by their advertisers. The decade could point to several proofs of this approach: *The Godfather, Jaws, Star Wars, The Towering Inferno, American Graffiti, Close Encounters of the Third Kind, Saturday Night Fever, The Deep, Grease, Superman, Heaven Can Wait, Kramer v. Kramer, Animal House*—all pictures that have grossed somewhere between five and ten times their cost.

In fact, after a steady decline from 1946, gross box office figures had picked up around the mid-sixties and risen sharply in the seventies, despite small setbacks in 1971, 1973, and 1976. Thus, the total gross for 1977 was nearly $2.4 billion and for 1978 about $2.75 billion. This should be set against a 1962 low of $0.9 billion and what was then the all-time high in 1946 of $1.7 billion (a figure not surpassed until 1974).

It is estimated that in 1946, with audiences buoyant and prosperous after the war, there were 100 million tickets sold a week to see the elegant gloom of *film noir*. But the average ticket price in 1946 was only thirty-five cents. The increase in box office gross is a trick of inflation. Whereas even in the years of the Depression, somewhere between 60 and 75 million tickets were sold a week, and whereas just after the war 100 million were sold, the "stability" of the seventies has been very hard pressed not to slip below the mark of 20 million a week.

Moreover, even though in 1946 the majority of films were both modest and profitable, by 1980 a terrifying spiral obtained whereby fewer films were made, more of them cost more, and a fraction were profitable. All through the forties, Hollywood was making around 450 films a year; in the twenties that figure had been nearer 750. In the seventies it hovered at 200. That progression marks the transition of moviegoing from habit to event. There are fewer theaters than there were, of course, and they seat fewer people. Still, there has been a marked shortage of product in recent years, which has made theater owners very anxious to get the big films of any season. Anxiety breeds faith, and so exhibitors are often required to blind-bid on a film—to make a financial commitment to it without seeing it.

When a film in the making bodes very well, or is talked up by an Elmer Gantry, then its costs can be guaranteed before it is even finished. That happened with Joseph Levine's *A Bridge Too Far* and Dino de Laurentiis's *King Kong*. The exhibitor may have to sign a deal that guarantees to the distributor a certain amount against as much as 90 percent of the box office after the "nut." The nut covers all running costs at the theater. In other words, even 10 percent of the gross—the toughest deal a theater can get—is straight profit that will be enriched by the lobby sales of food and drink.

Exhibitors protest the iniquity of being called on to measure a film without seeing it, and blind bidding is now outlawed in several states. They howl at 90 percent and guarantees: Someone had to pay for *A Bridge Too Far*, and when Levine could boast on the day of its release that he was covered, yet audiences didn't go to see it, then the burden fell on the theaters. But they are the most protected participants in the gamble just because of the nut. They pass on the agreed percentage to the distributor, and from rentals he then takes a standard 30 percent. But he has a nut of his own, not just his overhead but the promotion budget on a film. These days, promotion sometimes costs half as much as the film itself. Seventy percent of the box-office net goes back to the film's producers only after those costs have been covered.

Let us suppose that a downtown theater grosses $100,000 in a week. Its nut is $10,000, so that it passes $81,000 back to the distributor on a 90–10 deal. Of this amount, $24,300 is the distributor's due, leaving a notional $56,700 for the producers. In other words, on the most favorable terms a film can have, the gross figure is nearly halved before it reaches the filmmakers. On the far more common 70–30 split at the theater, the exhibitor passes back $63,000, and the producers can expect $44,100.

However, we are assuming that the producers paid for the film, and that they receive everything except the allotted cuts to the exhibitor and distributor. But, in most cases the distributor will have financed a large part of the film. And until that investment is repaid, he will pocket all the net income, claiming that the film is not yet in profit. This straightforward scheme can be complicated by some parties having a claim on the first dollar: For instance, Barbra Streisand has been able to get her profit points on a film put ahead of all other claims. Still, on a routine deal—if that has ever been struck—the point of profit is the production cost, the expenses of promotion, the exhibitor's nut, plus hidden or alleged charges that make accountancy the business's finest art. A movie needs to gross close to three times its budget before anyone can hope to see profit. In the summer of 1980, *Alien* declared a profit of $4 million, despite having grossed about $125 million and returning $61 million to the distributor.

That is why it is so hard to disprove the trade wisdom that only one out of ten films makes a profit. It also accounts for the gambling mentality of anyone investing in motion pictures, and for the various tax shelters that have made the venture more attractive. The people financing films are lured by what the trade press calls record gross figures; by the outstanding performance of a handful of films; and by the blockbuster code which believes in spending formidable sums to promote a few pictures. Investors have also always been starstruck. Whether they are conservative bankers, mobsters, or people who have made millions in dull trades, the thought of meeting stars, earning their gratitude, and being part of a national sensation only proves the ardor of imagination in those supposedly weighed down by Wall Street.

Now let us approach the business from the point of view of filmmaking. What does a film cost? Well, you can fill ninety minutes of screen time at a cost that would startle the industry. A competent, possibly entertaining student film could be produced for less than $25,000. In 1979 a feature movie, *The Return of the Secaucus Seven,* written and directed by John Sayles, was made for $60,000, and it ran nearly two hours. That sum covered only the costs of production: stock, processing, living expenses. Everyone involved accepted deferred payment. It was not a student film, nor was it exactly industrial. It did look professional, it was entertaining, intelligent, and interesting, and eventually it was bought for distribution.

That is a base for measuring industrial scales. A commercial feature is broken down into two budgetary areas: above and below the line. Above the line covers payments for the property and script, the producer, the director, and the stars—it is a way of saying such services are nobler, and it shows how great a class structure there is in pictures. As far as the property is concerned, Gay Talese's nonfiction book, *Thy Neighbor's Wife,* has been sold to the movies for $2.5 million. The musical, *Annie,* has been purchased for $9.5 million. To turn either of those properties into a workable script could easily cost another $300,000. And on such a large venture, you can expect to pay $1 million for the director, as much for the producer, and, say, $2 million each for two big stars. Thus, on something like the film of the Talese book (a prospect few readers of the book can see, so that we may suspect the purchasers never actually read it), we have potential above-the-line costs as follows:

Property   2.5 million

Script	0.3 million
Producer	1.0 million
Director	1.0 million
Stars	4.0 million
Total	$8.8 million

As yet, nothing more arduous than the scribbling of sig-
natures has been undertaken. Below-the-line costs are the
actual expenses of production: technicians, cast, equipment,
sets, costumes, travel, stock and processing, and so on. The
industry has great difficulty in reaching below-the-line costs
of less than $50,000 a day, or $250,000 for a working week.
That figure could easily be doubled if the film requires a
large cast, many special effects, or extensive location work.
Schedules can run anywhere from six weeks to a year, but it
is hard to consider a major movie being shot in less than ten
to fifteen weeks. Several have taken upward of forty weeks.
Then there is the time spent in post- and pre-production,
and the costs of release prints. A major release will involve
over 1,000 prints.

Suppose the Talese book needs twenty weeks at $300,000
a week (can it require many special effects, explosions beyond
the actors?), then there is another $6 million on the budget.
We have to throw in another $3 million for post-production
and interest charges. We now have a picture that costs $17.8
million. *1941* cost $40 million. *Heaven's Gate* cost $35 million.* *Apocalypse Now* cost $31 million. *The Blues Brothers*
cost $27 million. *Close Encounters of the Third Kind* cost
$19 million. *Star Wars* cost $9 million. *The Godfather* cost
$6 million. *Gone With the Wind* cost $4.25 million. *Citizen
Kane* cost $680,000. *Birth of a Nation* cost $110,000, nearly
three times its original budget.

The ladder gives the clue to the crisis. When *Gone With*

---

* As this book went into type, *Heaven's Gate* was opened, panned,
and withdrawn. At last, a giant project had gone from dream to disaster
in a matter of days.

the Wind opened, approximately four times the number of people went to the movies every week as do now. But moviegoers now pay about seven times the average ticket price of 1939 (though *GWTW* itself opened with seats in a range from 75 cents to $1.50). The chance of meeting costs that may have risen tenfold on deluxe productions, and twentyfold on "ordinary" pictures, is dependent on about 10 percent of the population and on ticket prices that are accelerating uncomfortably.

If we assume a continuing inflation of ticket prices of 8½ percent, then in 1985 the average price will reach $4.00. If, on the other hand, one accepts that ticket inflation might move more in line with overall figures, more in line with production costs, then the average ticket price could be $5.00, with $7.50 a normal amount for big city first-run theaters.

The above figures show that the costs of major movies have risen by more than 8½ percent a year. The increase from *The Godfather* to *Apocalypse Now* was 500 percent. Yet the number of tickets sold during the seventies has not risen. Indeed, *Variety* could only see a decline in May, 1980, as compared with the same month a year before—a decline of about 15 percent. Thus the trepidation as the year's summer season began. Suppose that in one season all the leading entries flopped as badly as *1941* did Christmas, 1979. You can argue that some will always founder if others are to prosper. *The Empire Strikes Back* opened more strongly than *Star Wars* did, as if to suggest that the steady decline in the appeal of all sequels might be averted. But *The Shining* did show an early falloff, and it was being laughed at in theaters in a way that promised word of mouth would cancel out the impact of its strong TV advertising. Suppose then that *The Blues Brothers* failed—because its stars had never really secured a large enough following from TV, and because its comedy was as crude as the reviews claimed and as uninfectious as *1941* had been. Then *The Empire Strikes*

Back owned the summer, and the business was left hanging on one young director-producer and the attraction of strip-cartoon movies, pretty effects, and animated toys for an audience between the ages of four and fourteen. The crisis of the movies in the eighties will be that they depend on an audience which can hardly distinguish between the shine of the picture and the proper buttery gilding on the popcorn.

There are other reasons for wondering whether this crisis might not bite deeper during the eighties:

(a) No audience is more fickle than the very young one.

(b) The rising ticket prices will add to the increased dubiousness of casual driving to make the evening out at the movies less compelling.

(c) For those who stay at home, the new facilities of television and video—on cable, casette, or disc— offer novelties and excitements that may be as profound as the onset of television, which loomed ahead of that bumper year of 1946.

(d) And if movies faltered, if the box-office gross began to decline again, then film distribution—the crucial arm of the business—could withdraw, since the distribution companies are now often the subsidiaries of conglomerates which are quite capable of rationalizing and are so interested in other home entertainments that they could shift their investment and their energies into the home video market, retaining only a handful of big city theatrical outlets.

There is another reason for believing that the movie imagination might slip away from theaters and large screens to the snap, crackle, and sunburst of video diversions. It is that so-called movies have been becoming more like diversions in the 1970's. Why not, when the audience has become increasingly concentrated in the teenage section, a group that has grown up consuming about 1,000 hours of imagery a year, most of it on TV? And the keynote of television is bland, distracting but undisturbing activity, an alternating stream of color, movement, music, pattern, and applause, a benign weather system that persuades the individual he is somehow in contact with that immensity outside him without ever having to puzzle over it. To turn on the TV is to participate in mass society: It registers presence and indifference, like being in a photograph on the wall. It is a crisis all by itself in that it mocks and betrays every other kind of imaginative attention that human beings have played with.

Video may be more superstitious than film just because it is so much less capable of conveying passion or beauty. It does not deal in narrative precision or plastic grace; it is not a medium that encourages us to detect authors or design. Looking at TV is like looking at the surface of the sea from a jet airliner—there is a trancelike emptiness of purpose, a shimmer of activity. Video is a light show that finally abandons those links with the novel which have haunted movies. You do not have to follow video. That unstoppable flow which possesses it excuses us from any labor or concentration. Indeed, in the home, television is regularly turned on but not watched. Surely it is the height of superstition to turn a machine on, as if it militated against loneliness and the dark, or against company and the duty to commune, and then walk away, hearing it vaguely from afar, feeling oneself in contact with it.

While purporting to tell stories, report events, and carry sequences—to be linear—television's real form is in the dial which permits arbitrary changes from one channel to another. Within its different channels, interruption is actually the dynamic of its structure. The medium has devised its own system of fragmentation to assist anyone turning on at any time and to flatter anyone too feeble to concentrate. A movie is about a wall that becomes alive with an overwhelming myth couched in the semblance of reality and propelled by the momentum of narrative. This is its chance at art, no matter that it risks corrupting our sense of reality. Television takes the same risk—and takes it more extensively in terms of the amount of watching we do—without threatening to move us. *It* will move instead, the fluctuations those of a drugged snake, so that we may be sure time is passing and everything is okay. Look at the TV: If it moves, you must be alive.

If the long-heralded revolution in video occurs, if the last-picture-show audience stays home with its library of discs and cassettes, then the new spectacle will employ the forms television has known for thirty years. The material shown will be less narrative than atmospheric: It will be whatever keeps the walls from being inert or boring—color shifts, pattern-making, the ebb and flow of light. Or it may be small fantasies, movies compressed into the length of television commercials, rapid evocations of sex, violence, terror, happiness, and comfort. These would be like pills taken to assuage every passing emotional ache or whim: the soul regimented into a set of symptoms, every one of which has its compensatory fantasy. Or it might be a kind of film accompaniment to music, dreams, and patterns, an oscilloscope for melody and harmony.

You could claim that *Saturday Night Fever* was no more than that: a sketchy story, or merely a filmed synopsis, hardly troubled by director or actors, which is a pretext for an image track to go with the unending drive of the Bee Gees' music. It was one of the most successful films of the seventies, enshrining the flimsy personality of John Travolta on the large screen, but making him one of the first movie stars to be as insubstantial, ingratiating, and transparent as TV stars.

There are already plenty of movies that serve as the realizations of lurking fantasies. Pornography has been one of the largest areas of trade for the new videocassette technology, and in the seventies it became a subtext in supposedly respectable films. In the early seventies especially, there was more nudity and sexual action in movies. It seemed as if the business had at last thrown off censorship and recognized that the small audience deserved "adult" entertainment and a more frank admission that sexual fantasy had always been one of film's most potent appeals. But later in the seventies one could detect a change. As if films had become more conscious of that teenage audience and less willing to risk offense, so movies seemed to shrink from sexuality. There are clearly labeled pornographic movies, very cheap and profitable, playing late shows in suburban theaters. And pornography is available for home video, as well as the opportunity with a home camera to star in one's own pornography.

As for violence there has been no slackening or caution. There is as much extraordinary destruction in *Star Wars* or *The Empire Strikes Back* as there is in Clint Eastwood pictures. You could argue that such violence is happily contained by the playfulness of the genre. It is much less easy to be so tolerant of the emotional and psychological cruelty in films that set out to scare us. The present vogue for horrific suspense taunts our own unhappiness and implies that the torrential fantasy of violence and death is necessary to our real stability. But then that only confirms the most sinister message of the movies: that we are all mad who look at images and believe in them.

The supreme exponent of television on the large screen is George Lucas, the very man we looked to as being the last guardian of box office bloom for 1980. Lucas, of course, is the director of *Star Wars,* the most successful film of all time, with a worldwide gross of about $400 million. He now seems set to be the boy tycoon for a flight of films that pursue the *Star Wars* legend—one can scarcely call it a story. Lucas is uncannily composed of shrewdness and naïveté: He is a little like the child in *The Shining.* On the one hand, he has guessed what the public would like three times in a row: not just the two *Star Wars* pictures but *American Graffiti,* which cost only $750,000 and has grossed over $50 million and inspired such television series as *Happy Days* and *Laverne and Shirley*. But on the other hand, Lucas snarls petulantly at the moneyed interests and pressures of Hollywood and talks of an early retirement in which he would make films just for himself.

In Lucas that conflict looks schematic and nightmarish. He must be a sturdy soul to survive it. But it represents a tension that has always beset the movies in America. People long to make films, to turn reality into a beautiful, arousing set of symbols. They want to communicate. But they cannot abide the way filmmaking forces them to keep company with sharks and profiteers. They cannot endure communicated feeling being sold and spoiled by commerce.

Lucas is a kindly image to the young. Thirty-six now, he still prefers sneakers, shabby sports clothes, and a beard. He was a film student, and he harbors the utopian wishes of the eternal amateur, alone with his treasured equipment, filming his wife in slow motion in the dunes or the cat asleep in the sun. Had there ever been a still-life genre in cinema, Lucas might have reveled in it. No matter how much his features fizz and move, he has the passive sensibility of an onlooker. Throughout the seventies he murmured wistfully in interviews about going off into the hills to make personal films. The wish was strong in 1980:

> *No, I don't want to be a businessman. My ambition is to make movies, but all by myself, to shoot them, cut them, make stuff I want to, just for my own exploration, to see if I can combine images in a certain way. My movies will go back to the way my first films were, which dealt a little more realistically with the human condition.*[1]

It could be a student wanting to become Stan Brakhage or Michael Snow. Yet this Lucas is in the process of building his own studio near San Francisco, as if he also hankered after the tradition of being Irving Thalberg or David Selznick, believing in a studio where a band of brothers might work together in the same spirit of dedication under the benign eye of the kid boss:

> *The idea for this came out of film school. It was a great environment; a lot of people all very interested in film, exchanging ideas, watching movies, helping each other out. I wondered why we couldn't have a professional environment like that. When you make a movie, it really is a fifteen-hour-a-day thing, and you don't have time to do anything else. If you do it year in and year out, you become a complete nonentity. You need an environment that gets people excited about things, and they don't do that in Hollywood.[2]*

Lucas has been hurt by Hollywood, and one of the most remarkable things about him is that he still weighs that hurt. On *American Graffiti* especially, he was treated like a pushover kid; indeed, his production contract on *Star Wars* probably only gave him $100,000 as director. But he was wise enough to claim profit points and to have an interest in all merchandising and sequel deals. Today he is embarked on the eight other films he plans for the *Star Wars* series. *The Empire Strikes Back* was the first of them, and it is revealing that Lucas didn't direct it himself but supplied the story, the advice, and the supervising eye of a producer:

> *I hate directing. It's like fighting a fifteen-round heavyweight bout with a new opponent every day. You go to work knowing just how you want a scene to be, but by the end of the day, you're usually depressed because you didn't do a good enough job.[3]*

Lucas can be the most depressing of directors to listen to: His ambitions are so mundane and vague; his disposition is so self-stroking and half-hearted. The disconcerting fact is that he is the most successful filmmaker around, the prototype of a new industry. But the longer you study Lucas, the more you recognize the link between his own callow desire for feeling good and the vapid positivism of his films. He endorses the mythology of success. In *Star Wars* he has used advanced technology to dress up a confrontation of good and evil that would not have challenged D. W. Griffith.

I have never felt in a Lucas film that if I went out for a pee or a hot dog, I would miss anything. It is not in the nature of the films that there is anything so important there. Whatever I missed will be repeated, the same slight commotion. It is like TV, which leaves you disconsolate and fretful at the end of the night in the knowledge that nothing has happened. Being with a Lucas film is to know we are sieves that experience runs through. The purpose is to keep us clean and unclogged.

Lucas likes toys and makes pictures in their image, tranquil at being entertainment for children, heedless of the gulf between technical expertise and thematic shallows. He is too young to scorn, too earnest to attack. Yet Lucas's position of authority is itself a symptom of crisis. His work, his sensibility, his ideals, have led the potential for filmmaking backward. He personifies the film student who has not had to learn anything else but lenses and opticals. And he has created a world in which the seasoned director might have to try to become like a student to keep in work. There is no chance of Lucas ever bringing us a movie worthy of complex experience. His films, if they do run on to the end of the century, can only encourage the young to believe that experience is a pretty, pat commodity, no more complex than chewing gum. The gravest limit to his attitudes is that he cannot see the smothering effect of his pictures, but despises the manners of the Hollywood system to which he, more than anyone, contributes life and breath. This is the pitiful lament of the rich who need to feel good and can sometimes manage it by abusing the system that enriches them:

They're rather sleazy, unscrupulous people. L.A. is where they make deals, do business in the classic corporate American way, which is screw everybody and do whatever you can to make the biggest profit. They don't care about people. It is incredible the way they treat filmmakers, because they have no idea what making a movie is about. To them, the deal is the movie. They have no idea of the suffering, the hard work. They're not filmmakers. I don't want to have anything to do with them.[4]

3

Calling the Strikes

In the summer, at least, the strike was a ball. The pickets were getting a suntan, and the waivers granted to several productions denied standstill. For many members of the Screen Actors Guild (SAG) and the American Federation of Television & Radio Artists (AFTRA), the news coverage outside the studio and network establishments was the only film shot of them all year.

Wherever you went the strike was as good a topic for conversation as scandals or grosses. When SAG got the idea of picketing the Universal studio tour and sent Erik Estrada to the barricades, that only drew more tourists than usual to Universal City. There were pickets on roller skates, buttons, balloons, and T-shirts for strike souvenirs, and the public took snapshots as if the whole thing were an arranged entertainment. You had to wonder whether someone, somewhere, wasn't thinking of a musical for next summer—*Strike!*, just like *Fame*—with a producer's daughter in love with a striking actor, and the picket lines putting on a street show that softened the heart and negotiating stance of Lew Wasserman, the head of Universal.

But the strike was serious and threatening because it was a direct expression of the complexities of the business. Not many people involved thought it would end quickly, and some predicted inactivity till Christmas. If there wasn't widespread bitterness that was only because the strike was regarded less as a union-management struggle than as a contest for the power that has always been the preserve of a few.

But gradually the actors' stand was pushing up the layoffs among IATSE (International Alliance of Theatrical Stage Employees) members, studio cafeterias, and offices all over town.

The Teamsters began to hurt, and the unions for lower-paid Hollywood support staff began to murmur that actors are different anyway. They don't work like other people. It's ironic that labor action by screen actors should be the last to get public sympathy, no matter that SAG can have few rivals for membership unemployed, or "at liberty," as trade language prefers.

"The great majority of actors make only a modest living at best. All we are asking is that when theater films are televised—and hundreds of old ones are being sold or leased for television right now—the actors should get a reasonable percentage of the additional revenue." [1]

That could have been the cry of William Schallert, SAG president. But it was the policy position of 1948, made by the then president, Ronald Reagan. Sales of movies to TV were just beginning, and it's now a matter of history that they went ahead without proper regard for the actors and as if the studio negotiators were asleep. Packages changed hands, hundreds of movies at a time, at a unit cost of less than $100,000, sometimes for as little as $10,000. The prosperity of TV was built on such deals, and many of the movies are still running.

A much tougher fight was put up in 1960, when actors struck for six weeks in the spring. Once again, Reagan was SAG president, despite some feeling that he had a conflict of interests because of his production role on *G.E. Theater.* By 1960 there was more fear that a strike could permanently close some studios—the reasoning that had led to settlement twelve years before—but no one could overlook the previous sellout. And so, in 1960 SAG wanted residuals from the sales to TV to be backdated to 1948.

In the event, they got no back money and were fobbed

off with a $4.5 million payment by the producers to the pension fund. On all new deals the producers agreed to pay SAG 6 percent of the income from sales, after a 40 percent fee for distribution. That was the contract that ended on June 30, 1980, and which provoked the new strike twenty days later.

But no one has forgotten. Ronald Reagan now looks less than the ideal union spokesman, and some actors saw the 1960 settlement as the source of present discontent. What made many people anticipate a prolonged stoppage now was that the focus of altercation had shifted. Just as the possibility of TV running old movies seemed unlikely to some in 1948, so today we face another unknown which could change the status of network television.

Alternative television was heralded all through the seventies, but now it is actually taking effect. The Screen Actors Guild and AFTRA are intent on securing a part of the action that will accrue from pay TV, cassettes, and videodiscs. The producers did go so far as to offer a percentage—less than 6 percent—but only after the first two years of trade, a period which the actors expect will see the bulk of the action.

The actors are choosing to be technological optimists, saying that cable, cassette, and disc will revolutionize the business in ten years. Nothing was more likely to prove them correct than an extended strike, for then the orthodoxy that the audience was waiting, eager, and respectful for the new fall schedules would be put to a severe test.

The networks were tight-lipped about their emergency strategies. The revelation of who shot J.R. was in the can, but after that, most series had a small backlog of episodes. There were specials and TV movies on the shelf, but only because no one had been too excited about showing them in the first place. Old movies might get heavy usage, and old series could be rerun. But the economy of TV depends on buoyant fall audiences tempted by new shows. No executive could deny that with drama and sit-com series unavailable there would be an obvious effect on advertising revenue. You can discuss it as a small shift in business, but it could be a major alteration in the climate of TV. After all, does anyone really enjoy television? Who would miss any of the steady series after two weeks? Public Broadcasting Service (PBS) was openly exhilarated at picking up stray viewers, and the companies engaged in cable and home video were doing all they could to disprove the leisurely estimate of the rate at which the new facilities would penetrate American homes.

When the American Federation of Musicians came out in support of the actors, that was a vital reinforcement. Films shot and aimed at Christmas were still in need of scoring. It was also another reason for alarm among producers, for if actors deserved and won residuals, then every other craftsman could claim precedent. The dilemma points up an oddity: That although writers of books and songs have had their copyrights carefully protected, many creators on film have earned little or nothing after their first fee.

Those fees are large in terms of what the average American earns. But actors and directors have died broke while one of their films played on some TV station every day. You can feel the merit of the claim, no matter that you understand the argument of the producers: that they take the risk and usually get their rewards, or their losses, after the actors have been paid.

Actors are ten a penny—they have to be if they want to be stars. In August, SAG published a report on its membership. Of its 47,000 members, 3,152 earned over $25,000 in 1979; 39,023 earned under $2,500 and some 15,000 of those got nothing at all. A mere 500 earned over $100,000, and it's no surprise that some of them—Ed Asner, Alan Alda, Henry Winkler—were doing their bit on the picket line. The actors' strike hung over the entire business, but its settlement benefited only 10 percent of the SAG membership at all, and only 1 percent significantly.

After all, some actors are producers. Not in name perhaps, but Ronald Reagan wasn't a named producer in 1960. Anyone whose presence is central to a film or a series, and who is in for part of the profits, is a producer. The strike was one more demonstration of artists seeking control of the business and more guaranteed rewards in the accounting. In August the daily progress of the strike kept another story out of the news. George Lucas was at odds with ICM, his agent, over the percentage of his earnings that the agency could take on *Star Wars* and *The Empire Strikes Back*. They went to court over percentage points only, but the points were being reckoned on $100 million.

Strikebound Hollywood is the last place to seek evidence of the struggle between socialism and capitalism in America. There is no more political ideology involved than there might be in Warren Beatty's *Reds,* where the interest in John Reed and the Bolshevik Revolution will require a box-office gross of at least $150 million if Warren is going to stay cool. Politics in Hollywood lays down that if the actor playing Juarez has $2 million against 3 percent, then whoever plays Maximilian will want as much.

The system is terrified of revolution: Warren Beatty might dream of being President one day, but he is as apolitical as the Norma Shearer who turned *Marie Antoinette* into a bromide about being nice to sad queens and knowing that discontent was only a matter of aristos thinking they were Basil Rathbone. That bloated and inconsequential romance about the French Revolution was made only because Norma was the dowager duchess at MGM, widow to Irving Thalberg, and holder of some stock in the company. "When you have them by the balls, their hearts and minds will surely follow" is the high point of Hollywood political theory, and the peak of gangster eloquence.

The strike was a squabble over the loot, and such bickering has always comprised the politico-economic history of Hollywood. The myth that the American film industry capitulated in the fifties disguises this reality: That as the structure of the business changed, so those squabbles became more intricate, more widespread, and more important. A kind of status quo had prevailed until the late forties, and it was called the contract system.

Very briefly, it was a hegemony as sweet as Kodak's. A few companies produced films, which they then distributed and played in theaters they owned themselves. We should remember that the people who founded those major studios, and who dominated them, were invariably men who had made their start as the proprietors of nickelodeon arcades and storefront theaters. They only ventured into production to ensure a steady supply of cheap product. They had no more interest in it than the grocer who cuts open one orange to satisfy himself about a consignment.

Los Angeles was the city where film factories had to keep the production line moving. To that end, the studios had obtained the services of technicians and actors. They were under contract, for as long as seven years, at set annual salaries for which they would work as and when the studio said.

Stars might make $500,000 a year in the thirties, but a star might make two hit pictures for his studio and be loaned out to another for a third at a salary of $300,000—all of which went to the original studio, which regarded the actor as a property. MGM loaned Clark Gable to David Selznick for *Gone With the Wind* and put more than $1 million into the film. In return, they got the distribution rights and 50 percent of the profits. Gable got a good part, and what MGM would have paid him for that year, with or without *GWTW*. No wonder his character didn't give a damn.

Gable was a big star in the thirties, and his powerlessness was typical. Very few stars made anything more than their contract salary. United Artists, formed in 1919, had been an attempt to ensure that the leading creative talents had a lasting income from their work. That helped Mary Pickford, but Chaplin had learned some years before to retain control of his pictures. Chaplin's significance in the business was as a star clown and as a lone-wolf tycoon. The former won the hearts of the world, but the latter made him disliked in the system.

Contracts and the empire broke down in the forties: Olivia de Havilland won a test case in 1943. But there were bigger blows. In a judgment of 1948, Paramount consented to ridding itself of its theaters on the grounds that to own the means of production, distribution, and exhibition was a trust. As that decision took effect, so Hollywood faced its darkest years, with film audiences falling off as rapidly as the sale of TV sets rose.

It was not the end of the system, but it was a crisis. Contracts holding stars for long periods became less common, but the stars were just as important to the visibility of projects. So stars began to see themselves as producers, the people who set up a venture and took the bulk of the profits. In the fifties and early sixties, Burt Lancaster, Kirk Douglas, John Wayne, James Stewart, Elizabeth Taylor, and Gregory Peck started a trend that now involves nearly every leading player.

Actors were not always trained for so much business, or willing to carry it out. So some of the packaging and dealing fell to their agents—people who also represented other actors, writers, and directors. The monopoly that had been righteously denied—after twenty-five years—in the Paramount decision was replaced with a new model. Talent agencies started to move into the devastated landscape with plans to build.

There are about as many large agencies as there were major studios. The greatest in terms of rapid rise and power was MCA. The Music Corporation of America was a talent agency headed by Jules Stein. Lew Wasserman directed its motion picture dealings. He and MCA had a good share of major stars during the 1940's.

But it was the crisis and the ensuing rearrangement of influence that changed the agency. MCA moved into several fresh areas of trade, including the sale of old movies to television and the production of material for TV and theaters. You might have thought that to be a producer and to represent actors was a conflict of interest. After all, it was the apparent bone of contention in the 1980 strike.

Actors not represented by MCA, and not hired for their productions, might have felt the unfairness. But their union, the Screen Actors Guild, had made a deal with MCA in July, 1952, that gave the agency unrestricted entry into production. Some nine years later, another court decision affirmed that this had been wrong and that MCA should separate production from agenting. But in the interval, MCA had become the most powerful body in show biz. The 1952 arrangement was engineered by the president of SAG, Ronald Reagan, an actor whose agent was Lew Wasserman.

MCA formed a company called Revue, which made many of the hit TV series of the fifties and sixties. In 1961 it purchased Universal, and as of now, MCA Inc. owns Universal City, Universal Film, MCA Music and MCA Records, a Coca Cola bottling company, three book publishers, and the company that leads the field in videodisc manufacturing.

And the name common to both sections of this chapter is . . . Ronald Reagan, the actor we deserved, despite the wise opinion of Gore Vidal that "I wouldn't want a professional actor to be President, because he's spent his entire life being moved about like a piece of furniture. He's used to being used." [2]

4

Directors, Producers, and Studios

The presentation of the 1979 Oscars was rather routine, an evening in which nothing could resist the tide of *Kramer v. Kramer*. If you treat a subject—divorce—that is so close to two thirds of the members of the Academy, it is no surprise if they acclaim social responsibility and a sensitive treatment of modern emotional distress. Better still, even in this new, young Hollywood, *Kramer* is a thoroughly old-fashioned film with a placid structure and a set of performances that looked admirable in the fifties whenever Elia Kazan used them. Dustin Hoffman at last was allowed to rival our memories of James Dean and Marlon Brando instead of being asked to be a character actor. He and Meryl Streep took Oscars. Robert Benton won for adapted screenplay and for best director. Then, as a climax to the evening, *Kramer v. Kramer* won best picture. There *is* something higher than direction in Hollywood.

Next day there were estimates that that last Oscar could add $25 million to the gross of *Kramer*. Some thought that, even without the acting Oscars and the awards to Benton, the best-picture accolade would have given the film fresh energy at the box office. All over America, new posters and new ads were singing out *Kramer*'s triumph, and "best picture" was slapped across the middle, like the sash on a beauty queen. The old Hollywood faith that a good director is a nice try but best picture is the fat cigar held true. No one thought to reissue *Bad Company* or *The Late Show*, the earlier works of the year's best director. One day, perhaps, if there are Benton retrospectives, those films will be more honored than the very effective but very calculated *Kramer v. Kramer.*

Benton still wore a big grin. He had knocked around too long without securing his place in the kingdom to be proud. In the early seventies, in efforts to improve the reputation of the American screenwriter, Richard Corliss included Benton in a group of easterners who "may have composed a new Hollywood symphony, but it is still the conductor, the director, who takes the bow." [1] Benton had had successes: He wrote *Bonnie and Clyde* with David Newman, after which they went on to *There Was a Crooked Man* and *What's Up, Doc?* (written with Buck Henry) before writing *Bad Company.* It is still somewhat eccentric or cultish to call that picaresque, chilly western one of the best American pictures of the seventies. And although *The Late Show* earned warmer reviews, Benton was probably grateful that a much earlier piece of stage writing gave him credit and the chance to earn income from *Superman,* a film that has too little of the shaping skill or credible dialogue at which he excels.

But on Oscar night, Benton was revealed as fiftyish, bearded, happy, and modest, with a family in the audience charged with the relief that speaks of hard times and years when Dad was in a bad mood. Benton joined in with everyone else in admiring the "family" atmosphere which had produced *Kramer,* no matter that the film is about breakup and contested custody. He looked like a seasoned professional who had paid his dues and who was so utterly pleased to have the statuettes that he didn't realize he was playing the Hollywood game in which "team spirit" disguises personal ambition. Even in the moment of triumph, he was less an *auteur* than a jolly, humble *patron.*

That very night, Hollywood had turned its back on the man who, more than any other, personifies the power, the glory, and the mania of the new type of American director:

Francis Ford Coppola. Not everyone admires or understands *Apocalypse Now*. Hardly a soul has looked back fondly on the happy days and family atmosphere of its making—least of all Eleanor Coppola. But it was a work of dedication, independence, will, and rampant ambition. It seemed to fulfill the hopes Hollywood often professes, but which actually frighten it, of amazing us with the force and scope of the medium. And in his own way, Coppola had paid his dues: He had made two very successful films in the seventies. *The Godfather* had been a beguilingly slick meeting of genre entertainment and social commentary; and in Michael Corleone it had established a sinister role model for every would-be Caesar in Hollywood. In 1979 on Oscar night, Coppola had been on stage to rant and roar about momentous, but imprecise, things to come in the eighties; only weeks before Academy evening, 1980, Coppola would announce the purchase of the old General Service Studio and a dream of restoring the halcyon days of Irving Thalberg with a "family" enterprise. At that time, he said that there would be parks and companionship in his studio, and open house for the great directors of the world.*

There is a constituency for whom Coppola is the greatest hero. He is first among the "movie brats," the one to whom they all look for sound advice and impetuous inspiration. He is a ticket to the new world for such foreign directors as Wim Wenders, Hans-Jürgen Syberberg, Werner Herzog, Akira Kurosawa, and Michael Powell, the difficult young and the stranded old; all being welcomed into the heart of the kingdom. If anyone could enable Godard to make *Bugsy Siegel*, it is Coppola; after all, he has backed Wenders on

* By February, 1981, Coppola's new company was close to bankruptcy. His next film, *One From the Heart*, budgeted at $22 million, began shooting only because the director mortgaged most of his own property. Zoetrope employees were taking voluntary pay-cuts as Coppola rebuilt Las Vegas on sets. Gambling is always the manner, and often the subject, of movies.

Hammett, and must have a store of satanic American heroes for these directors. Coppola is also a beacon for the thousands of film students who have a stairway to heaven in mind that includes Corman quickies, major screenplays, directorial breakthroughs, Oscars enough to play candlepins with, millions, vineyards, and the sweet pleasures of patronage.

But, in truth, Coppola is equal parts Hollywood man and adventurous outsider, and no one in the kingdom quite trusts him or his goals. *Apocalypse Now* was regarded as a rogue film, just as any auteur has been, is now and always will be suspect in Hollywood, whatever splendor critics and academics see in him. We have lived through Sarrisian auteurship, the myth of the death of Hollywood, and the golden legend of kids taking over the kingdom. The truth is muddier and bleaker: Fewer films are being made; technology is more encroaching and craft is less satisfactory; subject matter seems bolder, but exploitation has not faltered in its ingenuity or shamelessness; and the position of director is as complicated, uncomfortable, and perilous as it was for Griffith, Stroheim, Welles, Nick Ray, or even for Red Ridingwood, that forlorn stiff who was coolly lifted off a film without the gracious Monroe Stahr breaking stride, and given his own coat—left on the set—as a limp going-away present:

> *It was a sorry mess, Ridingwood thought. It meant he would have slight, very slight loss of position—it probably meant that he could not have a third wife just now as he had planned. There wasn't even the satisfaction of raising a row about it—if you disagreed with Stahr, you did not advertise it. Stahr was his world's greatest customer, who was always—almost always—right.*[2]

Scott Fitzgerald had mixed feelings about that power play, and the ambivalence is still with us today. He was moved by the authority of Irving Thalberg even while he suffered from it. *The Last Tycoon* has as much love-hate for its hero as Coppola ever felt toward Michael Corleone. Coppola, no doubt, means to provide opportunities for young talent, but he cannot resist the imperative of authority—that you must sometimes be a shit and a bastard. Not that Hollywood has ever lacked its share of righteous malice or neglected the subtext that it is bliss to succeed but downright cozy if your friends fail.

We take it for granted now that Fitzgerald fell victim in Hollywood to company domination, ruthless box-office priority, and the philistine urge to humble genius. That explanation went very well with Scott's soured life, and he could point to the subservient role of Frank Borzage on *Three Comrades* as proof that even the director had been ground down to the level of an employee. Similarly, it is argued that the heyday of the director was short: It lasted from Griffith's definition of the significance of the job to Thalberg's humiliation of von Stroheim. Before about 1914, pictures had been a trade owned by exhibitors who were driven into production only to guarantee their own supply. After *Greed*, every studio copied Thalberg's search for efficiency and hired producers to regulate the "artists" and ensure that the factory floor stayed active.

As a historical outline, this is repeated in survey courses everywhere. But it relies too much on our allegiance to directors caught up in delusions of personal grandeur and the ideology of nineteenth-century melodrama. Just as Griffith is the lucky spokesman for a generation of naïve pioneers, and von Stroheim a radiant self-destructive whose pride required failure, so in the allegedly strict age of Thalberg there flourished John Ford, Howard Hawks, Ernst Lubitsch, Josef von Sternberg, Frank Borzage, Frank Capra, George Cukor, Gregory La Cava, Leo McCarey, King Vidor, and Raoul Walsh.

Those names come from the top two categories—Pantheon and the Far Side of Paradise—in Andrew Sarris's *The Amer-*

ican Cinema, published in 1968. That book was the culmination of an argument launched in 1962, the sum achievement of which was to promote the idea of the director as auteur; not just Buñuel or Truffaut, but Joseph H. Lewis or Cecil B. De Mille. Sarris always strove to avoid the wilder excesses of the approach: that because of, say, *Kiss Me Deadly,* any Robert Aldrich film, seen or not, must be extraordinary. (Realists rejoice that this inane law never deterred the boisterous Aldrich from going on to make quantities of junk as well as a few more good films.) Sarris hoped that the theory of the director would never be built into a regime, but he knew that American experience of its own cinema was still warped by the tradition that cherished Fitzgerald's demise and the very simplistic verdict that a man like Orson Welles had been driven out of work:

> *Ultimately, the auteur theory is not so much a theory as an attitude, a table of values that converts film history into directorial autobiography. The auteur critic is obsessed with the wholeness of art and the artist. He looks at a film as a whole, a director as a whole. The parts, however entertaining individually, must cohere meaningfully. This meaningful coherence is more likely when the director dominates the proceedings with skill and purpose. How often has this directorial domination been permitted in Hollywood? By the most exalted European standards, not nearly enough. Studio domination in the thirties and forties was the rule rather than the exception, and few directors had the right of final cut . . . In retrospect, however, the studio system victimized the screenwriter more than the director. It was not merely a question of too many scribes spoiling the script, although most studios deliberately assigned more than one writer to a film to eliminate personal idiosyncrasies, whereas the director almost invariably*

received sole credit for direction regardless of the studio influences behind the scenes.[3]

It has always been to Sarris's credit that he insisted on treating every film individually. Equally, the best—or maybe only the happiest directors—have been those who disregarded rules about what to expect and worked out their destiny from day to day. But the auteur theory soon leaped out of Sarris's control, its time was so ripe. The context of the movies was changing. The mass audience had already settled for television, and the old movie studios were in disarray. By the middle fifties, big stars had formed their own production companies, aware of the shrinking confidence of the studios and the vacuum that was developing at the center of the business. As they carried the risk, and took more of the profits, so studio space was turned over to the manufacture of TV episodes. Films were pushed into a strategy that was already current—shooting in real places. That was one of the lessons of the new waves in Europe—not just the *vague* itself, but the films of Michelangelo Antonioni, Ingmar Bergman, and Satyajit Ray, all of which impressed America at about the same time. *Film noir* gave way to *Lucy,* and, awkwardly and nervously, American movies entertained a little European influence: *8½* meets *Alex in Wonderland.*

That process succeeded least of all in Hollywood, a community so dependent on exiles and escapees from Europe that it has always been suspicious of un-American ways. The audiences were the principal subscribers to the new intelligence. As more avid and knowledgeable filmgoers comprised a larger portion of the crowd in theaters, so they and their children began to receive an education in "film studies." That's where the auteur theory triumphed. For it appealed deeply to teachers who had grown stale or weary with Milton and George Eliot. They reckoned to prove their hipness, increase their enrollments, and have fun in class, without compromising their own ideals about Great Artists, if they moved over to Fellini and Alfred Hitchcock.

Hero worship had always energized the *politique des auteurs*. In France above all, the young critics hailed distinguished veterans because they wanted to be like them: Howard Hawks, for instance, was not just an admirable filmmaker but a dry manner and personal style to aspire to. The definition of the role of director was the description of a task, and a splendor, that Truffaut, Godard, and the others wanted for themselves. It was backed up with a very thorough defense of the potential of direction, despite restrictions of script, budget, and odious producer. Thus, the French distinguished the narrative conventions from the plastic beauty in Anthony Mann, Vincente Minnelli, or Nicholas Ray. The account of film as a heady audiovisual experience was vital and original, but it was clouded by a hero worship which, in time, constituted respectability in academic programs.

In the sixties, this critical argument was fought out against a background that prejudiced the result. The success of *Psycho*, the mass of writing on Hitchcock, and his own deft riding of the wave established a model hero for the new perception of film. Hitchcock's own dwelling on the engineered image encouraged viewers to bask in great moments of *mise-en-scène*. Lesser directors—in terms of visual brilliance and business chutzpah—took over their own films from the increasingly feeble studio system. Several European directors—Antonioni, Polanski, Truffaut, and then Milos Forman—ventured into the English language.

Film became an entertainment predicated on the names of directors. In the early sixties Otto Preminger followed the stately career of an independent producer-director and used elegant Saul Bass credits to establish a Preminger feeling. Jerry Lewis became for a few years the darling of some critics and the salvation of Paramount. Stanley Kubrick decisively abandoned America, as if the country were unworthy of him. John Boorman came the other way and, with *Point Blank*, revealed how far American genres had become international idiom. And a bevy of new directors lit up what was, in fact, a dull decade: Arthur Penn, Blake Edwards, John Frankenheimer, Sydney Pollack, Richard Lester, and several English directors who had a vague air of angry young men and/or swinging London. By the end of the decade, Coppola and Bogdanovich had emerged. Bob Rafelson had made a film, *Head*, which no one noticed, and helped produce another, *Easy Rider*, which "everyone" saw. Even Abraham Polonsky made a second film, and it was rumored that Joseph Losey might return to America.

Bonnie and Clyde was the pivot of those changes. It was conceived and written by Robert Benton and David Newman, stimulated by the jostling proximity of laughter and pain in Truffaut's films. They offered the script to Truffaut and Godard—which only hints at how many youthful illusions have fallen from Benton like scales. But it ended up a producer's film, the vehicle for Warren Beatty, who is one of the most reticent but prosperous figures of the seventies, the star as existential millionaire. He put himself in the film, along with the late-sixties anguish of the young. He got Penn to direct: Together, a few years before, they had made one of the most glaringly European, financially disastrous, and intriguing films of the decade, *Mickey One*. The "French" script for *Bonnie and Clyde*, its jittery mix of thirties folklore and sixties mood, Penn's rapture, and the chic bearing of the cast made a box-office coup. It promoted fashions, challenged our feelings about violence, launched Faye Dunaway, impressed the critic Robin Wood, and raised lines outside theaters. It also profited Warner Brothers, convinced Warren Beatty to be more than an actor, and augured a new phase of movies that dealt in the experience (i.e., the thwarted fantasies) of the predominantly young audience.

Of course, Penn was never quite as striking again. As intelligent and concerned as Robin Wood asserted, Penn didn't cash in. He made movies more dismayed by Americana, stranger and more offhand than the seventies wanted. *Night Moves* and *Missouri Breaks* have been condemned for obscurity and opportunism, respectively. I suspect they will survive better than films that were big hits in the seventies— *The Sting* and *All the President's Men*, say, whimsy and corruption smoothed together by the bland alarm of Robert Redford. Penn is exactly the kind of man who deserves the new respect for directors. But the seventies were a time of faltering for his career. He went back to the theater, and he was fired from *Altered States* before it had even begun to shoot: On that project the writer Paddy Chayefsky had become boss and would remain so until the replacement director, Ken Russell, ousted and mocked the script with lavish visuals. In the end, Chayefsky called himself Sidney Aaron in the credits.

You might not think it to hear the rhapsodies about Roger Corman's training ground for the young, the formation of BBS, the brotherhood of Lucas, Coppola, Milius, and Spielberg, but directors were still fired, out of work, and miserable. Monte Hellman barely worked, Polonsky slipped back into oblivion, and even Bogdanovich had to start his career up a second time. Jerry Schatzberg tried to be experimental, then he had no work at all, then he settled for the glum safety of *The Seduction of Joe Tynan*, a movie written by and sold on the predigested mush of Alan Alda. Even godfather Corman gave up directing to produce and distribute. It is likely that the average age of directors working in the seventies was lower than at any time since the early twenties. One can argue that more of those directors were their own screenwriters than ever before, and that they triumphed over problems and interference. When John Travolta dropped out of *American Gigolo*, Paul Schrader was left with half a budget and the uncertain blessing of Richard Gere. But he went on with the film and made something more complex than Travolta could have sustained. Coppola was able to make *Apocalypse* on his own, whereas any competent and conscientious studio executive would have cancelled or forbidden it. The system consented to Spielberg directing *Close Encounters* secretly and *1941* expensively— for over $60 million between them—and seemed prepared to take the fat and the lean that resulted with equanimity. The seventies was a profitable decade for Hollywood: Plenty of films flopped, but enough made fortunes, and the overall decline in attendance begun in the late forties was reversed. Periodically, there were waves of euphoria, none greater than the years in which Coppola set Lucas up with *American Graffiti* and made such a triumph with *The Godfather* that he could offer *The Conversation* as a bonus— gravity and responsibility paid for with the profits of a blockbuster.

It's a self-deceiving and youthful mind that can be pleased by that glib rationalization. No one should forget that young directors have made adolescent films—lively and appealing, but inexperienced in terms of complicated lives and camouflaged with technique. They may mature if they can face failure as the most fruitful means to that end. They could also come to resemble that other generation of elderly spoiled children: Mayer, Zukor, Cohn, Schenck, Laemmle. Coppola's wish to own a studio may involve the helping of friends and the easing of difficult and worthwhile projects. But it is also the wish to be a studio boss. On the west coast of America, pictures are still a business, and no one can survive there without devoting his energies to the acquisition of power.

Meanwhile, we should appreciate how far the changes in Hollywood practice that developed in the seventies have deprived us of an earlier generation. There is a terrible irony in the way belated critical acclaim, in France in the late fifties and in America in the early sixties, coincided with the withering of so many careers. It need not be tragic or surprising if old men work less: Thus, Alfred Hitchcock, Howard Hawks, John Ford, and Raoul Walsh went into semiretirement. But King Vidor, I suspect, would still welcome the chance to direct if it came along. He remains one of the most socially active veterans in Beverly Hills. But *Solomon and Sheba,* his last picture, was made in 1959.

A slightly younger generation had a far sadder story to tell. Vincente Minnelli is now just seventy, but in the last decade has made only two films—*On a Clear Day You Can See Forever,* a calamity, and *A Matter of Time,* worse. Nicholas Ray finished nothing after 1963. Douglas Sirk went back to Germany and teaching. Fred Zinnemann lost a major project. Joseph Mankiewicz stagnated, Richard Brooks seemed lost, and Jerry Lewis's career came to depend on the annual muscular dystrophy telethon. Alexander Mackendrick gave up the business. Budd Boetticher went south to become the sort of vagrant-poet that Sam Peckinpah might make films about. Elia Kazan turned to writing. Orson Welles roamed, yarned, and mocked TV commercials with his flatulent dignity. George Cukor apparently lost confidence. Billy Wilder worked on—*Avanti!, The Front Page,* and *Fedora*—but with loss of heart and good humor. As he started making *Fedora,* a testament that so few would appreciate, Wilder said:

> *I am, I trust, off the hit parade only temporarily. I'm going through a dry spell, that's all. I did not suddenly become an idiot. I did not suddenly unlearn my craft. It's a dry spell. Occasionally the vineyards produce a bad vintage. They say Wilder is out of touch with his times. Frankly, I regard it as a compliment. Who the hell wants to be in touch with these times?* [4]

That sounds alarmingly like Norma Desmond, the past resenting the present because of its drab or lazy expectations. *Fedora* is not well made, though that need not be all Wilder's fault. It required a certain kind of grandiose star, and none was willing to risk it. But what could be more poignant than a senior director anxious to vindicate the well-made film, yet no longer able to make it all fit together? Samuel Fuller did nothing in the seventies but *Dead Pigeon on Beethoven Street*, in Germany, and *The Big Red One*. It seemed wonderful that he should at last get that opportunity—in America, for Lorimar—set up through the help of Peter Bogdanovich and with Lee Marvin in the central part. The film was shot, but for a long time nothing happened. Studio rumors reported that Fuller was unable to edit it. He asked for help, but no one could make it coherent. One day a novice asked if she could try her hand at it. In the event, she turned that footage into the movie that was released. Youth gets a chance! Yes, but the pantheon crumbles, leaving the grim sight of old men less than they once were.

One could argue that Wilder's grievance and Fuller's dilemma were brutal evidence of their age, unkind time, and the movies' interest in new subjects. But the thematic novelty of recent films may only be a matter of greater frankness, or extremism, with sex and violence, and of less precision as far as intricate narrative mechanics are concerned. Is the medium as technically nimble as it once was? Lorimar, where both Wilder and Fuller sought help, is one of the newer, small, independent production outfits. It rents studio and office space at Culver City and only employs technicians for TV series like *Dallas*. Cameramen, editors, art directors, gaffers are all freelancers now. They work less often than their forebears did in the thirties and forties, and they can expect fewer of the team situations that flourished when the production-studio factories had a body of craftsmen under contract. When you make a film today, you have to pick up your top technicians as best you can. The significant number of foreign cameramen on major American films— Vilmos Zsigmond, Laszlo Kovacs, Vittorio Storaro, Nestor Almendros, Giuseppe Rotunno, Sven Nykvist, Robby Muller, Bruno Nytten—suggests that uncertain movie work is less appealing to American cameramen. It has made for a gradual dilution of "American style." Studio house style died away in the fifties; and in the seventies it became harder to identify an American picture by its texture. Very little study has been made of this, and it is not a thing Hollywood talks about, but I suspect the quality of craft work in American film today is flattered by the technological advances in photography and sound. Walter Murch, at Zoetrope, is an artist, or a magician, in sound without whom *The Conversation* might never have been made. Dolby and digital sound permit new depths of clarity and density as well as a more felt silence. But it is harder to hear dialogue than in the forties. Photographic and processing expertise have reached such a stage of fidelity and ingenuity that "lifelike" color has become an automatic, bland norm, while the laboratories can rescue all but the most devastating mistakes. Photography is more correct and more "real"; but is it less expressive? Among editors, too, is it possible that younger, less experienced cutters, and directors allowed to supervise the editing, have contributed to slacker, longer films? I wonder whether the scripts of *His Girl Friday*, *Laura*, or *The Awful Truth* could be made today at the original running lengths.

That much is speculation. But the new vulnerability of the director cannot be questioned. He has to find his crew and then train it to his ways, whereas an Anthony Mann or a Mitchell Leisen had the advantage of a unit in which there were only occasional changes of personnel. They also had the studio's paternal administration, cafeteria, pensions, and producers. From 1943 to 1963, every film Minnelli made was at MGM; his decline happened to coincide with the need to scout around the town for work.

All those directors who fell by the wayside in the 1960's had been brought up in a system in which the studio carried the weight of hack work on a film. If Fitzgerald saw Frank

Borzage as a stooge, and if we treasure the personal tone that Borzage still put into *Three Comrades,* it may be because the director was free to direct. He had only to envisage the scene and handle the action. He did not struggle with the script, audition actresses, and fight over casting. He did not argue for time and money, negotiate with every actor over terms, worry about lunch for the extras, or have to handle anxious calls from investors in the company. Those tasks fell to the producer, a figure the director was able to despise, resent, and blame if need be.

There are still producers functioning, people who package, fund, and sell others' films. They may be self-effacing admirers of their directors, or uninhibited profiteers. Their task may be to float all the money, resources, and talent for a picture, or merely to take the administrative load off the director's back. They may be movie addicts, showmen, or cold-blooded accountants. They are very seldom "line" producers, the kind of people who ride steady, vigilant, and even interfering herd on every stage of a picture. At best today they are sponsors or patrons. Charles Joffe has produced most of Woody Allen's later pictures and helped make Allen's "seriousness" commercially viable. Clint Eastwood, an outstanding businessman, who engages in nearly as many areas of movie work as Allen, keeps Robert Daley as executive producer at Eastwood's company, Malpaso. Irwin Winkler and Robert Chartoff brought *Rocky, Rocky II,* and *Nickelodeon* to the screen. Michael Douglas, a flimsy actor, seemed as dynamic as his father when it came to getting *One Flew Over the Cuckoo's Nest* or *The China Syndrome* made. Alan Pakula is one of the few directors who was a producer first. Robert Evans has ranged from *Rosemary's Baby* and *Chinatown* to *Black Sunday* and *Players.* Bert Schneider, once a crucial innovator at BBS, has put his name to only *Days of Heaven* recently. Frank Yablans has kept very firm control of *The Other Side of Midnight, Silver Streak,* and *The Fury.* On the last project, Brian De Palma seemed to be content with so rugged a producer, but he and Yablans later parted company, and De Palma went back to the semiunderground pictures he made in the late sixties before restoring his box-office reputation with *Dressed to Kill*. The shortage of hit material and the circling around of many would-be entrepreneurs can lead to the top-heavy credits of *The Sting*. That has five named producers—Tony Bill, Julia and Michael Phillips, David Brown, and Richard Zanuck: as crowded a scam as the movie itself describes.

More often than it might seem, however, directors do the work of producers. Since every film is set up now as a unique deal, and since most films involve directors far sooner than was the case in the thirties and forties, those directors need to be negotiators, businessmen, and managers. I interviewed Bob Rafelson a few days before he was to start shooting *Brubaker*. It was a film placed at Fox, with pre-production working out of a bungalow on their lot. But it was owned and produced by Ron Silverman, who had bought the original book years before, advanced to a script, and only then hired Rafelson. As for Rafelson, he had directed two exceptional pictures, *Five Easy Pieces* and *The King of Marvin Gardens*, for BBS, the company that he and Bert Schneider had founded with Steve Blauner. *Brubaker* was his first picture for a large studio, evidence of his own uncertain box-office record and of his famously aggressive integrity. But even under the cloak of a major studio, Rafelson, with a secretary and an assistant producer, was still working on scripts, budget, and casting, *and* making arrangements for the company's accommodations in Ohio. The panic and the excitement were not fulfilled. *Brubaker*, still with Robert Redford in the lead role, ended up as a Stuart Rosenberg film. Rafelson was fired after a week or so of location shooting because of an angry argument with a Fox executive who felt that the picture was already slipping behind schedule.

These are all cases in which someone other than the director is credited as producer. But Paul Mazursky has been co-producer with Tony Ray on his recent films, as part of his wish to operate out of New York City, away from Hollywood pressures. Robert Altman is generally his own producer, and at Lion's Gate, his headquarters, he has fostered one of the closest bands of collaborators in front of and behind the camera. Michael Cimino was one of the producers on *The Deer Hunter*. Beatty is his own producer, his own secret empire. James Toback only made *Love and Money* because he held on to it against all delays and obstacles, including the departure of original owner Warren Beatty, the coming and going of notional producer Pauline Kael, the transfer of the project from Paramount to Lorimar, and his own eventual burden as producer when no one else was left.

You can deduce from this that the new filmmaker must be not only capable and durable enough to handle that much paperwork, but actually inspired and aroused by it. Distributors and financiers are still very powerful, if push comes to shove, but they do recognize the extent to which the dynamic of the business has moved in favor of young hustler-artists. Chartoff and Winkler did yield to Sylvester Stallone's conviction that no one knew the concept of *Rocky* better than he did. And so a small-part actor had the kingdom thrown open to him. But Stallone is sly enough to please such men. John Travolta has made every bit as much money, but he is neither as aggressive nor as self-confident. Businessmen now take for granted that the young wish to be the center of the business. They have only contempt for, and fear of, a would-be director who cannot weigh his own film as a commercial operation. The artists have gained ground by acquiring the manners and the language of the traders.

Close friends Gary Kurtz (producer) and George Lucas (director) made *Star Wars* together. Kurtz had this to say about his duties as line, or working, producer:

If you want to categorize the function of the working

producer, it is to provide all the tools so the director can do everything he wants, or, at least, everything within the limits you are trying to work. I also function as a sounding board to discuss everything that comes up.[5]

But Lucas's own confession, or boast, shows how little scope that may leave for the producer beyond being a friend in need:

I come up from the film-makers' school of doing movies, which means I did everything myself. If you are a writer-director, you must *get involved with everything. It's very hard for me to get into another system where everybody does things for me, and I say "Fine." If I ever continue to do those kinds of movies, I've got to learn to do that. I have a lot of friends who can, and I admire them. Francis [Ford Coppola] is going through that now, and he's finally learning, finally getting to the point where he realizes he can't do it all. He's getting into the traditional system: "Call me when it's ready, and it better be right, and if it's not, do it again and spend whatever it costs to get it right." But you have to be willing to make very expensive movies that way.*[6]

There are so many lessons of the seventies in that: the near impossibility of low-budget films, the Selznick-like need to know and command everything, the sense of film being for its creators a process of management (and gambling) as well as of making. But even then, *Star Wars* was regarded skeptically by Fox, which had funded it; on first viewing, they thought they had a loser. It took critics and the public to persuade them they had the biggest grosser of all time. Even so, early hesitation meant a failure to get spin-off toys on the market by Christmas—a film is also T-shirts, records, and behavior fads.

Lucas's assessment of himself did not exactly work out.

So, rich from *Star Wars*, he has set up his own special-effects factory for producing sequels that he will not direct himself. He has become a tycoon, much like Coppola, who actually appeared to be overwhelmed by the problems of delegation and organization that blurred creative decisions on *Apocalypse*. Friends once, rather more distant now, it is conceivable that Coppola and Lucas could combine their production resources and become virtually a major studio—but only if they could guarantee themselves distribution. United Artists, too, sounded like a fine idea in 1919. Yet business and creation have always made for turmoil, and now that storm may wreak havoc all in the mind of one man.

The film director in America is still both more and less than an artist if one compares him with the range of painters, writers, and musicians. The depth of experience in films is less, but the audience is so much larger. Still, the moviemaker, and essentially the director, is a more prominent cultural hero exactly because he gives promise of spanning the business jungle and the precious delight and consolation of our imaginations. He is as idealized a figure as a president who might manage to be both efficient and wise. Far more people than go regularly to the movies regard directors as spokesmen for the times. Now, as much as ever, the director is lured by the chance of making a compelling entertainment that will be a subject of conversation and the means of impact across the country. He can seem, to others and to himself, as titanic as the Coppola who made *The Godfather*; as passionate as the Scorsese of *Taxi Driver*; as diverse, tolerant, and amused as Altman with *Nashville*; or a boy wonder, like Spielberg with *Jaws* or Lucas with *Star Wars*. This is an eminence that very few Americans can hope to enjoy—even if it lasts but a week. At different times, Coppola, Woody Allen, Altman, and even Warren Beatty have been held representative of the country. Orson Welles, I think, was the first to discover the huge fun, the glamour, and the authority of being a movie director, and of doing it all yourself.

But that strain can be killing. There were as many disappointments in the seventies as there were promising debuts. It is harder than ever to build a career as gradually as art requires. Too often, a young man finds himself overwhelmed by the project of the year—make or break. One day during the near decade of *Apocalypse Now*, Eleanor Coppola found this message from the darkness in her husband's typewriter —it is a cry of dismay that suggests how far the beleaguered Kurtz would be a portrait of the film director at the end of his tether:

> *My greatest fear—I've had for months—The movie is a mess—A mess of continuity, of style—and most important, the ending neither works on an audience or philosophical level. Brando is a disappointment to audiences—the film reaches its highest level during the fucking helicopter battle.*
>
> *My nerves are shot—My heart is broken—My imagination is dead. I have no self-reliance—But just like a child want someone to rescue me . . .*[7]

5

To Write a Movie

One of the best introductions to movies published in the 1970's was James Monaco's *How to Read a Film*. But what does "read" mean in that title? If the camera bears dumb witness, can its product be legible or is it merely phenomenal? If they will be read, must films be written first?

Monaco used "read" to describe something other than the methodical and imaginative tracking of words on a page. He argued that it is so natural to apprehend a film that we do not easily comprehend it. His book set out to train the viewer in observing his own process of watching. "Read" can also mean scanning in order to understand, looking so that we may "see." People say "I read him" to indicate that they have studied someone's appearance and performance, assessed all the levels of evidence, and come to an interpretation. Reading in that sense is close to our experience with movies: opening our eyes, ears, and selves to "signs" that will enable us to grasp the "scenario."

That word, too, has been misappropriated. Scenario once meant the written script for a drama. Today it also covers whatever pattern of significance (or narrative) the observer may fish out of the murky waters of life. It is a way of taming disorderly experience with the hope of containment, and it admits our fear of being overwhelmed by chaotic, incomprehensible action. Ironically, that anxiety is a consequence of our gradual retreat from reading's potential for articulate knowledge and reason's ability to describe and argue about experience. Movies often forsake those strenuous disciplines and instead encourage us into the pipe dream that looking *is* adequate, albeit helpless, understanding. "I see" may mean I understand, or only that I let anything happen under my eyes.

To write a movie became a topic of major theoretical interest in the fifties and sixties, while writing one's way into pictures became a reality in the seventies. And yet we are talking of different things. It was actually in 1948 that Alexandre Astruc proposed "this new age of cinema the age of *camera-stylo* [camera-pen]. This metaphor has a very precise sense. By it I mean that the cinema will gradually break free from the tyranny of what is visual, from the image for its own sake, from the immediate and concrete demands of the narrative, to become a means of writing just as flexible and subtle as written language." [1]

By 1980 Astruc's name was nearly forgotten, and his achievement as a director (*Une Vie*) had passed out of sight or release. But I'm sure Paul Schrader still knew the name, and in 1980 he was one of the most prominent screenwriters in Hollywood. Schrader was trained in a film school and through intense involvement as a critic in non-American film sensibility. He had been to UCLA, edited *Cinema* magazine, and written a book on Ozu, Dreyer, and Bresson. Then he broke into the kingdom: He wrote *Obsession* for Brian De Palma, *Taxi Driver* for Martin Scorsese, *The Yakuza* for Sydney Pollack, *Rolling Thunder* for John Flynn, *Old Boyfriends* for Joan Tewkesbury, and three movies that he would direct himself—*Blue Collar*, *Hardcore*, and *American Gigolo*.

In the first weeks of its release, it was reported that audiences were laughing at *American Gigolo* all over America, but the picture did remarkably well nonetheless. Of the films Schrader had directed, it was the first hit; and maybe in the nick of time. The man who startled Hollywood with his rapid rise, his intelligence and personal abrasiveness, and the $300,000 fee for his least impressive script, *The Yakuza*, had been near the end of his rope. *Gigolo* is a very serious picture; solemn, some would say. Yet it was laughed at. Did people find humor in it? Was it a success because of public derision, or did that only signal how Schrader had touched on a sensitive nerve—the separation of glamour and narcissism from love?

Gigolo was patently authored. Like a Firbank priest, it attempted to reconcile the aesthetic and the spiritual. It lifted lines and scenes from the work of Robert Bresson. And it was written on the screen, in the air, on the wind—however we try to define it. *Gigolo* had a look and a sound. When I saw it, it seemed to me that people embarrassed by or scornful of the "plot" were also disconcerted by the tawdry spirituality of the picture. On the literary level, *American Gigolo* is trash. But as an experience in the dark, drawing upon that especially zealous commitment to sight and sound that the dark demands, it is more profound than either claims of trashiness or attempts at explanation.

All of which is commentary that horrifies an older school of screenwriters and adds to their righteous indignation that for decades, unscrupulous actors, producers, and directors have been filching the credit for movies. Historically, the writers in Hollywood refused to see the mood and tone of pictures. They claimed to believe that directors simply transcribed their scripts onto celluloid. Gore Vidal has interviewed out too often for his reputation as an original wit on the indignity of discovering *The Best Man* advertised in France as "un film de Franklin Schaffner." Vidal has asserted that he could comfortably have directed the films made from his scripts, and that it was only an unfortunate and rather bored oversight that kept him out of the Pantheon:

> *I had a chance to direct in the fifties, and I turned it down. In those days, nobody who was a serious novelist would have dreamt of directing. And a great*

many successful screen-writers felt the same. Directing was for the hustlers. Then along came the Europeans with their theories, and suddenly directors were ennobled. We novelists who had been central to the culture began to float out to the far perimeter where the poets live, and I now think that, perhaps, I missed a chance.[2]

It may be pretty for Vidal to reflect on the cinema's loss, but his languid superiority only exposes his aversion to the necessary vulgarity of the movies. To bring a film to the screen is to wrestle with monsters dressed as clowns. It involves crawling, business mayhem, walking backward, and wholesale interference with fine ideas. Cut off from that perimeter of poets, you can only dive in your pool instead to get clean. In his novel, *Myra Breckinridge*, Vidal can observe that process from the outside with scathing enjoyment. But he is squeamish about looking ridiculous himself—it is the one thing that keeps him from major achievement as a writer, too; while the movie kingdom, rowdy and coarse, does not understand the fervent self-respect that Vidal is unwilling to risk.

That's why so many screenwriters once disdained directing and the squalid traffic of pictures. Vidal is only the last and most dandified figure in the line that has Herman Mankiewicz cabling Ben Hecht in 1926:

Will you accept three hundred per week to work for Paramount Pictures? All expenses paid. The three hundred is peanuts. Millions are to be grabbed out here and your only competition is idiots. Don't let this get around.[3]

and William Faulkner pocketing the money as he judiciously returned to Oxford, Mississippi, to get on with his "real" work. Incidentally, Vidal believes that Faulkner could have directed Renoir's *The Southerner* without strain, an opinion that makes one wonder whether he can appreciate either the wilfully intransigent achievement of the novels Faulkner wrote or Renoir's enthusiasm for compromise.

The Hollywood writer was once a lowly and abused form of life, bemused that he could earn so much more holed up at the Garden of Allah or the Chateau Marmont than working on a novel, a play, or an article for New York magazines. The bitterness he swallowed in the thirties and forties he threw up as anger when auteurism started assigning conceptual credit to people the writer had known as jerks. More recently, in the seventies, the writer has been very highly paid by the movies; he has found it easier to become a director and possible to own a piece of the project. Yet, perversely, the new status for the writer has coincided with a developing sense in America that movies need to be read experientially. The old virtues of construction and dialogue are less rigid or evident than they were when, say, Ernest Lehman wrote *North by Northwest* for Hitchcock. The two most vital words in *American Gigolo*—its literary triumph— may be the title itself.

Once upon a time, scripts were documents that had an internal use: They gave the studio hierarchy the confidence to make a film in an era when planning had supplanted inspiration; they appealed to a star under contract to the studio; and they reassured the managerial forces that the project could be made on schedule and for the allotted budget. The script was a thorough blueprint, to be followed scrupulously in the shooting and to serve as a model for the editing. Of course, some films turned out very different from the script; and sometimes if the script was lagging behind, the movie still had to be shot. But the approval of the script was the studio's ratification that the story "worked" and that the product should be put together in its agreed numbered sequence. No matter who ended up with the credit, scripts removed blame—"we filmed the script" was the defense when a picture flunked.

Films felt thoroughly constructed because of that systematic emphasis on sensible preplanning. Over a period of years, that made intricate plot construction one of the dominant characteristics of American film. In the forties, and in *film noir* especially, there was an implicit ideal by which the system looked for plots that were as complicated as possible but still under the control of accomplished lighting, tidy cutting, and adroit performances. You can argue that it led to a sterile ingenuity, exact but claustrophobic, which reaches its daft peak in *Sunset Boulevard*, in which the story is told by a corpse.

With the breakdown of the studio system, and the need to set up every movie individually, the script becomes a far more dynamic, external instrument. There is no factory now intent on stringent blueprint scripts. But there are distributors, financiers, agents, and stars who need to be convinced about joining in a project. That's where the two words "American Gigolo" may have been decisive, for they are an instant, commercial concept—like the name of a perfume or a restaurant. When you remember that originally Paramount had to say yes or no to "John Travolta in *American Gigolo*," you can see how far movies may be summed up in a slogan. Those five words are enough to ring box-office bells—a current star of exceptional appeal who is well suited to a title as blatant as it is enigmatic. Paramount surely asked to see the script—the parent company, Gulf & Western, would tolerate only so much superstition. They may have read it carefully and suggested sensible changes as befits responsible entrepreneurs. But when Travolta dropped out of the project —leaving the script intact but vacant without his rubbery strut—and was replaced by Richard Gere, the expectations and the budget were cut in half. Moreover, the Paramount attitude was not so very different from the manner in which Paul Schrader had first conceived of the project:

Well, American Gigolo *began in the screenwriting*

class at UCLA. In one of those round-table discussions I was suggesting occupations for a character: What does this person do? Is he a salesman? Is he a writer? Is he a gigolo, an American gigolo? I made a joke and then said, "That's an interesting subject." Then, after class I thought, "Well, that is an interesting subject."

The next day I was at the shrink's office, and we were talking about a problem of giving and receiving love, the difficulty of receiving . . . Sometimes it's easier to give than to receive. And as I was leaving the office, that little spark occurred, the crossing of two unlikes—which is Arthur Koestler's whole thing about the act of creation: two different things hit and spark, and bam! you've got something. The notion of the gigolo as a metaphor for the man who can't receive pleasure hit me, and from that moment on I had a metaphor that was uniquely representative of that problem. Then it was just a matter of plotting it out.[4]

"Bam!" is the giveaway, even if its dressed up as a Koestler synapse. Travolta plus "American Gigolo" is one bam! —enough to excite Paramount—and it is entertaining to see how far for Schrader the bam! bridges the classroom and the analyst's sanctum, a cute selling phrase that redeems a paining personal problem. (Did the shrink endorse the picture as therapy?) Schrader wrote five scripts in the year he wrote *American Gigolo*, so the need for an urgent bam! is more important than emotion recollected in tranquillity. Indeed, a screenplay labored over is almost by definition unviable; the rapidity of writing is in direct relationship to the screened intensity. A movie writer ought to be able to write a script in a month and still have time to kill at pinball. Most good movies are conceived as quickly as babies.[5]

Now, I do like *Gigolo*. It is the best picture Schrader has directed, as ambiguously touching and distressing as *Taxi Driver*, as worldly and adolescent. But I do not believe that it really clarifies the problem of receiving love. Perhaps that is too painful or too tangled a problem to ride the celluloid slipstream. The movie only sketches or asserts its themes with the speed that makes "American Gigolo" instantly fundable. This point is worth exploring because it says a great deal about the role of the writer in movie-making and about the anatomy of a film.

You could argue that the problems of giving and receiving love are among the most serious and worthwhile projects for an artist or a storyteller. (Although that claim does have the earnestness of someone proposing to eradicate typhus.) They are certainly novelistic, worthy of the extended prose fiction that we categorize as the novel. They are all the more seemly material for novels if those books can manage to be about good sentences and paragraphs first. *Anna Karenina, The Portrait of a Lady, Mrs. Dalloway,* and *The Moviegoer* all worry about them in one way or another. One could propose that just about any novel ever written touches on these problems. Prose describes and embodies the perplexities of thought. But how could anyone believe that the script of *American Gigolo* is not meretricious compared with those books, or that its aura and effects are not specious when measured against what a novel could do with the subject? No writer could leave Julian Kaye as emphatic and as vague as Schrader insists on making him. Words will not permit it, but pictures only allege deeper issues with the innuendo of a lewd wink at a marriage service.

American Gigolo does not inhabit that area of his own life which drew Schrader to the subject and title. It hovers around it like a gossip. Lack of tranquillity might explain this, but it could owe more to the slippery restlessness of movie as a medium. The picture actually presents a sleek, shallow character—the person as image, or as "glossy," to use a photographic term—who is only agitated by the plot's cunning tricks. He has no inner life; he seems desperate to avoid any risk of it—when he is alone, he sculpts his muscles and studies shirts to avoid reflection. What makes the movie so exciting is exactly the sensibility that realizes the riveting lack of materiality or substance in imagery. Indeed, it is a very helpful step toward defining excellence in movies to say that the form seems to require fascinating images caught up in such crises of external action that *we* provide them with an inner life.

There is hardly an internal crisis—of spirit, mind, or feelings—in film, though Schrader's idol, Bresson, comes as close to it as anyone and in the process makes films that leave most people cold and uninterested. All the fret and agony is in the image, and *American Gigolo* is more a rhapsody to surface than its glib disapproval of modishness realizes. It has a tranquil narcissist as one character and a fashion model as its leading actress, and it is infatuated by its own re-creation of svelte L.A. interiors. The plot crisis is resolved by an action that implies a moral decision, and which borrows the language and gesture of Bresson's *Pickpocket*, but this is the dynamic of comic books or silent films in which every point must be spelled or mimed out in action. Schrader, I'm sure, feels Julian's dilemma, and something of its dread is conveyed. Because the characters are so hollow, we can fill them out with our imaginative play. But there is a direct correlation between the instant enchantment of *American Gigolo* and the speed with which it fades. The picture is the terse conceptual novelty of the title plus Schrader's considerable success, cinematically, at giving it atmosphere. Real moral or psychological development has been sacrificed to the disco bam! of provocative password and suggestive ambiance—like "Rosebud" and the palpable, deep-focus regret that fills Xanadu and helps us accept *Citizen Kane*'s self-pity as existential fatalism: No Trespassing as a hard-boiled version of leave me alone.

Schrader would not necessarily dispute this. In his *Film Comment* interview, the longer he talks, the more you appreciate what the film has omitted:

To be perfectly honest I didn't end up exploring the theme in the film the way I had hoped but just sort of became interested in the young man who had made something of himself, a sort of Horatio Alger of sexual fantasy, who had made himself into this desirable object, and as a result of it had found an identity in pleasing others and had lost a sense of accepting anything real. And though it's not exactly a problem that many people face, it touches on a problem people do have. It's the whole problem of when you give something, you can distance yourself from it, just stand above it. When you receive something, it calls for more participation with the person who's giving, to deal with a one-to-one relationship, to show appreciation. It would be very easy for me to pick something off the wall and give it to you, but that is not an act of generosity, it's an act of ego. It's not an act of ego to take a gift from someone and relate to it. So that's really what it's about. It's about sex as ego on his part.[6]

However contradictory Schrader's comments are, no matter how far viewers could recognize the film from his description, he is unquestionably the auteur. It could be that his very volatility is what produces the unique and rather creepy ambivalence of the film. But his urgings and longings have written a film in which the writing harnesses the straight-faced narcissism of the cast, that basking lizard called L.A., the sumptuous production design whereby glamour verges on grace and chic seems sacramental, and the sensual nagging of the Giorgio Moroder music. *American Gigolo* was not hindered by two tracks getting into the Top Ten, or by a look that beckoned and denied imitation just as surely as the poetic torture of fashion photography.

The film was the poster, an iconographically definitive design which combined ecstasy and anxiety in its silver-gray sheen and which thereby illustrated the title—one of the

most suggestive the movies have known, with that faint hint
of impossibility underlying everything—as if the public were
hoping that one could not be both a gigolo and American.

I don't mean to be dismissive by saying that the title is
the best piece of writing Schrader has done. Such packed
simplicity is the essence of pictures. Steven Spielberg testified
to the same thing when responding to a question at an
American Film Institute seminar about whether his search
for material favored short treatments or finished scripts:

> *What interests me more than anything else is the
> idea. If a person can tell me the idea in twenty-five
> words or less, it's going to make a pretty good movie.
> I like ideas, especially movie ideas, that you can hold
> in your hand.*[7]

There are ideas and ideas, and anyone desirous of having
them all reduced to palmable size may only need ball bear-
ings to play with. One can imagine the delicate dismay of
Gore Vidal at that declaration of principles from a modern
American in communications. But it's too good a game not
to play, and you don't have to pursue it for more than half
an hour to test its validity. I worked at it for ten minutes
and came up with these—I don't think any readers will miss
a title:

> *Older guy comfortably in love meets perfect girl. Pur-
> sues her. Realizes she is stupid as she shows no hesita-
> tion in fucking him.*

> *Man keeps stuffed body of Mom. Believes she is inside
> him. Protects both of them from intruders. Keeps motel
> as trap.*

> *Taxi driver lives alone, looking for love. Fails. Finds
> child whore and kills five to save her. Is he talking to us?*

> *Huge shark appears off resort coast. It eats people.
> Three men go out to fight it.*

Hairdresser screws around.

Halloween.

All of those were substantial hits of the last two decades, and all of them had a novelty of plot situation that bordered upon impossibility or the liberation of dreams. Not even the last one is intended as a joke. You could easily give a twenty-five-word synopsis for John Carpenter's compulsive B picture. But the one word is all we need, and brevity is always more intriguing. Halloween cannot promise anything sedate, and *Halloween* is to menace as sugar is to gratification. In the same way, I'm not sure that "Shampoo" isn't better than "Hairdresser screws around," because it is shorter and because it conjures up the froth of ejaculation—a sort of sperm rinse.

The significance of these short-form descriptions is that they capture the literary haste and impulse with which films are set up today. A movie script is generally a typescript that works out at about a page for every minute of screen time. Over the years, every effort has been taken to make them easy to read: Their format provides a narrow, central area of type—hence the notion of reading down the middle of the page, the ease of falling as opposed to the effort of lateral scanning. You can speculate over the reasons for this, but if scripts are aimed at people who believe in speed-reading, is it any wonder that a phenomenon of speed-writing has evolved to accommodate them? Producers, stars, and distributors have too many scripts to read. Therefore, they will be impressed by a script that reads quickly and fluently and in which crucial things happen early. There are decision-makers who like to boast that if they're not gripped by page 20 then they read no further. Another, rather scurrilous interpretation is that many of the people who have to read scripts do not read with comfort.

The nutshell idea can launch a blockbuster. David Brown and Richard Zanuck read Peter Benchley's novel, *Jaws,* in manuscript. The novelist's agent may see film rights looming larger than any publishing deal, and in the last fifteen years more and more novels have been written in a styleless style and about situations or locations that may appeal to the movies. Some novels are sold to the movies long before they have a publisher. Zanuck and Brown bought the book in twenty-four hours. They worked with Benchley on the first-draft screenplay and then hired the two-fisted Spielberg to direct and to push the script into a tighter second draft. Far later in the day, John Milius added Robert Shaw's long speech about the sinking of the *Indianapolis*—the most "eloquent" writing in the film and a sequence that structures the picture by providing an extended, hallowed pause in which the mythic context of danger is deepened.

But the mechanics of suspense on paper always depended on whether the shark could be made plausible on screen. *Jaws 2*, a greatly inferior film, suggests how much Spielberg's dynamic vision—his movie writing—and his identification with the two "ordinary" men had to do with the success of the original. Nevertheless, there must have been an hour at which Zanuck and Brown decided that the essential scheme of the book—that the shark acts with intelligent malice—would work on screen. They fired one director on *Jaws 2* to get what they wanted, and would surely have thrown Spielberg overboard if necessary. Sharkishness is a trait that movie men understand.

Moreover, two years later Spielberg himself wrote the screenplay for *Close Encounters of the Third Kind* more as a storyboard than as a written script. When so much of a movie lies in the fulfillment of visual wonder or the close-cutting of suspense, no wonder a "script" turns into something a prospective buyer can see, spread out on the table, and comprehend. It's like reading a comic strip. The influence of Alfred Hitchcock is enormous here, for he always preferred to spend months with his scriptwriters before emerging with a storyboard script that the actors and crew could execute simply. Spielberg might argue that the action of *Jaws* on the page could sound neutral. Its excitement lurks in the charged framing and editing, and in the Cassandra-like music, which lets our involvement transcend the framework of impossibility.

So the script must be a means of selling a project, the thing that will stimulate investment confidence. There are writers so aware of that issue they will not trust reading when a more direct story-selling is available. James Toback had a script that several studios had turned down. He decided to let Warren Beatty have a chance at it—to hope that Beatty might read it would be negative thinking. But: "I know there is nothing harder than getting an unsolicited script read by people who have several hundred a day delivered to them. I knew Beatty's office was stacked with them. So I told him, 'No, I've got to read it to you.'"[8] Beatty pulled back from such hustling, but then he conceded and bought the script over dinner. For all he knew, there was nothing as yet on paper. If Toback waved paper in the air, that would only be a tactic pioneered by McCarthy.

And it's not so far-fetched. A lot of scripts get talked up and contracted long before they're written. Even beginners can sometimes get "development money" to proceed with a five-page treatment. The few top writers can command large sums on the promise of a script, or a book, by the end of next year. There are people who have earned a living as screenwriters for ten years but who have had only one picture made in that time. The competition is intense: Several hundred scripts in Beatty's office need not be an exaggeration. Most of those that are read come by way of the best-known agents. Scripts out of nowhere are sent back unopened, simply to protect the producers against legal charges that any film they do make owes something to a script they might have looked at years before. Beatty and Robert Towne had such a suit over *Shampoo*, and they only reversed the first judgment (a six-figure damages fee) on appeal. It all confirms the adage that there are only so many stories and that all movies recycle them. And the old Hollywood still believes that you can't pull anything off without a sound script, while the new reckons that writing is the most promising route into the industry. Whereas once upon a time it was very hard for writers to get out of their own special trade, in the last twenty years the ranks of directors have been kept supplied by ambitious writers.

Robert Benton has come all the way from *Bonnie and Clyde* to *Kramer v. Kramer*. Michael Crichton turned into a director after first selling novels and scripts to the movies. John Milius wrote *Jeremiah Johnson* and *The Life and Times of Judge Roy Bean*, and then stepped up to be a director. Some time before those scripts, he had written the first draft of what would become *Apocalypse Now*. Joan Tewkesbury wrote *Thieves Like Us* and *Nashville* for Robert Altman, and then made *Old Boyfriends*. Buck Henry did script work for ten years and now seems on the verge of a directing career. After a long period of writing (*Heller in Pink Tights, The Molly Maguires, The Front, Semi-Tough*), Walter Bernstein directed *Little Miss Marker*. Toback wrote *The Gambler* for Karel Reisz before making his own first film, *Fingers*. Walter Hill had four screenplay credits before he directed *Hard Times*. Michael Cimino wrote *Silent Running*, wrote and directed *Thunderbolt and Lightfoot*, and then exploded into prominence with *The Deer Hunter*. Both Woody Allen and Marshall Brickman wrote scripts before graduating to directing. And Francis Ford Coppola helped Gore Vidal write *Is Paris Burning?*, and then scripted *Patton* and *The Great Gatsby* in his early days.

There are times when it seems eccentric to want to do the one without the other. A few leading directors have no writing credits—Hal Ashby for one—but reports about the prolonged birth pains of *Coming Home* make it clear that Ashby contributed several ideas and a great deal of scripting attention. Some directors are like Hitchcock in that they feel insecure without the presence of a writer and the opportunity of bouncing twists and lines back and forth. Still, a few directors remain content to make the films scripted by strong writers: Sydney Pollack, George Roy Hill, Herbert Ross, and Sidney Lumet, who probably kept very quiet during the making of *Network*. That diatribe against television was the personal triumph of Paddy Chayefsky, and this was one of the few films of the seventies with which it was possible to sit back in the wash of elegant, rhetorical dialogue. That may only have constituted a crust of "intelligence" on a soap opera film, but it reminded us of how seldom today's dialogue has wit or a rhythm of its own. When people talk in pictures now, it is to promote the action and pocketsized ideas, not to revel in the rich sounds of language as sometimes seemed the case when Hawks, Sternberg, Lubitsch, Mankiewicz, Hecht, Raphaelson, Furthman, and Wilder held sway. Woody Allen's dialogue is funny, to be sure, but I doubt if it would read better than a stream of one-liners, all the more desperate because of the lack of literary momentum. No one in pictures talks like Gore Vidal—even if he sometimes sounds like George Sanders.

No, the best dialogue writer at work on film today is Neil Simon, alas. Alas because the films he works on are among the most depressingly safe, commercially cozy films made. Simon is an industry, or a genre, so successful that he has not had to alter or stretch his theatrical attitudes or exceed the veiled banter that passes for emotional seriousness. The limits of Simon as a screenwriter were made clear in the BBC-TV presentations of Fredric Raphael's *The Glittering Prizes* and Alan Ayckbourn's *The Norman Conquests*. Their interplay of wit and real life, style and experience, farce and pain, revealed all the devices that cushion Simon against raw feelings. His people are always dialogue-smart. The singular shortage of good movie comedy—and I include Woody Allen —is the result of too many writers who seem driven by the medium and by the fear of upsetting audiences into movie conventions and away from experience. Perhaps they have simply not had enough experience.

Among writers who have not directed, or dominated a film like Chayefsky and Simon, we should note William Goldman. His credits include *Butch Cassidy and the Sundance Kid*—a crucial mixture of western genre and hip humor, apparently sufficient to crush the western—*The Great Waldo Pepper, All the President's Men* (a sly rendering of political mess as tidy *film noir*), *Marathon Man, A Bridge Too Far,* and *Magic.* There could be a prize for anyone discerning character there. Alvin Sargent has a worthier body of films to illustrate his skill and human sympathy: *The Stalking Moon, I Walk the Line, The Effects of Gamma Rays on Man-in-the-Moon Marigolds, Love, Pain and the Whole Damn Thing, Paper Moon, Bobby Deerfield,* and *Julia.*

But probably the most respected among other writers is Robert Towne. He has been out of sight since *Chinatown,* apparently working on a project about the infancy of Tarzan —literally being brought up by apes. Before that, Towne had several credits for scripts as economical and atmospheric as that for *Chinatown.* In addition, he was prized as the best script doctor in town. In that capacity he worked extensively on *Bonnie and Clyde* and *The Godfather;* among other things, he wrote the final conversation between Brando and Al Pacino. He also completely revised the script Schrader had written for *The Yakuza,* shared credit with Warren Beatty on *Shampoo,* and wrote Hal Ashby's *The Last Detail.*

Towne's prestige does not appear to have inflated his very practical sense of how a writer on an American movie must endure rewrites in the process of collaboration and compromise. Towne argued with Roman Polanski over changes in *Chinatown.* No one can say who was right, but Towne acknowledges the decisive weight of responsibility and power that rests with the director. Like any writer, he knows that sometimes directors get the credit for things the writer invented. But, unlike Vidal, he doesn't sulk over that fact of life or construct a theory whereby movies could dispense with directors.

I don't know if it's true of any other kind of writing, but screenwriting has two levels, really. One is when you're initially working on the script, doing it in isolation, away from all the mechanics of the making of the movie, the presence of the actors, the production problems. Then you finish and bring it into the real world, the real-phony world which is the movie world. That's a whole different process, and I think you've got to be schizophrenic about it. At one point you're more or less the creator, and then you're part of the group of people who are trying to bring something to life. It's difficult to make the distinction sometimes, but not all that difficult if you're working with people you trust and really care for. Then it can be very exciting.[9]

The writer in that situation is yielding his or her integrity (along with the loneliness), and if Towne is an outstanding example among Hollywood writers, then he does seem to rate craft, conceptual vividness, and on-screen workability above everything else. That is one way of saying that the American movie has not risked narrative structure in the last twenty years. The needs of the market, especially the pressure to be understood quickly, have restricted new possibilities.

In Europe in the same period, the films of Jacques Rivette have encouraged a process of rehearsal and improvisation in which the players become the writers. Rivette has also broken through the supposed time limits and suspenseful rhythms of the feature film. His best pictures have been about fiction, duration, and coincidence, not just machines for selling stories with handy meanings.

Jean-Luc Godard is another of the most radically innovative "writers" of modern film, partly because he so rarely had anything resembling a script. He wrote with the camera and

the dialectic of editing. In *The Discreet Charm of the Bourgeoisie* and *That Obscure Object of Desire*, Luis Buñuel and
Jean-Claude Carrière composed films that were satires upon
the well-made film and profound celebrations of the clandestine shapes in life and dreams. Eric Rohmer actually
wrote a series of novellas and then went on to film them.
Hans-Jürgen Syberberg, with *Our Hitler*, discovered a teeming collage of fact and legend that makes every modern
American picture seem old-fashioned.

Continental practice suggests that either the director must
be the writer, or that the film can emerge from a new spirit
of group enterprise. In America, too, we can see the roles of
writer and director falling to the same person. But the
Rivette approach—of liberty allowed to the actors and of the
film being less a refined, finished toy than an "attempt" at
film—has been tried in America only by Robert Altman. On
Nashville Joan Tewkesbury's script was the springboard for
the actors' work on their parts. Many more hours were shot
and edited than were ever released. Equally, Tewkesbury
had written lives for the characters that never showed on film
but which helped inform the performances. In her introduction to the published script—actually the cutting continuity
—Tewkesbury gave this defense of the elements of any film
that are a matter of theatrical experience above and beyond
literary comprehension:

> *As you read the screenplay, remember this was writ-
> ten for a visual medium capable of giving assorted in-
> formation to our perceptions on so many levels and in
> so many layers that we can't systematically record it.
> With that in mind, all you need to do is add yourself as
> the twenty-fifth character and know that whatever you
> think about the film is right, even if you think the film
> is wrong.*[10]

It was more than twenty years ago that Nicholas Ray said
that if everything had really been in the script then there was

no need to make the film. *Nashville* in script form is a dull read; as a film, it is hectic, confusing, random, musical, creative, and an affirmation of the ordinary. But film tends to make everything extraordinary, and scripts are already tributes to the value of system. American movies have rated the sensational, organized image above ordinary experience—commerce has ordained this more than the minds of the filmmakers. As a result, we have imbibed as an ideology a set of dramatic subjects and a totally dramatic context that need not be exclusive. Film itself writes, with or without authors, with or without concepts or subjects. Film is a process, a sequential observation, more sensitive to time and change than susceptible to literary coherence. Large box-office movies show no sign of adapting to that, and they may find themselves farther and farther behind the sensibility of the times. It is a glum epitaph for the seventies that Antonioni's *The Passenger*, despite Jack Nicholson and Maria Schneider and an adequate thriller thread, was a flop.

Film offends and disappoints our best writers and people who believe in literature. But that is because of its banal efforts to ape the novel, the play, or the essay. It cannot match writing's ability to struggle with ideas, complex feelings, or moral distinctions. But film is an atmosphere, a presence, and a deceit that reaches millions and affects them in ways they hardly notice. It is like air. The future is in films that write in that atmosphere. English director Nicolas Roeg sees this task and opportunity, and it is one that will erase the distinction between writer and director:

> *I believe film is an art. I believe it, I truly believe that. Thought can be transferred by the juxtaposition of images, and you mustn't be afraid of the audience not understanding. You can say things visually, immediately, and that's where film, I believe, is going. It's not a pictorial example of a published work. It's a transference of thought.*[11]

6

Lies Allowed

I have lived in L.A. all of my life. No, not all of it. Whenever I lie, I'll tell you. That's only proper if lies are going to be allowed.

The idea of Los Angeles has always intimidated me. Perhaps I honored the city as the Oz beaming out all the daydreams of my childhood, and did not want to explain or dispel them. Did I think once that L.A. was a mountain, a lion, a globe, an eagle on a rock, searchlights on an obelisk, a radio beacon, and the letters WB made into a shield? Fantasies rely on the absence of verification, and L.A. knows it could be a shabby hell without its aura of wondering. Who has gone there without having to acquiesce in the mystique? So every newcomer contributes to the reputation. "It's too big for a city," inhabitants sigh, inferring that it must be a state of mind. That is how "space" means so many things in L.A. and why mystical journeys are respected as much as a weekend in Maui or going over to the Valley for *sushi*.

The plane going there does not seem drawn by the force of enchantment, even if the airline speaks of the friendly skies. But how many people on scheduled flights can explain what is keeping the ponderous entity in the air? Flying there begins to furnish L.A.'s character. Going west across America, there are two thousand miles of evidently occupied land. Then the turmoil of mountains, where the ground's disorder speaks through the quilt of snow. And then the desert—like Antonioni's *Zabriskie Point*, the model of deserted land. Does it require a European to appreciate L.A.'s relationship with that pink-ocher wasteland, scratched with the trails of exhausted insects? It looks as if no city could survive there. You remember Death Valley, von Stroheim's *Greed*, and the futility of gold in that roasted wilderness.

L.A. materializes after two hours of this desolation. There it is, a metropolis, for sure—a dense stubble by day and spilled glitter at night. But between the straight line of peacock sea and the desert, L.A. looks isolated and arbitrary from the air. As the plane sinks, and my ears flutter with metamorphosis, I cannot shake the feeling that L.A. is somehow removed from nature, unreachable except in one of these flying machines, the invention of which approximately coincided with the trick that turned L.A. from a village into a city, with the pioneering of movies, the theories of relativity, and Freud's *Interpretation of Dreams*.

From the balconies of the Chateau Marmont on Sunset Boulevard, a hotel that prides itself on being a link with the old Hollywood, you can look up at the mauve crests of hills, rough rock with scrub covering. North of Sunset the land rears up steeply, and you feel the instability of its geology. Could fire, snakes, or Mansons help from spilling over the dry slopes?

These hills to the north are for beasts to hide in. They say there are deer there and coyotes, and there is also Bel-Air, an estate for the very rich. Their houses are couched in the slopes, held firm by the vines and creepers of the golden years when it was routine to remake the ground. There are tourist maps of Bel-Air, and anyone can prowl around its narrow, serpentine glens and lanes, checking off the homes of stars. No one but gardeners ever seems at home; there is never a sign of lived-in untidiness, a car door left open overnight or a body collecting dew on the lawn. Just as the houses are often hard to see, so one wonders if they are not deliberately elusive "homes" for the visitor's camera, not lived in but official residences.

Higher up, the hills are as crumbly as cake. There are slopes where lions seem to have clawed at the ground. Many houses sit on stilts or are wedged into escarpments. Great rains sometimes loosen them, and fires can pour over ridges like soda pop. The backbone of the hills is Mulholland Drive, a winding road with dangerous drives falling away to concealed houses. You must infer wealth from the cars you pass on the road, or from the discreet security systems as common as mailboxes. You can hear tales that rock stars live within a stone's throw, and you can pass this weird mock château or that inexplicably accurate example of the Japanese style, wondering if this is the dead end where Bugsy Siegel may once have lived.

Old photographs show how recently L.A. was a coalescence of villages in the midst of country. No matter that it is so modern, it feels as old and secretive as a Spanish city. Many of the styles on view are Spanish, and many of the people on the streets are Mexican. But it is especially Spanish that in the open, people make a *paseo* of a stroll, while houses are hidden. Movies play with great light and merciful dark, and a similar pattern of display and secrecy affects the city.

When I first flew to L.A. by night, I read a star biography: *Ladd: The Life, the Legend, the Legacy of Alan Ladd*—so much slimmer than its title—by Beverly Linet. It is a bad book, but part of its failure is a result of that chiaroscuro life-style, of being a star and being something else in the dark.

Alan Ladd grew up in the San Fernando Valley, having to walk several miles to school, and married a native of L.A. They had a son, Alan Ladd, Jr., until recently the head of Twentieth Century-Fox. The elder Ladd was a bit-part player for years: He is even in *Citizen Kane*, with a few words to utter from the shadows in that unexpectedly deep voice. His career only found momentum when an agent, Sue Carol, heard him on radio. She liked the voice and was struck again to discover that a dapper blond athlete went with it. She fought for his stardom and married him after he had got out of the first marriage.

Ladd had ten flawless years at Paramount and the box office; but he was seldom proud of his films. He got 5,000 fan letters a week and remained nervous of personal appearances lest people laugh at his height—something boosted on-screen with boxes for him or trenches for the actresses he had to kiss. He believed he was nothing as an actor, and he longed for good directors and worthwhile parts. He had children by Sue (one, David, is the husband of Cheryl Ladd), but publicity's white lies kept Alan Jr. out of any magazine portraits. The first marriage was never referred to, and the antagonism of fame and deceit made Ladd's face disconsolate. It helped in *Shane*, in which he nursed a silent load that explained why he had come out of the hills and would have to ride on again. *Shane* is a very L.A. movie in that it deals in the glamour of rootlessness, the poetry of being footloose and fancy-free. California still receives more migrants than any other state, and L.A. has more recesses, fantasies, and escapes for them if jobs fail to settle them.

At the end of his life Ladd drank heavily, languished in his second marriage, and apparently tried to kill himself. His is not the sharpest tragedy among stars, but even this cursory book conveys the wretchedness after stardom betrayed him. All that elegant menace enclosed his own sense of failure. How much he wanted to be a hero in pictures. How much he had sacrificed. Beverly Linet met him just before he died and asked him what he would have changed in his life.

"Everything," answered Ladd—it is the yearning of L.A.[1] that everything might be altered, and nothing is implacable. And yet Ladd was a man who had already made the journey from a twenty-dollar-a-week bungalow-court apartment to a magnificent ranch in Hidden Valley and a mansion in the Holmby Hills.

He spent his life in a city that has so many neighborhoods and so little sense of center. There is a downtown to Los Angeles, one scrappy cluster of towers. It could be a middling city in a midwestern state, a business district hemmed in by freeways. But downtown L.A. is ten miles from the sea, and just about everyone involved in pictures lives to the west of the alleged center. As a result, downtown is just one more locality, but one many Angelenos do not see. If you live in Santa Monica, Malibu, Beverly Hills, Westwood, or Hollywood, you might pass downtown on your way to Dodger Stadium but never enter it. The only means of travel located there are the bus station and the railroad. The bus station is a notorious danger spot, but the Spanish wonders of Union Station are unknown to many people who live in the city.

In fact, downtown is on the edge of areas where many Angelenos would not go—the barrios and east Los Angeles. At night, the downtown area is littered with drunks and derelicts, and if you are driving to explore, you can find yourself suddenly in streets that are empty and badly lit. The proximity of this harsh, threatening section is an assertion of how little L.A. wants a center. It is a gathering of villages, suburbs, and neighborhoods, as provincial as the city that was once arranged around the city-state studio headquarters.

The city's instinctive stance is to look toward the ocean with its back to downtown. All the great boulevards—Sunset, Hollywood, Wilshire—run east to west, the numbers getting into five figures as they near the sea. That series of horizontals is etched in by the steep hills to the north and the white landmarks along the ridge: the Griffith Park planetarium, the HOLLYWOOD sign, UCLA, and the Getty Museum. Of course, the megalopolis stretches much farther. There is urban complex a hundred miles east of the ocean, out as far as San Bernardino. Only then, but abruptly, do forest, mountain, and desert set in. There are layers of suburbs to the south as far as Long Beach, Anaheim, and Newport Beach, and there is sprawl all the way to San Diego. Beyond the northern hills, the San Fernando Valley takes over. But in the middle of all that, bounded by the Pacific, by the Santa Monica Mountains, by downtown, and by the Santa Monica Freeway to the south—that is the area that Angelenos think of as theirs.

The sea is vital and more than geography. On the map the coast is curved, but in practice it seems like a straight line, a promise of emptiness seen at the ends of all the streets going west. There are miles of hard, sandy beaches, nearly all free and safe. The breeze helps the western end of L.A., but the idea of the edge of the world refreshes and maybe deludes everyone. You can comprehend the dreadful threat of Japan in 1941 when you reckon that that shore was deemed so safe.

The city has always used the beaches, but in recent years their role as playground has intensified. To look at Venice Beach, you could believe that a Disney or a Selznick was its impresario. The action that has sprung up there is citizen theater; the beach, its surfing and its suntan, is the least attraction. There are roller skating courses. There is the enclave of Muscle Beach, where men and women push weights toward the sun and rub oil on their bodies. And there is the promenade, where, for a couple of miles, you can dip in and out of stalls and cafés, watching and being part of a parade of performers.

They are not professionals. Venice Beach is haven for all the people who have never made it in pictures but who can attract attention because of their clothes, their bodies, their deft sensual movements at roller disco, their outrageous stunts. There, as you watch—would I lie?—a mime show parts to admit a black woman, tall on skates. She wears a tiny rose bikini, and her eggplant body shines with lotion. Her feet and shins are oddly encumbered with the strutting boots that go with skates. She is playing a guitar, and she wears heavy earphones with stereo cassette players. The mime show goes on, two clockwork dolls. I doubt if there is another place in America where the races mix so easily unless it is in the professional theater. And that's the clue. For somehow, without design or script, the people who go to Venice Beach have seen that they are a show.

If you are visiting L.A., the beach is a cheering contrast to the great hotels. They are citadels of privilege and glamour, and their task is to provide comfort and insecurity: It is a measure of your status which commodity you respond to.

The Beverly Wilshire is one of several excellent hotels in town. It has an original building on Wilshire Boulevard, with red awnings and flags nuzzling the tops of specially planted trees. But an annex has been added recently, lower down on Rodeo Drive. This has permitted a road to pass between the two parts of the hotel. If you are staying there, you drive into a canopied, cobbled yard, and a valet will take your car to the underground garage. The valets are nimble agents for the dream, freeing you from parking. In the days before Christmas, the hotel arranges for artificial snow to fall in this driveway.

If you hang around, you will think you see everyone in an afternoon. Lee Marvin? Or does Marvin have a look-alike he sends out to divert attention? Would look-alikes and doubles qualify for a portion of earnings after separation? Do you see how the law is adapting to this city's shuffling of personality? The question of integrity hangs over an industry that uses stand-ins for long shots, and keeps picture and sound in separate cans.

Hollywood hotels are awash with celebrity. The Beverly Wilshire protects the really illustrious. No one pesters Marvin; he doesn't look like an easy autograph. But just because everyone is so alert, you and I can stroll through the mirrored lobbies, attracting our own quick darts of suspicion— it is the principle found on Hollywood Boulevard, where the sidewalks are measured out by star plaques set in the paving stones. Every second star has a show-biz name on it; but every other star is empty and available for you and me. Some walk that street gleefully trampling everybody from Fred Astaire to Adolph Zukor. Others step from one clean star to another, sure they deserve them.

I am talking about walking, a subversive activity in L.A. The city is so far-flung that no one has questioned the need for cars. There is no subway, but there are rumors of a bus system. I asked at a restaurant about a bus working La Cienega Boulevard. "I never use the buses, sir," the manager replied coldly—if he'd known about my nasty leanings, he'd never have seated me. But such a bus exists. In 1980 it's a sixty-cent journey made with blacks and elderly whites. Still, the industry goes by car, and visitors are expected to hire a car, one that can be bumped, left, or ground down without remorse.

Do you want to live in L.A. and work for the movies? The question dogs me and most of the people I see in the city. One day I learned that Orson Welles was working around the corner, jammed in a cutting room with assistants he sent out to fetch cigars and meals. I could have pinned him down to five or six buildings, and then gone through them like a health inspector. But the chance of meeting the man I most admire was daunting. Rescuing news comes that he has gone to Vegas—it's easier to believe in a magical transformation than in any available airline. That is a fantasy inaugurated by L.A.'s most characteristic artist, Howard Hughes, who eclipsed being with uncertainty. No influence is stronger in Welles's work than the shadow of Hughes: It is there in *Kane, Mr. Arkadin,* and *F for Fake.*

The last film is such a derisive evaluation of cinema that it debunks the need for earnest critics. Movies are séances: If they have been participated in, is there room for rational commentary? *New West* had an article on the awkward position of film critics who are really anxious to make movies. It alleged several close contacts between critics and filmmakers that would seem to compromise praise or attack.

The focuses of the story were James Toback and Pauline Kael. Ms. Kael had recently taken an indefinite leave of absence from *The New Yorker* to produce for Warren Beatty and to develop script material. She had known Toback for some time and reviewed his debut, *Fingers*, with qualified enthusiasm. So Toback and Kael found themselves on different floors of the Beverly Wilshire, trying to cast *Love and Money*, his next film.

I have seen Pauline Kael at her home in Massachusetts, and I wondered how much the new world would aggravate her. Her house in the Berkshires is a series of unusual spaces flowing together with a definite program of working and being alone. Could she live for long in the Beverly Wilshire, and could her zealous sincerity endure all the changes in direction that Toback's subjunctive soul accepts? Kael would dream a film, and want it exactly so. But Toback is closer to the impermanence of films and L.A. No casting possibility shocks him as much as it might her, because he knows the screen will confer authority on the dream. He guesses that films are not authored in the way critics like to believe. They become the trips of the audience, just like a freeway drive.

That is why L.A. is still the nerve center of the movies. For most people—for Pauline Kael and Alan Ladd—movies are the means of change, the gamble that has crowded California. I do not mean that you have to believe yourself capable of starring in pictures. It is enough that you can see them and participate in their rapturous escapism. If America ever welcomed outcasts, then movies would be the creed of the country and L.A., the site of the religion. L.A.—Lies Allowed: And so Samuel Goldfish could become Sam Goldwyn, and Archibald Leach could dissolve to Cary Grant.

"Soon to be a Major Motion Picture," the city says everywhere, and "soon" is the key word, as uplifting as the rattle of the ball on a roulette wheel.

It sounds like an imaginary place, but only because I want it that way. City Hall or the Police Department could describe a city of mundane realities. I have felt that likelihood myself walking west along the drab, factual wreck of Washington Boulevard, which could be any street between New Jersey and Detroit.

But then the street crosses an open culvert, the size of a canal, and you can see the causeway, the slick of greasy water, the flotsam of broken branches and supermarket detritus. Is it the culvert from *Point Blank*, where money could be delivered and assassinations quietly performed? "It's just a sewer," reason claims, but imagination prefers the tributary of the Styx. Lies Allowed encourages the mania for inner meanings. So many of the buildings have glass walls to ease that vision. The largest metropolis in California is a mirage in which cement and stucco are as flexible and impermanent as studio sets. It is Fritz Lang's *Metropolis* and the universe conjured up by Dungeons and Dragons.

But the exotic underworld still lurks beneath real space and lives which must try to distinguish between the creativity of fiction and the havoc of irrationality. Throughout this book I reproach myself for being captivated by the moving image. A part of me wishes that there had been no photography, no film, no television. But I am moved by the energy in fiction. American movies may harness that too rarely, but they have entertained me all my life. Is it insane to live and work in that mode while still urging caution?

Reality and imagination are not separate forces in our lives. They haunt and mimic one another, and properly so. Our most debilitating condition would be if either one overpowered the other. But if we must live paranoid, or in the discord of two ways of understanding, then we must expect extremes of dismay and exhilaration as the struggle goes on.

The L.A. I feel is a labyrinth, with a blind master at its center, too intuitive to need to see. Even the argument that the city acquired that legend from the manufacturing of films is beyond proof or disproof. To write about such things is to advise lucidity, argument, and evidence. Yet the urge to write may come from an unwarranted conviction not far from pathology. Is it dishonest to argue over the nature of this compulsion? Is it especially irrelevant to describe L.A. rather than be there? The legacy of photography is that we no longer have to evaluate the world; it is enough to witness it. Photography erases complexity and analysis with the instant recording of a new language—appearance—which has no referential meaning.

But I have hopes for explanation and remedy . . . like any teacher, Paul Harvey or Charles Manson. In the late sixties, that invalid didact, Joan Didion, wrote a short article on the force of Howard Hughes, someone she had never met but who lived in her thoughts. In those days she lived near a building Hughes kept, locked and deserted, at 7000 Romaine, in "the underside of Hollywood, south of Sunset Boulevard, a middle-class slum of 'model studios' and warehouses and two-family bungalows." She meditated on the whereabouts of Hughes, his life or death. For his last twenty years, he had reached and kept to the territory of fiction so that without having to appear, he left people talking and thinking about him. He does seem like an example of happiness, but he had undertaken that pursuit more ruthlessly than most people.

"Why do we like these stories so?" Didion asked herself. "Why do we tell them over and over? Why have we made a folk hero of a man who is the antithesis of all our official heroes, a haunted millionaire out of the west, trailing a legend of desperation and power and white sneakers?" [2]

Her answer begins to allay my own fears at feeling haunted by conflict, for it clarifies the pact that sense and sensibility have to keep in the environs of L.A.:

> *We admire the Adlai Stevenson character, the rational man, the enlightened man, the man most dependent upon the potentially psychopathic mode of action. Among rich men, we officially admire Paul Mellon, a socially responsible inheritor in the European mold. There has always been that divergence between our official and our unofficial heroes. It is impossible to think of Howard Hughes without seeing the apparently bottomless gulf between what we say we want and what we do want, between what we officially admire and secretly desire, between, in the largest sense, the people we marry and the people we love. In a nation which increasingly appears to prize social virtues, Howard Hughes remains not merely antisocial but grandly, brilliantly, surpassingly asocial. He is the last private man, the dream we no longer admit.*[3]

7

The Mythology of Achievement

A story from the thirties, told by a "serious" writer lured to Hollywood from the East: He was a novelist or a playwright, and he was uncomfortable in Los Angeles. It was so much more thoroughly cut off in its heyday. The industry had gone west to get away from eastern monopolies, and the writer felt marooned by the four-day journey. But he had already picked up part of L.A.'s style, the entertaining cynicism—which may have sounded like self-denial in his memory when he dragged himself back to the Malibu bungalow that he always loathed. The sourness makes this story funny but deadly. The writer's nib was turned into a weapon against himself. You only hear it as an epitaph after you've stopped laughing.

"They bring you out here where you have to endure the monotony of the beach and sunshine." He told his story to a circle burnished with both those gifts of nature, but still proud to have a celebrated patio jester scold them. California's placid assent does more to damage the critic than ever a yes-man does to a tyrant. One day the critic wearies: Heartless agreement has made him ripe and dull, and so he sinks into suntan. This pale protester is still talking, though: "They take your work and cut all the life and personality out of it; they get you to collaborate with scoundrels and illiterates; you write lines that will be candies in the mouths of actresses stupefied with self-love; your command of structure is demolished by one brutal question, 'Does it play?'—in Oshkosh or Oxnard; you are told your irony is 'sick'; ambiguity is smoothed away by the happy ending; they expect you to say you like it out here, and to be cheerful and available; you are deprived of intelligent company, news, politics, the theater, music, good restaurants, sports teams disturbed at losing—and what do you get for all this? A small fortune."

"Count your money outside."—a line from *The Conversation.*

Another story, from the seventies. An actor gets a call from his agent:

"I have good news and bad news for you."

"Give me the good news first." (An easterner would probably take them in the reverse order.)

"You know that house on Copa de Oro? The one you've been after for the last year?"

"What about it?"

"I think they'll take one point two million dollars."

"That's sensational. I thought they wanted one point six million."

"They have difficulties."

"What's the bad news?"

"They want ten thousand dollars cash down."

"You're right, Mr. Thatcher. I did lose a million dollars last year. I expect to lose a million dollars this year. I expect to lose a million dollars next year. You know, Mr. Thatcher, at the rate of a million dollars a year . . . I'll have to close this place . . . in sixty years."—a line from *Citizen Kane.*

Toward the end of the seventies, film culture in America addressed itself with suspicious diligence to the business of Hollywood. The trade was booming, and a new wave of young people seemed to be enjoying its plenty. Movie magazines ran columns on deals and trade gossip. Perhaps for the first time, anyone interested in the art of the film began to examine the thrill of a contract's fine clauses. *American Film Now* by James Monaco and *The Movie Brats* by Michael Pye and Lynda Myles were based upon the sensible but fashionable view that film criticism had been neglecting the pressures which business—its excitement, its grapevine blooms, and its unscrupulousness—put upon the very movies that received such fond interpretation in the romantic light of the auteur theory. The word had been mounting in university film departments that it was all very well to be taught the ontology of the image or the semiotic analysis of *Young Mr. Lincoln,* but how does one get into an agent's office and grab him in a minute and a half?

If there was a radical energy in would-be filmmakers in the seventies it settled for the old show-biz game—Dungeons and Dragons. Instead of pursuing problematic subjects and new forms, it took on the epic task of "making it." Censorship was in retreat, so it was possible to kid yourself that the subjects were more bold. Films were longer, and that made it easier to hope that narrative was finding novel journeys. But the films were only slower, more brutal, and more alienated from experience. *Taxi Driver* has an ending that startles a viewer trained in the thirties. It mouths and sports a sexual violence possible only in the seventies. Yet it is more fully devoted to the dead-end fantasy of the marketable product than most films from earlier decades. Its bravura morbidness shows immaturity isolating itself in the terrible beauty of paranoia—a commodity that is the essence of photography and all its forms.

That mood may be a response to the ordeal that faces new talent in Hollywood. Suppose the writer or the potential director goes out there intent on doing original and personal work. The climate of achievement warns him how difficult it is to make anything, how few ever get any credit. His projects gradually imitate the films that are made and slip closer to the market. Between poverty and such lurid rewards, the young person's hopes imitate the chameleon. He can tell himself that a compromise now may be redeemed by a more honest film later. He persuades himself that "energy" is the true subject or "force" of America and its films, and so his hero becomes a killer. He begins to think of things people will finance instead of pictures he wants to make.

L.A. coaxes that insidious slippage. Paul Schrader wrote *Taxi Driver*, and made *Blue Collar*, *Hardcore*, and *American Gigolo*, all in L.A. Recently he announced that he was leaving the West Coast and would live in New York:

> *I've lived in Los Angeles for 12 years, and I can feel the level of my conversation slowly deteriorating. I've got to go back to the well . . . In L.A., you get so far away from real people that you stop thinking yourself. And I've just got to do some thinking.*
>
> *I've realized something about myself, which is that I've stopped thinking in terms of ideas and now think in terms of premises. For example, there was an item in one of the trade papers the other day about a new project at one of the studios: a black boxer on the skids whose career is saved once he's managed by a young white girl. And I said to myself: 'That's an interesting premise, I wish I'd thought of that.' Then I realized that it was nothing more than a twist on a remake—just a variation on* The Champ.

The discontent is a beginning. But its expression is so flatulent. Maybe anyone prepared to talk about "real people" or "the well" has yet to take the first steps in mature education. "Real people" sounds horribly like the "just folks" who stand around in Capra films. *Taxi Driver* and *Hardcore* suggest that Schrader's most damaging ignorance is of people altogether. His work is so much the projection of someone who has lived alone or in the dark, trusting that life is like the movies. Yet Schrader is an outstanding example of someone who made it, who went to L.A. and negotiated himself into six-figure fees for screenplays before he began to direct himself. His woeful realizations about L.A. still stop short of the way its practices shelter his naïveté. The diagnosis is still content to take a caption form. It is something a character in a film might say at the moment of disenchantment, giving up Faye Dunaway and Bel-Air for some wholesome girl back east. The man may teach school, or write books about iniquity in the West.

The books and the articles on the movie business have been as accurate and as useful as reconstructions of Napoleonic battles. You can trace the deployment and the decision, but there is no smell of cordite or any panic. All accounts are compromised by a set of problems that make the movie business the source of mythology rather than a subject that can be understood from reading company reports. The business, like the pictures, demands an instinct for spiritualism and image. There is still no better way to evoke the role of money in Hollywood than by telling stories—they at least honor the perpetual conflict between reality and imagination in the ideas and actions of the place. Word of mouth is the industry's own analysis of society: It clings to a gossip culture.

The business of pictures has never been businesslike: It is neurotic, theatrical, legendary, secretive, the proper subject of both criminal allegation and Babylonian dream, but not fixed or rational. When Twentieth Century-Fox previewed *Star Wars*, they were apprehensive about their product. It took the uninhibited enthusiasm of the critics they had invited to the preview to warn them of success. But within a day they had imperial plans for T-shirts, stunts, and toys to support their winner. For a few months George Lucas could have raised money to film Kant. The trembling exhilaration of gambling is everywhere.

Not many people work hard in Hollywood. Picture moguls have been long-lived as a breed. The local cult of health regimes guards against overdoing it. But they hope with an intensity unsurpassed anywhere else in the developed economies. They are not well organized or methodical—anyone who suspects that Hollywood cooks the books should first discover whether it ever learned to keep them. But their nervous system is so attuned to deals, double crosses, and magic packages that the unstinting energy for association transcends failures of planning. Terrible films that flopped at the box office are still revered today because of the grace of the deal that put them together. The ideal bringer of order now is the agent. His vision can survive creative failures. The need for immaculate conception is part of the lust for decorum.

There is a recurring shot in American films—a religious image—of someone opening a case neatly filled with wads of money.* The cucumber color is pleasing, and the uncountable amount is sweet, but it's the tidiness that is most satisfying. Cash itself is recognized as less potent or real than the aphrodisiac attribution of money. It is more important to have the rumor spread of what you have been paid than actually to be paid for that amount. For a week in L.A., the city shook deliciously on hearing that Bo Derek—$25,000 and a supporting part in *10*, but central to the promotion of that moderate hit—had been offered $1,000,000 for another film. There was a huge billboard on Sunset Boulevard on which the cardboard figure of Dudley Moore swung like a pendulum across the continental body of Bo. No such scene is even hinted at in the film—which encouraged those people who believe in advertising as a creative art. You cannot understand the faith in money simply by tracking down the figures and the amounts. But you cannot quite grasp a film unless you appreciate the force of the faith for anyone who makes or wants to make them. The inscription "Soon to be

---

* In February, 1981, Frank Sinatra was being examined by the Nevada Gaming Control Board. He was asked about the folklore that he had once carried an attaché case holding $2 million to Lucky Luciano in Havana. To which he replied: "If you could find me an attaché case that can carry $2 million, I'll give you $2 million."

a Major Motion Picture"—on books, lavatory walls, or bod-ies—invariably notes two things: that a picture is being made, but that it will only assume full life and power when it is released and when it becomes major. Minor motion pictures are certainly less desirable than skin disease. There are peo-ple in L.A. for whom the only pictures that exist are those in their first weekend of release—the moment of majorness. In November, 1979, I heard misgivings in L.A. about the $40 million *Star Trek*; but on the first day of its release, a Friday in December, I saw people being turned away from a full house at a small New Hampshire mall theater. That's all the prophets need to know, and some of them never bother to see the picture. Word of mouth is the wisdom of the money superstition. No picture had ever had a better opening weekend than *Star Trek*.

One large embarrassment about the books on the film business is that their authors would like to be part of that business themselves. Their historical sense, their investiga-tive perseverance, and their stamina with awkward discov-eries are already colored by their wish to make great films and earn a fortune doing it. The small fortune is a thing of the past. Today you have to be negotiable to lease a condo-minium. Hollywood is so treacherous an illusion because it says great movies and big hits can be accomplished at the same time. In the end its cultural legacy has been to blur creativity and success in the gelatinous haze of L.A.

Monaco, Pye and Myles, and I, too, always want the film to be as good as any other art might be. It burns us to learn that the system producing them has the baldest sense of what quality is. We look away from evidence that movie-makers will veer from one dumb novelty to another in the panic to feed the public's fickle tastes. The books observe the same circumstances: the end of studio empires in which the major companies produced and distributed films and had artists under contract; the dismal decline in the quantity of films made, from around 700 to under 200 a year; the daunting increase in budgets (*Citizen Kane* in its entirety cost two thirds of what Bo Derek can ask),* and the greater dependence for fiscal viability on a very few pictures, helplessly expensive and necessarily generalized in their subjects and their demands on the public. The books see the same newcomers taking over the business: the corporate structures of Gulf & Western, Transamerica, and MCA treating Paramount, United Artists, and Universal as subsidiaries; the clutch of agents, lawyers, and accountants who have gone from being service men to power brokers; and the generation of "movie brats," film-school kids who have managed to direct films.

You can be cheerful or foreboding about the shift in the landscape. It is easier to be encouraged, though, if you see the high flight of George Lucas as proof that *you* might soon be making a major motion picture yourself. After all, the more jaundiced could respond, if a deft, mindlessly happy kid can get so far and have two movies in the top ten of all-time box-office grossers, as well as a personal fortune of over $2 million for every year of his tender life, why then, surely you could do it, too.

I should declare an interest, or rather an experience, for the very lack of concern or interest is what made the experience depressing. The largest check I have ever received in my life came from one of the most important agencies in Hollywood for a screenplay that will never be made. Looking back on it, I suspect that the chances of it being made were always tenuous compared with the business angles it opened up beyond my vision. There may have been a week, or a half hour, when I was "sexy" in someone's mind—someone else had talked about me, and susceptibility to rumor did the rest. That let me become the beneficiary of a lavish gesture, so long as I took care not to believe in the screenplay. "Learn not to care" is industry advice when so many

* Yet technically watchable films are still made in other parts of the world for one fifth of what *Citizen Kane* cost in 1941.

certain bets are only old press releases. It is another reason for cynicism, for no one does too much without the saving writeoff, "I never thought it would happen." I cannot guess at the network of fantasies and hunches in which I was briefly a part. But I have seen them mislead others. What was a large sum for me was a trivial amount in the business, and since the most urgent currency is belief and only large fees inspire great faith, it was always likely that this scheme would trail away to be reassessed as loss or expense in another part of the accounting forest.

I do not intend to be bitter, or to stop trying. Without proven credentials, I was given the encouragement to write something that might be filmed. Untried talent can now worm its way into the business, it is so full of holes. The seventies were marked by the career explosions of newcomers, and hysteria has only made the industry hope for a quicker crackle of fresh artillery. Newcomers are better for word of mouth. No one knows of a track record to challenge the immense claims. The greatest deals involve beginners, for they appear out of nothing. Among directors, studio heads, agents, and writers, it is rarer to find people over the age of forty. You must get used to meeting potentates younger than thirty-five. You could become sentimental about this if you felt that the emerging pictures were worthy. But you may be more impressed by a panorama of celluloid dreams that unashamedly disclose immature experience. Sometimes a movie is thirty talking to twelve, unsure whether it is Svengali or downright envious. The craze for toy spinoffs, for posters and T-shirts, fits a generation of tycoons in sneakers.

Suppose that nearly every picture of the last decade has been overestimated in the surge of box office. You cannot adequately gauge the generosity of critics and teachers in their search for artist-heroes until you inhabit L.A. and feel the cult of youth in business. It is as if the aim now was to make movies that felt like trailers. Promotion budgets often rival production costs. A kind of inversion is at work: better that a movie's selling campaign be good, than that the movie be good itself. The worse the movie, the more scope there is for exaggeration and deception. The focus on deals fosters sharp practice. I am not talking about the few surfacing scandals, the David Begelman affair, or the everyday abuses in blind bidding and cost rigging. They are not very different from the devices that Hollywood has always used. But they do mark a trade in which the coup of selling at least equals the art and craft of manufacture. Hollywood trusts deviousness and is the foundation of modern advertising. *Citizen Kane*, forty years ago, felt that reckless excitement and could not repudiate the charming manipulativeness of its hero. Kane guessed that the weight of headline indicated the state of the news. He excused a line of business that would prefer to succeed with palpable junk. Making a hit out of *The Deep* is more admired in L.A. than managing reasonably with a difficult picture.

Business is profiteering. It adjusts quality to dividends. It evolves its own bureaucracy and its own morality, and it knows enough Darwin to foster unhindered competitiveness among its employees. But if we give way to the hope that a business might also be capable of serving what we think of as art, a rich stream of communication, social change, or a heightened sense of being, then we are victims of a damaging fallacy and of people in Hollywood who have never been tempted by it.

I want to test one area of the fallacy. It seems localized, but it should prove an excellent guide to the limitations of the system as a whole and a warning about the pervasive threat of Hollywood thinking in America. It seems to be a theme or preoccupation in certain pictures, almost a condition of the American dream—like credit cards or blue cheese dressing—but it is a direct consequence of the business ideology. American movies have always consoled the people who ran the industry.

Let me call it the mythology of achievement. It draws a

broad parallel between the hopes of Americans and the dynamic of many movies. America was so recently the second chance for failures, refugees, or the disadvantaged that the schematic pattern takes the breath away and replaces it with the posed struggle of a game. So many American cities resemble Monopoly, with numbered grids. L.A. is only the most fanciful, catering to all those immigrants; the city where structure, geography, and atmosphere seem devoted to the transformation that will save all blighted lives. Once at Universal, a man moved into an office, got himself a desk, a sign that said "manager," and a say in making or breaking pictures before the company realized that no one had ever hired him. He was David Selznick's father, blown in with the wind. Alexander Korda's strategy for Hollywood was to arrive, establish a base in a hotel you can't afford, eat out at restaurants that are too expensive, overextend yourself as flamboyantly as possible, and wait for offers.

America has worked as it has, a brittle but compulsive socioeconomic miracle, because in real terms the lives of enough immigrants were remade, while in the mirage of wistful futures, enough reckoned that theirs, too, *might* make it. But the cultural stress on whether it all worked made progress, putting it together, or getting on, the most distinctive measure of America. Such newfound status breeds terror—the quickly gained may be lost at savage speed—and it equates well-being with materialism. The imaginative energy that had been restrained for so many generations could not be calmed or satisfied with such rapid worldly success. The hopes and dreads of the country flailed around, and still do. The American middle class is a bitter study in the tension between having "made it" and remaining uneasy. Very early in their industrial history, films saw the need to reassure fears that position could be lost if the unstable weather of America continued. No country advertises insurance so much, or so vividly. Thus, the rabid fantasizing of Hollywood pictures is part of their ideological conservatism. If anyone doubted this in silent movies, then the gangster pictures of 1930 onward were the clincher. They luxuriated in slaughter, the destruction of property, and the luster of outlaws, and they repeated the slack proprieties of law-abiding decency. "Don't enjoy this mayhem," they pretended to say, but "The world is yours" flashed a sign in *Scarface*—a masterpiece of sardonic contempt—and the people of America have struggled for fifty years not to notice the scorn that their most treasured medium holds for them.

The American movie was a demonstration of achievement, however demented and nihilist its tone. The happy ending might not always be counted on, but even the unhappy ending was conclusive. It accomplished the action and resolved problems that the film had set up. Never did a film trail away or end with the uncomfortable pregnancy of enigma. Harry Cohn said that when a film lost it, his arse started to itch, and so endings had to be as emollient as hemorrhoid relief. The shaping of films encouraged us to believe that the world shown in the dark and the world struggled with outside were different. It did not ask us to carry the line of thought formed in one over to another. Movies righteously labeled themselves as pap escapism. They proposed distraction in movie theaters. "It's only a movie," the industry shrugged to critics. But to itself it urged a care with the lifelike image that would make audiences believe in the pictures. The secret of the riddle was in making the fantasy so lifelike.

No one alive in America in this century can believe that the distinction was observed. People have been confused, not least the filmmakers, men like Martin Scorsese, who expect Charles Manson every time they enter a taxi. They have been stranded by an entertainment form that refuses any responsibility for the larger context, but which preys upon our need for gratification and resolution. Films promoted a dream in which human figures achieved things—love was defined as a state of social duty waiting to be occupied:

a desirable, well-built property with the structure as security and the pool an orgasm. Once in it, characters were left— happy, asleep, or inert. Achievement was all. Thus, wars or conflict on screen were to be won or lost, never explained or remedied. The political analysis of war and the human experience of love were discounted. They had to be if the conflict was to be uninhibitedly violent and the lovers put to sleep as the film ended. The Vietnam War is the most available example of an historical reality inflamed by the principle that action speaks louder than words. Similarly, the mind's hope of dealing with reality is bypassed by the slogan—thrown around in script conferences and advertising meetings—that a picture is worth a thousand words. To this day, divorce is admitted in about one in ten of the films that proscribe love, no matter that divorce affects half of our marriages and is testament to Americans' still vital and ingenious craving for metamorphosis.

I want to consider two films—unquestioned classics and preeminent box-office triumphs but more than thirty years apart—to show how far the achievement fought for in film stories mirrors the narrow search for accomplishment within the industry: *Gone With the Wind* and *The Godfather.*

David Selznick's 1939 picture is more convincingly the work of one man than Coppola's recent film. Indeed, Coppola was something of a gamble as director and was always obliged to observe the wishes and whims of Paramount, the production company. He claims that he made *Part II*, with more liberty, to redeem some of the concessions he had had to accept on *The Godfather. Gone With the Wind* may be a less adult, less socially accurate, less intelligent picture—it may be. But it is a flagrantly personal film. No one has really thought of Selznick as an artist, but he was clearly the auteur on *Gone With the Wind.*

He had his own company and enough money and support from his fellow directors to play his hunch. Selznick purchased the rights to Margaret Mitchell's novel. He went through writer after writer to find a script that would "play" without offending readers who expected a faithful translation of the book. He pursued his ideal cast, and he hired and fired directors as he needed them. If you read the memos, you know that no one knew more about the details of the film than Selznick. He built it piece by piece. He beseeched but he never trusted; and he had the energy to keep track of all the talents he had hired. The way he rode herd, the cattle turned sheepish. Just as no page of the script was without his alterations, so no scene of the film went against his browbeating vision of what it should be. And this determination grew naturally into obsession.

The film took longer to make than anyone expected, and it cost more. But no one could restrain or deter Selznick from that extravagance. The more prolonged the venture, the more clearly he was engaged in vindicating himself and not just proving the idea of *Gone With the Wind*. Had the picture failed, he would have been called to order and left with the debt. He would also have been mocked by a business which had humiliated his father, and which was led by Selznick's own father-in-law, Louis B. Mayer, whose crocodile tears were trained to drop with the force of acid. That only increased the drama of what Selznick relished as the greatest venture of his life. Making the giant project work —at four and a quarter million dollars and three and a half hours—became the crux of his being. Achievement has seldom been more on the balance with a film, and that is what makes for such an affinity between David O. Selznick and Scarlett O'Hara.

Margaret Mitchell's novel is called a romance. It is often described as a fantasy for female wish fulfillment. But it has more resonance than that, and the moving film has no equal as a form capable of carrying submerged symbology. *Gone With the Wind* was an entertainment of the thirties that traded on the comparison of two American ordeals—the Civil War and the Depression. Its deepest energy is less romantic than the longing to hold on to order, stability, land, home, and property despite a climate of danger and loss. There is love in the book and the movie, of course: glamorous but thwarted love stories to torment the audience's desire for contentment. (Love only works in a movie so long as it is blocked or withheld. Full sexual reward on screen has expelled love, and probably sacrificed most of the tension that was once so delicious.) But in the end, *Gone With the Wind* subordinates romance to achievement and even suggests that a woman is better advised working for property than twisting her heart. Like so many American movies, it entertains the daydream but guides the distraught imagination of the viewer back into solid things. Scarlett is rejected, and Rhett quits the house, but the house has been held on to, and Scarlett has proved herself as a businesswoman. The shrewdest fantasy appeal in the picture is to comfort viewers plunged into dull work that their romantic unhappiness or vacancy is honorable. The picture knows something every small boy writhes over—that movie love is silly compared with power and ownership. *Gone With the Wind* is the monument of a man who worked every hour he could. It may be sentimental and melodramatic, but we would be unfair to Selznick if we belittled the blazing statement of self that he suspected he would never match. Its passion grows out of working yourself to death to build a house, a kingdom, and a legend of achievement. It may not be art, but it is ego broadcast as entertainment and turning into money—and that is Hollywood. The pretending required of audiences only worked if it had first captivated the filmmakers.

Selznick's pretense may have been so heartfelt that he was never conscious of it. But no one doubts that Francis Ford Coppola measured the resemblance between himself and Michael Corleone. *The Godfather* is a meticulous allegory on the need for strong-willed genius in the young businessman. The defense of sacrifice is better articulated than it was in *Gone With the Wind*, and more cynical: The compromises required of a young filmmaker had become crueler in the years since 1939. Selznick had far fewer inhibitions about what he was doing, and there is more zest and energy in his picture than in *The Godfather*'s remorseless emphasis on self-pitying control. The catch phrase of *The Godfather*— "We'll make him an offer he can't refuse"—is Coppola's rueful acceptance of his own hard-pressed career need to make so delicate a project. Young filmmakers now joke brazenly about the deals they've made and the armorplating of commerce that weighs down their conception of a picture. They sneer at their own helplessness. One can only describe as chronic indecision the inability to clarify, comprehend, or challenge *The Godfather*'s pusillanimous endorsement of both the cinema's glorification of gangster violence and its habitual handling of underworld money. But the romantic pressure of *The Godfather*—that which makes us want Michael to prevail—was a ripening fruit in the selfhood of a director confronted with such a major project and so many obstacles to his authority. To be in charge, Coppola had to have a clearer vision of the movie than anyone else. He had to know exactly what he was doing. It is no less than the task facing Michael, who must impress the more seasoned members of the family with a drastic decisiveness that lets them know a new age is dawning.

Step back six inches, and Michael looks like a little boy pretending to be tough. But the movies always pull us *in* that six inches and so dominate us that we are hypnotized into missing the masquerades. Like any gangster bluff or scam, the trick relies on detailed preparation. The shooting of McCluskey and Solozzo over their dinner depends on stringent composition, a half hour of gradual gut-tightening, and the delicate surgery that can implant little gobbets of blood and plastic flesh so that they burst out and fall in the unfinished pasta. The "setup" in movie-making is an isolated moment in the screenplay that is treated with all the craft required of a corner in the blueprints for a new building. And this is where the pulse of achievement is always deep within a film, not just in its skeleton but its DNA; the American film has itself been the realization of a comprehensive plan. It looks like a theorem come to life, and that is what promotes the doctrine of material accomplishment.

We can trace this process in a way that shows how businesslike it is. The deal, the package, the project, today and at any time since the early 1920's, depend upon a script and the judgment of anyone reading it that it will work. It is as if a painter came to his patron or client before he began to work with a painting-by-numbers outline of his dream so that anyone could see what it was going to look like. Hitchcock prepared a script and a storyboard to fulfill that purpose exactly. It may be just because he had surrendered to the financial demands so fully that shooting itself bored him. But all scripts aspire to the clever, close-fitting fluency of a new plastic knee joint in the leg of a sportsman. They number their shots; they use a kind of engineer's code to describe them. They predict and require instants of spontaneity, spasms of chance, and lively animation in the filming.

The script is a mark of monetary nervousness. When budgets are so high and when so much hangs on a venture, it is against the nature of businessmen not to plan for any detail they can isolate. But that means that filmmakers back into a film with their eyes on a script, endeavoring to make the picture fit it. They are like nervous strangers in an unknown land, only anxious that the terrain fit the map so that they can believe they are safe. A script is a protection in the middle of the night if one suddenly doubts the whole enterprise, and it is a vehicle for carrying the blame if the picture does not work. "It was all in the script," you can say, leaving the listener to imagine the perverse way in which fate undid that carefulness.

Of course, explorers who go by the map at all times are seldom lost. They will generally reach where they had planned to go. But do they experience the wildness of the places no one else has seen, or are they like those camera-tourists of the twentieth century who spend so much time snapping the view from the indicated vantage that they have hardly been there themselves? Are their minds filled and changed with the beauty and mystery of remoteness? Apply the metaphor to film, and you may begin to understand the dauntingly premeditated air of American film, the scarcity of either the unexpected or the ordinary. Movies are so often made up of predictable but extraordinary events. Creatively that is of the highest importance, for one of the implicit duties of the medium (and one of its richest opportunities) is to let duration work or unfold with as little interference as possible.

In the mind of an American movie financier—and that is always the mind the movie brat is trying to imagine—that smacks of improvisation, risk, and a hole in his pocket. The novelist lets time write his novel, or he lets the difficulty of what he is attempting take its time and suffer his own pass-ing doubts. A filmmaker knows in advance that he must shoot in seven, thirty-one, or 109 days, or suffer penalty. You can regard that as a stimulating discipline, a test of the artist's power to cajole and urge his crew to do it his way in time. But the pace to be kept up with is so rigorous that it may be wiser not to take on difficulty. The script and the director's plan may decide in advance on the easier way out. Most directors know exactly how their work will end before they set out. They can look it up in the script. Very few novelists, painters, or composers have that limp advantage, or could endure it.

Does this sound like a small point? I hope not. It is re-sponsible for the signal lack of difficulty in American films, the thing that keeps them from being as complex and prob-lematic as the most demanding art, and which pushes them into the bloody, maudlin, cynical, and sweet extremes of filmmaking game plans. You will meet writers in L.A. who have great endings, brilliant beginnings, or single jokes that they are trying to work into full-length offerings. That is a way of creating that submits to the fragmentation of factory filmmaking. It is the insistence that every minute in a film should "work" that evades film's natural readiness for doubt. Draft scripts converge on their final, paralyzed tightness—a pleasing effect but not worth repeating—in response to objections like "It's not clear," "That doesn't play," "It's not strong enough," or "That's not right."

Many scripts will benefit from that nagging. It is a method that will produce neat, effective entertainments, taut suspense pictures, smashing impacts, lines that jab you with suitability, cuts that quicken the pace, a stream of action that never loses the viewer's nerve-racked confidence, a code for us all to connect with. There is virtue in that: No filmmaker could fail to learn from the well-made Hollywood picture, which was at its peak in the years 1935–1950. But a climate of such movies is oppressive, and the vaunted "new" Hollywood is abject and servile if it cannot look beyond the feeble need for tidiness or retrieve many of those technical skills that enabled tidiness to function. Today, despite the riot of special effects, the technical expertise of filmmaking is in decline.

The end of the studios has deprived us of the standing corps of technicians who knew exactly how to design, photograph, and compose music for the prescripted blueprint movie. Those men were no freer than mechanics in Detroit, but they had skill, experience, and pride. They created the look and the stylishness of the classical Hollywood film. It was lovely to look at, as easy on the eye as it was on white lies. In addition, it was so widespread and so hard to escape that it both caused and excused the great shortage of personal style. You can describe it in craft terms, which is only half an answer. All those craft skills were bent toward getting it "right": The plan was to be realized exactly—the script's outline put on film, on schedule, and under budget. Unswerving attention to rightness soon amounted to an ideology: The elimination of mistake bespoke the hope of an ultimate orderliness.

That culture of professionalism dominated our experience in several ways. No one said anything wrong or inaudibly in movies. A fluffed line was thrown away along with inadequate recordings. Every image was ideally lit and exposed, ideally in the sense of some feeling, mood, or action waiting to be illustrated. The look of films—happy or unhappy—was lustrous and paradise-like. The lights were arranged to produce a mood, and the camera's aperture was adjusted to the lights. Shots would be filmed again if an actor was a foot out of line so that the frontier shadow on his face did not fall exactly where it had been intended. People tiptoeing into unfamiliar rooms actually had white tape crosses on the floor for their peripheral vision and nervous feet to hit. After every take, the camera crew were asked, "Was it all right?" before the shot was deemed to be "in the can." This is the language and the mentality of tight-lipped banking.

Hitchcock, and many others, simply put their coinlike pieces of shot film in order, tightened, trimmed, and . . . refined. Editing can be an opportunity for creative appraisal. There are writers who throw out entire drafts; painters who burn early canvases. But the movie process cannot allow itself the creative danger of such adventurous, and demanding, thinking. It is a trimming operation, leaving less of what you had, but financially unable to jettison the most expensive things you filmed—the leading actress, the earthquake in Peru, the war, no matter that they all look trite. Hal Ashby was an editor before he was a director, and this heads-down admission shows the unavoidable servility of editing: "The first time you see your film cut together, you deal with what bothers you the most. You stop to edit in every scene on the way through. The next time you deal with what bothers you the next most. You refine it and refine it and refine it." And if your head is filled with such thoughts, you can believe you are Mondrian or Bach, not a sugar manufacturer.

The viewer is supplied with "rightness" in other things—the aura of the places where action occurs, the overall philosophy of casting, the appropriateness of atmospheric music breaking the silence. All those things conspire in the comfort and idealization of our experience. But the most forceful of all is the one that we can most easily fail to detect: composition, the way in which the medium perceives the action. For a stable camera can tell us that the most dreadful events are manageable.

Of course, you cannot film anything without framing it—and, as that word suggests, you cannot simply surround action without seeming to contain it. A great part of the authority and the coldness of film as a medium is in the grip that framing constitutes. But framing and composition—which are not exactly the same, though composition's exuberance increases with framing's determination—can work with degrees of discretion and domination. I cannot explore styles at the length they deserve, but the films of Altman, Renoir, Antonioni, Mizoguchi, Godard, Rivette, Rossellini (at least) have the subdued compositions of a withdrawn, tolerant, and open-minded camera, so that we can let our eyes roam and discover the elements and the contradictions in a shot. Just as briefly, Hollywood has always encouraged mannered camera angles and unique points of view, dogmatic, interpretative, and visually cute. *Citizen Kane*, the work of Hitchcock, and the general style of *film noir* are obvious illustrations of the tendency.

There are outsiders even in Hollywood. But the American system of making films has seldom doubted the expressive power of framing. That confidence has carried over into the way advertisements are photographed—still or moving. Desirability can so easily be assisted by framing that it is worth noting the apparent affinity between this visual acuity and commercial interests. It exists in fascist art, too, where brilliance of design cries out with the nobility of force.

The industrial pursuit of rightness is the heart of the mythology of achievement. When every shot strikes us with its accuracy, then the movie is already accumulating its need for targets and goals being reached. But it is a desperate earnestness, and it often discloses the insecurity of the interests involved in filmmaking, the terror of giving an audience something else, and the helpless acquiescence in their own inexperience of the young people who now make the major movies. Nothing has betrayed American film more than its horror of mistake, its mistrust of a movie experience that might transcend "rightness" or partake of something more complicated.

8

The Pied Piper of the Las Vegas Sahara

Ritual sacrifices mark the closing of seasons. A swoon of good will sighs from the television as summer ends, enough to bring steel leaves to the ground.

"Why is it called Labor Day, Daddy?"

"Well, son, that's the day Jerry Lewis goes to work."

Some such exchange occurs in American households, but work is hardly an adequate description. The telethon would not have lasted if it consisted of ordinary labor or regular charity. The curiosity has grown into an institution because of its freakishness. It is an orgy in which money and sentimentality thrash about together, just as rats and children change places in Browning's cool horror poem about Hamelin. We cannot tell whether the love and money invoked are friends or enemies—the orgy is too involved. But the spectacle is awesome and exhausting. It leaves us stripped and changed for fall. We hope and trust that it licenses "Jerry's kids" for another year.

This is not an attack on Jerry Lewis's integrity. It is an attempt to grapple with the escaping balloon of his performance on Labor Day. What does it say for our values? If ninety million people watch him for some portion of that day, then we are involved, not just bemused onlookers. Give us a festival or disaster, better still the two together, and we will huddle over the magical box. The one thing to top soap operas on daytime TV was the lies, revelations, and melodrama of the Ervin hearings in that summer of 1973. The ebb and flow of Jerry's energy, the spasms of pity and exultation on the program, and the haphazard way in which millions turn it on and off are like the traces TV leaves on our souls every other day of the year.

I do not question Lewis's persistent claim that he is not paid. But I am unnerved by the piety and anguish with which he brandishes his altruism. In 1978 he read a statement about his monetary cleanliness a few hours before the end of the telethon. Some hours earlier he had announced the coming of such a statement and warned us to be ready. We were being promised a communiqué from his inner soul, inadvertent proof that there were parts of him that were closed off from sight. The testament and its trailer were not just portentous. They were as vital to the dramatic shape of the telethon as the last hour's rush of money after the stagnant night and the cold morning. This was not an incidental squeezed into the schedule; it was like a crisis, a transfiguration, before the climax of the ceremony. It showed us the Jerry who wants to be a saint. As a drama, the program holds back the money deluge until after Jerry has taken his vows. He needs to establish his virtue before the national slot machine cascades.

There are religious glimmerings throughout the telethon. The Love Network is an electronic hot gospel sparked by soap opera passion. I had the odd luck of encountering it first in 1975 on the day after I had come to live in this country. Stunned by travel, I appreciated the shrewd focusing of the telethon on anyone already depressed or ill. The program's aim is health, but its tone is heavy with sickliness. It equates disease with flaw or guilt, especially in Jerry's challenge to the parents of sound children that they send along some protection money for a merciful fate. Not only the Las Vegas setting but Jerry's solemn threat—"I'll get you"—to potential sponsors made one think that after McDonald's, organized labor, and the Jaycees, a Godfather might arrive with a kiss for Jerry and a discreet donation. The program is styled after the thirties movies in which hoodlums collect pennies to get operations for blind children—so they can watch the movies.

I had treated the telethon in subsequent years as something to avoid, the best reason to get out into the sun. But in 1978 I submitted to it for most of fifteen hours. Early on in the show, I said to myself that I must be sick to be watching it. Its interweaving of hysteria and monotony seemed a revelation of television's raucous nature; it arouses fear and loathing, but it smothers the strength of will to resist. And now I see the program as one of the best guides to America any newcomer could ask for. The telethon's agony is the country's, for it depicts the remoteness of altruism and charity in a society as self-conscious and compromised as ours. Don't mock or deplore the twenty-two hours. Just marvel that so much is conveyed in so short a space.

I still know more about Jerry Lewis than I do about muscular dystrophy. The program does parade sufferings: There was one shuddering, gaunt man on film, scarcely able to hold up his head, who died two weeks after he was filmed. There are reports of the research paid for by the money collected. And there are poignant victims of the disease, notably the "poster child." But the explanation of the disease is sketchy—as if evil did not merit substance—and the experience of those who have the disease is not really attended to. The majority of screen time is filmed with bouncy people and sums of money as sterile as surgical tools. The action is positive and dynamic; the creeping total fights with the despond in Jerry's spirit. He is a surly depressive, but he goes manic at every fresh million. And he is only downcast sometimes because his great, flabby heart suffers more than most. The corporation men who file before him with checks, the college kids who had rolled beer kegs across Iowa, the firemen whose boots are filled with dimes—they are all worthy but dowdy soldiers in a fight that has this goal: one dollar more than last year. "That will satisfy me," the domineering Jerry concedes, infatuated with progress and the insane vision of an entirely healthy, undying society.

It is easy to think that breaking the record will absolve us, too. The blitz of a twenty-two-hour appeal seems to guarantee a year's supply of concern, weapons to hold off the serpent disease, and the virtual gathering of all diseases in MD. At one point the freewheeling Jerry, tottering through words with the giddy momentum of fatigue, said, "It's like cancer"—he heard his own words—"and that's another thing we've got to deal with." It was a weird reminder. His desperation had suggested a one-on-one confrontation—Jerry versus MD—that embraced every other struggle. It made his ownership of the blighted children seem much odder. Does every saint have his team? Why should one disease monopolize Labor Day? Why doesn't every cause have its twenty-two hours? Why only twenty-two hours? Is late money counted, or is it called for ineligible receiving? And why the Jerry Lewis telethon? Would we abide by the Jerry Lewis Superbowl? The Jerry Lewis moon landing? The Jerry Lewis House Select Committee on Assassinations?

I am not just adding to the criticism that the telethon has swollen as Jerry's career has dwindled. The telethon seems to me his greatest twenty-two hours, the purest strain of what has always been a garish and turbulent personality. It is the outpouring of a soft-hearted tyrant and a cunning simpleton; it is admirable and nauseating at the same time— but Jerry has always unloaded his confusion on the audience.

For the best part of twenty years he was a comic idiot— first as a contrast to the cool, sleepy Dean Martin, and then as the speeding jerk in films he directed himself. In the fifties he was often called "spastic" or "demented": He gibbered, he moved as if with impaired control, and he behaved on screen with a self-righteous lack of adult reason. His screen character came as close to retardation as film has ever ventured. Jerry could have been an aberrant or a robot with

faulty wiring. Some people were offended even then, but
the saving framework of comedy helped him get away with it.
We know now how calculated the stammering wreck in a
grown body was. Dean Martin was nobody's fool—he was
becoming one of the wealthiest people in show biz, and the
shrewdest of stage drunks. But he was browbeaten by the
stooge kid he protected on the screen. Jerry devised their
partnership, their routines, and the direction of their careers.
He revered such earlier comics as Stan Laurel, he studied
the engineering of laughter, and he longed to make films
all on his own.

So, was his goofy kid a fake? Were the eyes of innocent
catatonia behind blastproof lenses really scheming their own
antics? I don't think self-consciousness detracted from the
cult of primitive emotionalism in Jerry. In every movie he
had grave interludes of "sincerity"—like the love stories in
Marx Brothers pictures—and a four-year-old's lecture, plaintive with the humbug that children are simpler and purer
instead of young human beings. What he wanted from the
world was love—for himself, to be sure, but also for everyone. An awful childish hope affected him: You can't be
happy unless every last soul feels good. He wanted people
to be nice so that idiots like him wouldn't be laughed at.
He could conjure up a blanket sweetness with fascist gusto
and pull it over the troubled heads of humankind. He offered it as shelter, but it was a shroud. The philosophy was
stupid and just as dangerous as the contemporary thought
that America would shape up if it only rid itself of un-
Americans. But because the sentimental savage, Jerry, uttered it, it was regarded as charming and respectable. After
all, it is very close to a widespread American faith: that
everyone should like everyone else, that there be no acri-
mony to spoil Utopia. Jerry was in direct line of descent
from King Kong and Dumbo, a tribute to the irrelevance of
mind or discrimination if the noble heart beat strong. It is
also the pattern of many trading relations in this country,

where critical thinking is blinded by the willful amiability of seller and buyer. That, in turn, attests to the grace of money, purchase, consumption, and profit. Jerry often squeaked to the mercifully selfish Dean, "Be nice." It was a prelude to "Have a good day" and "Have you hugged your kids today?" And if the squeak is less piercing now, Lewis is still making us guilty about niceness.

But on Labor Day it is the insistence that impresses. Jerry has grown up. Sometimes, half-heartedly, he wheels out the freak of the fifties and rehashes an old routine, stumbling after his former finesse and enduring the clumsiness that has replaced it like a sober citizen supporting a drunk. Lewis has come out of the closet of his partnership with Dean. It's as if Stan Laurel turned on Ollie with "Beat it, you creep. Who needs you?"

Jerry Lewis had triumphant years in the sixties. He became the hero and chief support of an ailing Paramount, clown and businessman combined. The films he wrote, acted in, directed, and dominated are among the most inventive comedies ever made in America—*The Bellboy, The Ladies' Man, The Errand Boy, The Patsy, The Family Jewels,* and *The Nutty Professor*. The last is the most alarming version of the Jekyll and Hyde story ever filmed; it is also the family link between Martin and Lewis and the telethon. Jerry plays a scientist, the kid's looniness given adult rein in the stereotype of inept genius, ready for a Nobel Prize but falling on every banana skin in the fruit store. He is especially helpless with women, though bashfully hopeful that Stella Stevens will be "nice" to him, as if he might get to be her lapdog. (Marriage in all of Jerry's films is a dreadful fate for the women and a return to the safe womb for him. Jerry would be good as *Alien*.)

He drinks his own potion and is transformed into a creature called Buddy Love. The arrogance, sexual swagger, and gloating nightclub smoothness of the alter-ego singer have always reminded many viewers of the ultimate Dean

Martin—as if Jerry were avenging all the screen put-downs by his brilliantined partner. Jerry denied that and said Buddy represented other ghosts. In *The Nutty Professor*, Love is as demonic as any Hyde, and the movie is unequivocally fearful of him. But it is Buddy Love now who often stalks the Sahara stage, snarling to technicians, then pretending it was only a comic whine. Sometimes the tired eyes go flat as if he means to torture us for being the meek audience. Years later, you look back on *The Nutty Professor* and see how mixed its maker's feelings were toward his monster and the business of being on show.

If "Buddy Love" was coined originally to satirize sexually narcissistic crooners, the name now coincides with the lament of the telethon. When Jerry read his statement of clean intent, he prefaced it with the admission that he needed to be loved by everyone. That's what he said, though it's never easy to know what he thinks and means. His speech is as ponderous and clotted as Nixon's. The example he gave had nothing to do with love, and everything to do with applause and reassurance. Love exists between individuals; Jerry's emotions are always aimed at the crowd. He referred to a recent appearance at the London Palladium when 4,999 people gave him a standing ovation, but Jerry had seen only one stubborn dissenter sitting on his hands. Even the solitary sinner is worthy, and the star wants the crowd to be a single force without deviants or individualism.

Language is being abused in this situation in a way we see all around us. Audiences do not love performers, just as people do not love possessions. They enjoy them, they idealize them perhaps, they may live through them. That is no more love than when a performer "breaks down" at a standing ovation and says, "You're beautiful . . . I love you." What occurs then is only a surge of approval and satisfaction lapping over the performer's insatiable insecurity, and a misleading aura of community settling on the show-biz transaction of getting the act you paid for.

Lewis bullies on the telethon, not because he is mad or unscrupulous about money, but because he is helpless with the thunderous possibility of love. Of course, the program aligns the two things remorselessly. There were proud donors coming in with checks, but they were unable to give the necessary identification of whatever corporation or event had raised the money before Jerry ripped open the envelope to get at the figures. "Just give me the numbers," he said, trampling upon any dignity which donors or generosity might deserve. Jerry had the shameless need for gifts and attention that consumes some invalids.

The protestations of sympathy or gratitude are never as persuasive as the spectacle of Lewis's own glorification. He hogs screen time, and ensures that the money, the compassion, and the frenzy all flow through him. Charity is as spoiled by his personality as political activity is by the presence of a dictator. The TV spectacle centers on the way Jerry's volatility reacts to the total figures: He writhes with urging, staggers with plenty and disbelief, and then is called to order by the solemn guardian of the total, that model of respectful attendance, Ed McMahon. Jerry turns into a witch doctor when he discovers his own lucky number, thirteen—luck for the unlucky—hidden in each new set of digits. It is Jerry's demand for love, his eventual tearful collapse, that drags at the pockets of the masses. *His* peace of mind is at issue. The hysteria of the campaign obliterates the everyday experience of dystrophic suffering with the drama of salvation. There is, I suppose, a Christian echo in this, but it is hard to hear because of the undisguised brutality of Jerry's triumph. This is not a sublime act of saintliness, but the reckless glory of a show-off.

Both the pathetic "nut" and the thug, Love, are in evidence on the telethon. Jerry picked up a healthy infant and mimicked the expressions on her bewildered face. He went into maudlin chatter with the poster child, assuring him of love even if he got his name wrong once. That little boy guessed he was an icon of pathos, but he could hardly deal with the wound of yearning in Lewis. The professional performer in the child seemed grimly pained that Jerry had stolen the greatest travail from him. But as the program progressed, and fatigue stripped away defenses, so Jerry came more and more in line with the sulky petulance of a spoiled-child emperor.

His bow tie fell loose. The incongruity of baby face and fifty-two-year-old features became more pronounced. He chewed on the scepter called his hand mike, pretended to doze on people's shoulders, lounged, pranced, and veered about in the certainty that the camera had to follow his whims. His drooping face had a leaden, deadpan stare, and he smoked like a gangster, no matter that health was the light at the end of the tunnel. He grew impatient with the technicians producing the program, he hurled challenges into the vague dark—why shouldn't he exploit a kid if the cause was good? He told donors to get on with it and sometimes flaunted his contempt for their dull rehearsed speeches. Sincerity and disillusion rage in his head. Does he realize how visible his sneers are, or are they unconscious? Is the aggression so flagrant because Lewis guesses it preys upon the most likely donors, or is it the neurosis of a show-biz one-man act who has not had a picture released since 1970 and who is excited by this exaggerated wrestling with the people?

Some $29 million were raised in 1978, though I remain confused about how much came from the public and how much from corporate sponsors or groups identified with the muscular dystrophy campaign. Still, the summoning up of so much money is breathtaking; it comes with so many stories of ordinary dedication and painstaking service that it maps a plenitude of good will and casual resources in America, underlined in the following week when the $5 million tab for the House Select Committee on Assassinations was put in question. Yet it is only about three quarters of what *Cleopatra* or *Star Trek* cost.

It is a measure for good if some of that money goes to treat muscular dystrophy patients or to find a new understanding of their disease. The telethons have built hospitals, prolonged lives, and brought relief. No society should refrain from that effort. But the telethon exposes our crude ideas about charity, illness, and happiness. If a disease is so dreadful, should it be left to Jerry's frenzied care? If there is $29 million for muscular dystrophy, what is there for every other organic failure our bodies face? But must we be so fiercely, morally disapproving of illness? Is virtue or value secured if death and handicap are averted? Life may be a sharper pleasure and a more responsible course once death is respected. Lewis makes death a taboo. He also overshadows men and women who spend their working lives in charitable pursuits. When he deplores assertions that he gets 10 percent of the take, he undermines people who may earn less than $10,000 a year running charities and raising only five or ten times their salary. When the country leaves its sick so much to chance and free enterprise, and yet has such qualms about admitting sickness and death, it should honor the everyday, humdrum work of citizens employed by charitable institutions.

The telethon is a theatrical gesture that diminishes reality just as Lewis's agony/ecstasy of rising total would be dashed if a Howard Hughes, say, called in moments before the deadline and said he'd match the telethon's collection with one stroke of the pen. The telethon is a demonstration of how the fevered arena of TV has corrupted generosity, sentiment, and happiness. The event may be shaped by Jerry Lewis's own turmoil, but it is a natural development of the medium. Far from a unique occasion, and the one instance in which television puts aside steady habits, the telethon is the summary of the treacherous medium. The poison is more concentrated, but it is there every day, another stealthy weakening of muscles and values.

The telethon's ingredients make this clear, as much as its form. It has a floor show of TV stars, and it is based upon personality as a disguise or recompense for everything else—the maelstrom of news crystalizing as Walter Cronkite. The corporate sponsors are still buying advertisements, but with the added prestige of community service. Just as game shows are the flowering of the promoted prizes, so the telethon puts a shine on the amiability of big business. The twenty-two-hour flow is a model of any day's TV: song and dance, jokes, commercials, talk shows, soaps, documentaries, game shows, live action sports, moral uplift. All these pseudoforms are ripped away from their living reality and reduced to the listless furor of the small screen.

The telethon is a ghastly sign of our culture. It is preoccupied with dread of disease, unhealthy emotions, and credit-card salvation. And its package is so steeped in vanity, melodrama, and tacky sensation that our most widely used communicative experience, TV, is revealed as a symptom of debility more sinister than the deaths of children.

9

Waiting in the Lobby

Will the movie live up to the gathering in the lobby? Will it be worthy of this unwholesome collection of hot and bereft people who must wonder why I am describing them? Can the movie match their lounging variety, be as sharp as their new-made jokes? Is the picture that will face us soon in the dark compatible with our untidy spectacle? Or will it leave us regretting the unscripted caprices we give up in the dark? Shall we sit in well-behaved rows? Does that reassure our dread that there may be no other order? We are so much more engaging in the lobby, cartwheeling this way and that as our imagination explores the throng. I would as soon stay there and let the film pass by like a train not taken.

I am at an urban movie house, where three auditoriums surround a lobby as large as any one of the theaters. The design has created the impression of legs supporting the body of a crab. This lobby is not just a useful waiting place, large enough for one house to empty out without colliding with the 8:45 line—after all, it is astute for the management to keep those who have seen apart from those about to see—it is itself an amusement arcade.

Inside the theaters the floor may be uncarpeted and the seats made of a gutty plastic that hides its shabbiness in the dark. The lobby is worthy of a hotel for teenagers—its garishness makes them feel at home, for they want some mild shock to let them know they are awake. Its carpet has an inane pattern that boogies wall to wall, too busy for the space. There are seats like those in airport lounges, for one and a half people. The rest rooms are located in the lobby, and they are bowers where you can repair and beautify your person. There are tissue dispensers (paper as yet, not the fine leaf of new skin), portrait mirrors, and the cosmetic sheen of pink tile from which, maybe, the very sweet rose scent may exude, with just one prick of disinfectant in its humid swoon.

Sometimes in my rest room you will find dudes carving their hair and piously touching their softest recesses with deodorant lollipops. I wonder what sights there are in the other rest room: fifteen-year-olds caressing themselves so that nipples will be unequivocal through the sheer cling of halter tops? Gatherings like that of *The Women,* rating the studs who are outside humping and heaving at Space Invaders? Juliet in the closet making sure a borrowed diaphragm fits, or bent over a fragile pyramid of cocaine on the mock-marble vanity slab?

You can dream those questions in the lobby, it is so alive and pressing; and the coterie of the powder room emerge so alert they must know we are thinking of them. Or is there a risk here of wordy Humbert not noticing that the Lolita of his gaze—some Cheryl from Sherman Oaks, or even the fabled Paula from Portuguese Bend—has no vocabulary and may make love as hesitantly as if her grammar were being examined?

The illuminated waterfall in that corner may not be in the best taste. There are cigarette ends and Styrofoam coracles bobbing in its froth. Are the green plants beside it rubber or flesh? Is the earth only brown plastic nubbins? Do the chandeliers grow as slowly as camellias, or does a truck from Pomona deliver them whole and stiff and ready to be strung up? What is that smell that will smother Juliet and hyacinth body lotion but the sickly fallout of popcorn, the least romantic climatic condition of the American movie house?

Wherever you look there are collections of particles—

available handfuls to stop boredom or avert concentration. Those dry nuggets of fake earth for the potted plants and the droplets in the waterfall are beads on a necklace that also contains the exploded kernels of popcorn and the flickering symbols of Space Invaders. There is a rain of noise: the bleeps and farts of the video game, the shoveling of corn, the scatter of the waterfall, and the multitude of conversations. The one thing the movie will offer that is not provided in the lobby is the accomplishment of an unbroken ribbon, two hours long, in which the same granular nerviness of so many separate frames—172,800 in such a film—will be lost to sight.

But if the lobby's catering to spasm is so successful, can films lure people into the dark? This lobby is a gathering of kids, and while you wait for your movie to come out, you may see some spend twice the price of admission on video games or refreshments. It is possible to enter and use the lobby's diversions without paying to see a film. The theater management would prefer that you chose from among its amusements than buy a ticket of admission on which it must pass a substantial portion to the distributor.

So why not bring in more video games? There are usually gangs at every screen waiting a turn. Why not add pinball machines? Or seats at the counter so that hot snacks could augment popcorn and candies? They might install a few television receivers and have the movie play on them, or some infinite overtime Rams game. Or they could convert one area of the lobby to a disco, playing the music from the movie and having scenes from it fluctuate on the stucco walls.

The theaters could be converted to make extra lobby space. Why not an intimacy lounge or a roller rink? Anything left over could be freed for car parks, where crime might be localized. How long before ingenious management puts a glass wall between the lobby and this marauding ground, clear for the lobby-ists but dark as privacy from the outside? Then we could observe the quick acts of mugging and rape, as serene as when we watch such actions in a film. The lobby is ready for the living theater of Venice Beach.

It may be that we now watch films as little as we do because the medium has taught us a way of seeing life which we can practice all the time. That's why I wonder if I might not prefer the erotic views of the lobby to what any actress may lay bare on the screen. In the same spirit, doesn't the stupefying mass of 1,000 Picassos (another granular assembly) tempt one to study the flamingo steps of the ten thousand moving past them? See the spectator's face duty-aimed at Pablo, while the profile wonders what expression to arrange, what knowing small talk to provide. That is the origin as well as the demonstration of Cubism, seeing and being seen in the same moment, the face splitting with the strain of simultaneity. By comparison, the painted faces look staid and asleep.

But the movie beyond the lobby is worth examining today, for it is so attuned to the lobby's ambience. *Urban Cowboy* is supposed to occur in Texas, and John Travolta is alleged to be a rugged oil-rig worker. Do we have to prove that implausibility is now a vital part of the entertainment? The people in the film wear cowboy hats, like J. R. Ewing, the crowd at the 1980 Republican Convention, and the Dallas Cowboys cheerleaders. Tough, self-sufficient men who want to be liked and envied in advertisements for cigarettes wear them: They are the costume of schizophrenia, like T-shirts that flaunt a message to bypass talk or doubt: "The guy in this shirt is OK" or "I fuck, I suck and I tell."

The western is dormant today, trampled upon by its camp availability for advertising. *The Long Riders* is a studious re-creation of the countryside and the bearing of the James Gang such as a banking commercial might employ. If only the boys could have seen any of the films about them, then that last bungled Northfield raid might have been kept from tragedy. The latest movie about them is so earnest, it casts real brothers as the families in the gang. But it is helplessly archaic. As if underplaying and taciturnity could any longer stand for the rural nineteenth century! Why strive to re-create a world that most of us now think was bogus? That most intense American myth, the West, may never be be-lieved in again except as the breeding ground for fakes, shams, and actors, like Altman's Buffalo Bill. There is the same cheerful strut and leer of lying in J.R. and the cheer-leaders. Texas has settled for being a huge back lot, where fiction lives in the melting air. The Lone Star State: It sounds like the sublimity of every man in his own photo-graph.

Urban Cowboy is that paperback Texas. At one point, a character looks out of a penthouse window at Houston by night—or a black cloth speckled with stars—and says she loves the energy of the city. We never take her at her word: We know Texas can't fuel or feed America on anything but dreams. Her character, a socialite who is sleeping with Travolta's oil rigger and making him beef Stroganoff, is preoccupied with the transformation of identity that energy's meltdown might allow. She is a fake longing for another charade, and her wistfulness comes from shampoo ads (the place where you suspect you first saw two out of any three young actresses today).

She comes on as an adult, and the actress is fully grown, like everyone else in *Urban Cowboy*. But the real pitch is toward teenagers. The story of *Cowboy* has Travolta as a country boy who comes to Houston and gets a refinery job: It's a homily of our media that anyone who works at a refinery is a natural roughneck. In fact, he goes to live in Miller-Lite land from a backroads home out of Country Time Lemonade. After work, he visits Gilley's, a real tavern in Houston but the ideal of lobbies everywhere.

Gilley's is a spacious, perhaps infinite, interior that defies its squat, unimpressive outside. It has bars, live music, games, and diversions. But its newest feature shows how far all its areas lean toward the promise of fulfilled fantasy. This is a mechanical bull: a headless, black-leather juggernaut worked from controls, surrounded by mattresses for soft falling, but so much more pliable than real Brahma bulls. Of course, the "old" rodeo, from Buffalo Bill to *Junior Bonner*, was already the nineteenth-century cowboy life turned into show biz. This is one step further, the rodeo of Rodeo Drive and Neiman-Marcus.

Travolta rides the bull, and wins one of the girls at Gilley's (Debra Winger). Without it being stressed, the tavern is a sorting house for sexual liaison, and the girl sees Travolta a while before he notices her. She is more aggressive than he is, more intelligent, more awake. But she is not as glamorous as many of the other Stetson models there. This credits Travolta with ordinary tastes. But it also points to the quality of Debra Winger as an actress, something that accounts for the imbalance of the project. Travolta is efficiently upstaged by his partner, someone as sexy as Colette and pretty in a mean-faced way. Once upon a time, she would have been lucky to make waitress at a studio cafeteria. Movies today can appreciate her abrasive character and the uningratiating sexual personality. It is something you could notice in any crowded lobby, and it is not a belittling of Debra Winger to say that the streets are full of people who could be as striking on the screen.

The couple marry as swift as winning at a game show. That action, and their reaction to marriage, shows how entirely childlike they are. Not that the movie rebukes them or even notices, but *Urban Cowboy* is unaware of mature reflection or anything but instant reaction. You might hope that its bald emotional dynamics are being parodied. But nothing in the picture threatens the adolescent's own scale of emotional values and energy. Meet, spark, marry on impulse, be depressed and bewildered by the first situation that requires compromise or patience. It is strip-cartoon film, with reading-book techniques applied to adult situations. The couple are playing at marriage because their culture has required nothing but spasm response from them. Gilley's may be real, but marriage is a set of labels: one on the car, His and Hers on the towels, and twin T-shirts. *Urban Cowboy* has no footing in real life, save for that very precarious actuality of living under the hat called John Travolta and having a not very wise or experienced young man wonder what the hat expects of him.

There is so little reality because Travolta is such a concoction. *Urban Cowboy* is derived from a nonfiction article written by Aaron Latham, but the movie is a package inspired by *Saturday Night Fever*. There is the same would-be dangerous but actually protective arena; a competition to display Travolta's starry movements; and the same climbing frame of character development in the material. Neither film is very far from the sort of after-school TV movie about how young people should make personal moral choices. The atmosphere is, theoretically, more sordid, but the analysis of problems is as simpleminded and as optimistic as honesty getting ahead and sweet breath earning a kiss. The pictures are torn between what their own terminology could only describe as "doing good" and "feeling good." You cannot hold the young audience without offering the latter, but Hollywood is still constrained by the conservatism that wants to promote the former.

In this film the virginal selfishness and the taboos of role-playing spoil the marriage. It would have to be something as instinctive or stereotypical: The characters have no other kind of life or resources. They sulk and they pick other bedfellows with all the spiteful whim of kids commanding new friends to jab at old alliances. Travolta meets a woman from *Dallas,* no matter that this is Houston, and Winger goes with a lean, mean, real rodeo rider. He's older, he looks like Clint Eastwood on food stamps, and he wears black—it's a tough, authentic world surrounding these babes.

Travolta measures up to this other man, iconographically, in the way Jeffrey Hunter did to John Wayne in *The Searchers*. But whereas that film accepted the earned hardness of veterans, *Urban Cowboy* sees a mysterious virility in Travolta that flatters his teenage following. When the bull-riding finale comes, Travolta wins, and for good measure he thrashes the man who has put makeup bruises on Debra Winger's wan face.

The pampered features of Travolta take their cuts and sadness, too. How woeful he looks, though no one on the picture seems to realize that the ten-gallon hat overwhelms him; he looks dwarfed and lugubrious as if the hat were made of lead. He also looks like a soft kid in whom the generous or the gullible could mistake innocence for sensitivity. Travolta is well into his twenties, but the secret of his appeal is that he does not disconcert a teenager watching him. His own vision of adult life confirms the highly colored inexperience of the kid in the audience. That he can play such parts without irony can only mean that he is still caught up in the kid's sensibility.

James Bridges directed *Urban Cowboy*, the man who won praise for that browbeating, muddle-headed melodrama, *The China Syndrome*. Praise from the media, that is; in a Hollywood indifferent to politics, the movie attracted the awe that smelled magic in the coincidence of its release and the actuality of Three Mile Island. One of the two producers on *Urban Cowboy* was Robert Evans, among the most astute packagers of film today. I have to stress the significance of the package because someone surely recognized that the commercial potential of *Cowboy* required the triteness of the story. And just as Gilley's resembles the urban playground of the theater lobby, so the film has many of its characteristics. There is a hazy atmosphere, a perpetual restlessness— part action, part a fear of depth or slowness—the provocative manner and gestures of people playing sex like a game, and the steady background of music. If the action ever flags, there is music to ride along with.

As we imagined the future of the lobby, so *Urban Cowboy* is like leafing through a photographic comic book, the pages turned by the throb of music. It is a picture that asks the teenage audience to dance and sing-along with it, registering its skeletal emotional scheme and retreating now and then to the rest room to make themselves facsimiles of the stars. It's a wonder no lobby has installed its own mechanical bull, though very few of our young could deliver the unbridled pantomime of sex that Debra Winger achieves in a gratuitous set piece. Travolta's face at that moment is a study in mortification and inadequacy. Teenage sex is an act overshadowed by its reputation, but in that passage of play, Debra Winger establishes herself as a woman. Travolta and his character look on as shocked as spoiled kids witnessing pleasures beyond their capacity.

Urban Cowboy doesn't have the box-office charge of *Saturday Night Fever* or *Grease*, but that's not because of its defects. Although Travolta's great hits opened only three years ago, you can believe that that moviegoing generation has already passed on. In the summer season especially, movies rely upon an audience in the eight to fifteen range, kids free from school, addled by heat and bored enough to try a movie. When *Grease* did such remarkable business in the summer of 1978, it was because so many children went back to it more than once. Films are events or places where the young feel comfortable hanging out. Not even parents find it monotonous or unenterprising if kids go to the same beach every day. Wave after wave, stupidly the same, but it's supposed to be healthy and inspiring. There is more disquiet if the choice falls on an amusement arcade. But as far as the picture trade is concerned, a repeating audience only illustrates the disregard of the crowd for story line or moral suspense.

Grease was not strong on either, though it does play off the tension between peer pressure and independent action in a way that a summer-camp counselor could believe was conducive to betterment. Whenever I saw *Grease*—it was all repeat business—I was struck by the ease with which customers went back and forth from theater to lobby, to take in or release refreshment, or just to walk around. The big musical numbers in that film would bring the audience back: They were loud, active peaks that anyone in the lobby could hear calling.

It is too easy to be disapproving of that "slackness." The musical is among the worthiest film genres because of the directness with which it deals in pleasure. But not many of its practitioners believed in working to fit songs and dance routines to a strong narrative basis—would that have crippled the pleasure? That moment when action hesitates and breaks into song is so destructive of dramatic involvement, yet so delightful, that it points to the superior ease of opera or films like *The Umbrellas of Cherbourg* in which the entire action is sung, allowing no hint of a gap between talk and songs and never requiring that nervous laughter of collapsed dancers before the fade-out rescues them at the end of a routine. The "story" of many celebrated musicals can scarcely be remembered, it is so slight. Would anyone care to give the plot synopsis of an Astaire-Rogers musical, or stretch the "drama" of *Singin' in the Rain* beyond three sentences?

There are very few musicals as such today compared with those Arthur Freed produced in the forties and fifties at MGM. Perhaps the form depended on a studio system well-stocked with dancers, but just as rich in designers, choreographers, arrangers, and cameramen who could film dance ensembles. Perhaps the musical is too fanciful or sunny for our moods. The high style of Fred Astaire withered as he aged, but it was hurt more by the domineering "naturalism" of the 1950's and the supposed emphasis on "serious" material that went with it. The few attempts to rediscover the musical—like *At Long Last Love*—have disclosed the loss of faith in stylization, and the terror of such as Burt Reynolds when asked to attempt it. Astaire emerges from that comparison as an unaffected romantic, while Reynolds's most crushing handicap is the cynicism with which he tries to hide his timidity.

Yet the musical's waning also coincides with the growth of new music for the young—Rock—with long-playing records and the empire of disc-jockey radio. Music is more important than it has ever been as the cement in loosely constructed films and as the promotional instrument that reaches the young audience.

We should note that during the sixties, several film-distribution companies found themselves parts of conglomerates that also owned record labels. But this is not just a trend in the Monopoly of movies. In the sixties too, in the shadow of old-fashioned battleship musicals like *The Sound of Music,* dramatic films began to use music as more than the appropriate mood background it had been as far back as silent days. Even then, atmospheric accompaniment was provided live in theaters and on sets when love scenes were filmed. But by the early sixties, some films were known by their theme songs: *The Magnificent Seven, Breakfast at Tiffany's, Hatari!, The Pink Panther.*

Henry Mancini wrote the last three in the list, and was the leading composer for films of that era, more melodic than but just as lush as the music in high-class elevators and just as upbeat. His theme for *Days of Wine and Roses* would grace a love story, and it is like a breath-freshener on that grisly tale of alcoholism. "Moon River" for *Breakfast at Tiffany's* was arguably written to swell the slim character of Holly Golightly, but it was "laid on" the sound track of the film and not integrated with it. With *Hatari!* there was every suspicion that even the proud Howard Hawks had filmed an innocuous episode to make room for "Baby

Elephant Tango." Such tunes sold on records and were played on the radio. I doubt if the movies deserve credit for recognizing a vital method of promotion, but when it worked they at least learned from it. Barbra Streisand lamenting "The Way We Were," a rhapsody in nostalgia, cleared a receptive way for the film that had to have the same name. Many of the Bee Gees' songs for *Saturday Night Fever* were released in advance of the film, and the same practice was employed with Olivia Newton-John's "Magic" from *Xanadu*. Kids had heard songs long before they knew there was a movie attached to them. Thus, when the film materialized, it had less unfamiliarity to battle against.

Not only songs have worked. Music can be more than a mood, it can be as elemental in the film as the quality of the light or the presence of an actor. Bernard Herrmann had never written film music that did not alter a filmed scene if it was removed. But he won more than the admiration of his peers on *Psycho,* where the music is the track on which the audience rides the ghost train of suspense. When Alfred Hitchcock spoke of the "roller coaster" of a picture, he could argue the contributory merits of story, cutting, and camera angles. But the trapped-bird agony of *Psycho* cries out in the music, for that is what makes the expressive murders as much a release as an ordeal.

Music less close to the heart of the film, but as noticeable, distinguished *Bonnie and Clyde, The Graduate, Easy Rider, The Thomas Crown Affair, 2001,* and *The Sting.* In all those cases, moments of the music were introduced as ironic commentary—the package addressing itself—a directorial aside or as the source of the action. "Foggy Mountain Breakdown" in *Bonnie and Clyde* was an important way of supplying the film's fresh attitude toward its outlaws. The music was merry, and its momentum carried us into new, perilous moral permissiveness. "Mrs. Robinson" gave *The Graduate* a self-awareness that was not otherwise present in the strangely flat action of the movie; without the Simon and Garfunkel songs, it might have been too harsh, too distanced for the large audience. Scott Joplin's jaunty rags were shamelessly appropriated to endorse the cleverness of the intrigue in *The Sting*, while Strauss's "Thus Spake Zarathustra" gave Stanley Kubrick's stately images in *2001* the properly vague sense of eternity. Most organic of all, maybe, was the banjo-guitar duel in *Deliverance*, a scene that arose without undue contrivance and which foreshadowed the film's confrontation of cultures.

An orthodoxy was growing: that successful films used music; that movie albums were often worth releasing and might occasionally do remarkable business; and that a hit single from a film was a strong inducement to box-office success. The trade had no great expectations for *American Gigolo*: The material was thought of as sleazy, the casting change had halved the budget, and yet the direction was high-minded. But the film did very well, perhaps because of the regular radio plays given to the sinister, glasslike style of "Call Me," composed by Giorgio Moroder and its singer, Deborah Harry; and "Love and Passion" with music by Moroder and lyrics by the film's director, Paul Schrader. The score to *Gigolo* was as acute and suggestive as the best black-and-white photography in *film noir;* it provided the same ambiguity of glamour and neurosis.

The album for the film carried the design that Schrader had insisted on for the film's advertising. *American Gigolo* is an uncommon hybrid, full of ambition and personality, but to his many talents Schrader adds a thorough, Protestant respect for business. The packaging of his own movies gives him no offense. It may even be a source of satisfaction, and no critic should separate the creative from the commercial in the unexpected balance of sordid and spiritual in *American Gigolo*.

John Williams is a more conventional figure: he may become the Arthur Fiedler of 2000, urging patriotic bombast into the air above the Charles River on July 4. His music is never as insolent or heartless as Deborah Harry's. But he is the movie composer of the moment, concertmaster on some of the greatest hits of the last decade: *Jaws, Star Wars, Close Encounters, Superman, The Empire Strikes Back.* Williams worked on several other movies for which no one recalls the music—*Black Sunday,* for instance. But people who never saw *Jaws* can identify the bass warning of murderousness in the water. Still, there is something confident in that music: It is foreboding, but it is as affirmative as Jack Nicholson's ax killer in *The Shining.* More typical of Williams is the adventurer-go-forth robustness of his "space" music, a kind of disco Gustav Holst.

It's not unreasonable for deep space to be alive with the sound of music. When man found only emptiness there, so his films filled the void with futuristic apartments, surreal landscapes, and Muzak. Williams is as shallow and accomplished a craftsman as George Lucas. He writes music that a kid can believe is serious, but which is as digestible as the mushy texture of the visuals and the coded characters in *Star Wars* and *The Empire Strikes Back.* Indeed, George Lucas is the preeminent merchant of the lobby. *American Graffiti* is still the archetypal film in the genre. Motorization converts a California town into a kind of lobby, and suggests how far the drive-in was ancestor to this new public arena. It abides by the young person's dream of owning the night town, and it treats the diner, lovers' lane, the main drag, the radio station as ordained sites in the board game of growing up. Music is as constant on its track as circulatory driving to pass the time. There are no numbers. None of the characters sings. But car radios never cease; they are an empire and the oil that lets the young society slip along.

The Star Wars pictures make the universe into a lobby, or an adventure shopping mall. No distance is too great when you can time-warp on a cut. And the ultimate designs of space seem done by the same brisk, eclectic, and op-art eye that designs lobbies: silver-foil surfaces, sliding doors, plastic as a core building material, and the movement of video screens from inset panel to entire walls. The video game *is Star Wars*, a film that was very hard on the actors because they were always looking into areas that would be filled with electronics and special effects. Luke Skywalker, Han Solo, Princess Leia, and the robots are instant character types—plastic statues, gods of the week, in the lobby of America already living in the future.

As a projected series, *Star Wars* denies dramatic entity and resolution. We may not live long enough to see the whole story. So the buzz and prettiness of the moment must be enough. Such films make moments one more item in that series of particle collections. You watch *Star Wars* as you put popcorn to your mouth: one shiny taste treat after another —there is no order, no nourishment, no harm. The light show that the lobby is seeking has been made, and *The Empire Strikes Back*, the first sequel, is the perfect movie package, so much the same as before that it hardly needs a script. It was responsible for about a quarter of the national trade in the summer of 1980.

I have argued elsewhere that there is a crisis in American film, and it has to do with the industry's catering to this teenage audience and its most protective fantasies. It seemed only yesterday that parents were deploring the scarcity of films their children might see. Yet now we are witness to the industry as a whole dedicating itself to a fickle, underdeveloped part of the population. In the summer of 1980, as well as *The Empire Strikes Back* the young audience had *The Blue Lagoon, My Bodyguard, Foxes, Carny, The Island*, and even *Dressed to Kill* to offer possible self-portraits. Not that there is necessarily anything responsible parents could take their children to now without fear of having them alarmed, oversugared, or misbeguiled by dazzling careers of fame. *The Black Stallion* is still a rarity in that it is designed to appeal simultaneously to the awe of children and their elders' sense of loss. Sentimental, predictable, and picturesque it may be. The second-half recreation of a Norman Rockwell America is less novel but more interesting than the much-praised National Geographic desert island. But in the faces of Kelley Reno and Mickey Rooney—don't they sound related?—it has images of natural gravity and delight in which the parallel lines of childhood and old age writhe around each other like the strands of honeysuckle.

Better that than *Fame*, the nadir of films celebrating youth, if only because it is the most pretentious. *Fame*, too, has its album, for it uses the New York High School for the Performing Arts in the way that *Urban Cowboy* uses Gilley's. I will accept all the protestations that this is a real school, no matter that it seems like a screenwriter's invention, the place where a long-running TV series might live. What does it do but take Central Casting's notion of the hordes of New York and turn them into show business? *Fame* insists that its kids learn the dull subjects, too, but it never shows that mundane process, and it exonerates kids who seem to have learned everything they know from weekly exposure to the gilded egotism of Bob Fosse's *All That Jazz*, the work of another child who would rather die than grow up.

Fame is snappy, rhythmic, and cute-slapdash. It changes as often as TV and suckers you with the same myth that it's worth waiting for what comes next. Next-next-next—the stream turns into a chant or a neurotic tic. Several of its young people have the charm of unhindered superficiality, like kids in advertisements for Coca-Cola, assured that their well-being is a spiritual tan and glow. The director of *Fame*, Alan Parker, is very adroit: He knows just how to construct and cut his film so that we have a collage of incidents—fragmentation again—not one of which will strain the stamina of the audience. It is the oldest Hollywood wish for children —that they be greasepaint adults, falling in line with the scenario ideology of TV and advertising.

One has to concede the directness of the title. *Fame* is about celebrity, making it, being noticed more than the need to notice others, being drawn out of the crowd. Can you imagine a film called *Achievement* or *Work?* Moreover, no one fails once the audition process is over. And if life, moth-eaten monster, must dole out its unhappiness, why, then, let fame be your umbrella. It is as if the world, its chances and its dangers, had been given up for the glamorous idea that the young may carry a spotlight around with them. The disco already, and the lobby soon, will need roaming spotlights so that every kid can feel the phantom warmth of attention on him or her. Fame can override every other choice in life: It harnesses will and energy, it passes the time, and it could be the drive that leaves humanism as stranded as the Bates motel in *Psycho.*

But fame and *Fame* are also the offshoot of fad and craze. This fame is not really lasting, it is a hungry search that will be appeased by a brief moment of glory and the envy of others. Andy Warhol seemed to be identifying the new ubiquity of starriness when he said soon everyone will be a star for fifteen minutes. But isn't the quarter-hour life-span more suggestive? It presupposes not a mountain peak of prominence with dreary slopes of anonymity on either side of it, but a sensibility in which only peaks register. Thus, we are famous or we do not exist, in orgasm or dead, on or off like the TV set.

Movies are packages made for that culture. It is legend in the gullible film industry that the first weekend of any movie is enough to plot its fate, and the promotion for any film seldom exceeds a month. No one knows how to nurse a small success over a long period, or considers such success legitimate. The selling of movies depends on bursts of mania, not a prolonged, rational acceptance. That policy affects the initial decision of financiers to go with a film. The package now is increasingly a question of whether the film can work in that first month, not whether it can persuade people slowly. As never before, the title, the slogan, the poster, and that snatch of sound track—all capable of being delivered in a ten-second TV promo—are decisive in whether a movie is made. *Fame* is a sufficient, exemplary title: a monosyllable that says everything and nothing, and provides the urgent wail—so like "Me!"—of the title song, a whirl of kids dancing in a ragged street (urban renewal is the rosy dream hinted at all along—a good show could clean this city up), Rex Reed's bottle-opening fizz, "*Fame* bursts with electricity from beginning to end," and the overall atmosphere of the lobby, of narcissism turned into a soft drink.

I said that *Fame* had the carbonated exultation of Coca-Cola advertisements despite the apparent contrast between the vitality and salvation of Cola Youth and the double-quick sketches of unhappy home life, abortion, and pornography that help give *Fame* its sexy shiver. The "sordid" is an obligatory, unfelt script notation. The nervous haste ticks off several life "problems" to vouch for its heart, but the film has been put together like a marketable kit, not a living work of imagination. All that matters in *Fame* is the overdrive of atmosphere, the excitement of stardom, and the regular popping of electronic bubbles. Plot, characterization, and interaction have been fed into the package like production values. There was a time when Hollywood resented the charge that it dealt in so few plots, so many stereotypes. But now the industry and the culture act upon them and take comfort in the narrow range. Code has supplanted infinite variety. We, too, regard such areas as the wasteland of cliché, and in our lives seek the small explosions of bubbles. That a movie should be felt by its makers and welcomed by viewers as a package—the lobby instead of an intricate house that has to be explored—is not just the most depressing aspect of today's movies, it is the grimmest consequence of over eighty years of film and 150 years of photography. We are living in an age in which our sense of significance is affected more by the assertion of the photograph than by the attempt of the word.

10

Gigolos

The gigolo strolls by the Hilton pool, sipping his piña colada. He is a male human figure that might have come in a cereal packet. The burnished brown of his body must have rubbed off from those stained wheaten flakes. Not a shiver of surplus hangs from his body: It is as lean as a script treatment, and the only passage that has been fleshed out more fully can be imagined beneath the turquoise sateen of his swimming briefs, which a Dufy must have drawn on him just before he stepped into the sunlight. Look closely . . . and you see that the flush of moisture on the briefs has never known the pool. It is paint drying. Do not touch, therefore, only watch the languid pulse beneath it—like a shark's blunt head grazing in the waterweed.

Two hundred feet away, Wilshire is sideswiped by Santa Monica Boulevard. There is a seashore rush of noise that is traffic, and the towers of Century City peer over the palms to examine the hotel pool. All around this pit of exhausted ease the hotel is a railway station of tourists, clutching maps, ignorance, and foreign languages, waiting to change their money, waiting for bus tours or to spy someone who might be a star. The pool of the Beverly Hilton is an oasis for people who might be stars: Subjunctive fame occupies the sun trap snorting the sweet air of Ambre Solaire. It is the salt crunch that rims every margarita and the convex ebony of every lens in every pair of dark glasses confronting the sun.

You could believe the hotel employs everyone at the pool.

For these lizards are the opposite of tourists, who are forever tapping the pockets that guard American Express. They are inmates, intimates, and cognoscenti, and nothing they wear has anything as cautious as a pocket. They are an in crowd, a cult, meant to make visitors uneasy. Their knowledge must be as deep as their tan. They have the supreme ease and authority of letting nothing interfere with the basking process; their respect for vanity is sustained by bellhops and waiters who can make a canapé or a Reuben seem like Communion. When so many members of the Screen Actors Guild are out of work, why should a rather inferior major hotel not scoop up three dozen of the loveliest, at daily rates and all they can drink, to be a feature of the hotel?

What the poolside presents is what travelers from New Jersey or England would think was "fast." It appears to be an indolent pleasure ground where clay-dark bodies doze showily for one another, meet, chat, and saunter into the shady hotel for an hour of more furtive conspiracy. They look like gigolos, just as crocodiles look dangerous—if one was only sure they were alive or awake. The ladies resemble harlots, their heads full of Saks and sex, their slender legs tethered by gold anklets. The arena is as full of flesh as a wardrobe is with prospects for the day, and if you close your eyes you can hear the squeak of hot skin. But the act of the gigolo is all a matter of being seen and inspiring tourist dreams as he vanishes into the dark. This is a movie set for might-have-beens who can make Iowa Rotarian tours think they must be.

Yet for all we know, the burnt-umber bodies watch TV or play Hearts in a dowdy lounge that the Hilton makes available, with a perfunctory salad table on hand. Then, after an hour, they practice their slow motion, leave a slick of oil on their thighs, and ooze back to the pool area to take their silent curtain calls. There they simper to companions to say it was so-so. The gigolo is an icon of imagined abandon and voluptuousness. But so lovely, so lean, and so regular, he must be neuter to keep it up. He is a figure in the game, though, an official in the Church.

Nearly thirty years later, could Richard Gere's Julian Kaye be the offspring of Norma Desmond and Joe Gillis? This arc of association spans 1950 and 1980, from *Sunset Boulevard* to *American Gigolo*. The arc may be as elegant a curve as arcs are meant to be, a shape in history discovered by the light, but at either end there lurks a virulent, suggestive, trashy movie.

Julian Kaye is the young man in *American Gigolo* who hires himself out to bring sexual home runs to wealthy but arid ladies in Los Angeles. One of the women he has lately brought to climax is murdered, and Julian is the leading suspect. Why not? The moody husband who chose to watch did ask Julian to beat on his wife's unresponsive cunt. But Julian, harassed victim of circumstances, will be saved by Lauren Hutton, the wife of a senator, someone Julian has met in the Polo Lounge and who has herself begged for his loving service.

Joe Gillis in *Sunset Boulevard* is played by William Holden. He is a Hollywood screenwriter, broke, low on luck and plot lines. To save his car from repossession, he drives it into the fairy-tale lair of a witch who lives in retreat in that plush section of Sunset Blvd. between Copa de Oro and Benedict Canyon. She is Norma Desmond, or Gloria Swanson, the queen of silent pictures, hiding out until talkies blow over. Gillis lingers at the house, made cunning by the thought of sanctuary and cozy work. He is one more tourist tickled to see the rotting inside of a star's Xanadu. This star wants someone to freshen up the script that is to be a stately barge for her comeback. The spineless Gillis stiffens up enough to sit at the typewriter, wear vicuña coats she buys for him, and tango on a tiled floor where Valentino may have slipped before him. But in the end, lack of backbone tells. When Gillis tries to walk out on the lady, she shoots him: Did Tom Mix teach her aim? He manages the elaborate totter that will have him fall into the ironic pool. He manages more: He recounts the whole damned story from the same pool, dead but still capable of working up a movie.

The arc hangs there, as assertive and illusory as a rainbow. But I can fashion it for you segment by segment. *Sunset Boulevard* is too tasteful or too afraid of the monster's inner den to be clear, but we must believe that Norma Desmond has taken the reptilian Gillis into her bed. Without a spine, he may lie protected between legs encrusted with legend and bring a tingle from the past back to the old lady. Although he cannot go upright, he might stay hard long enough to throw out the seed of plot, the bend of the arc.

Sunset Boulevard mocked its own industry, so allegedly some pillars of the Hollywood community thought the film should not be shown. It had no qualms in exploiting the gloomy career of Erich von Stroheim or the glaring vanity of Gloria Swanson. But it could not risk thirty and fifty in bed together, or imagine what they might do to please one another. And because it could not witness sex, it could not conceive of love. The film is so appalled by its own central relationship that it has the petty nastiness of a child paralyzed on the threshold of its parents' sweltering chamber. The child wills itself to be cold, and finds ridicule the best cooling agent. Thus, it says its own conception was grotesque and disgusting, not fit to be seen.

Is that what makes Julian Kaye so cool? Was he the tadpole made in that terrible stew? But he was a fetus still when Mother returned the favor with a quicker, leaden sperm in Daddy's back. Julian was drawn from a womb incarcerated in an institution for the criminally insane, a place where Norma Desmond still lives and still toils at her comeback. But Julian was given over to the care of . . . Max von Mayerling, the butler and ex-husband to Miss

Desmond, and the alias of Erich von Stroheim, who had once been fired from his own movie by a Gloria Swanson who owned that part of the world.

Max could not keep up the moldering house. It was sold, and he moved to rooms in Inglewood, caring for Julian who was named and given every other asset by Max. There had to be a surname. "You have to provide the child with a legal name," explained the clerk. "O . . . K," drawled Max, and that was it. The boy's name was the essence of accent. Max should not have had the child, you will say with the civic resolve of a Phil Donahue. Of course not, but in a movie not every plausible nicety is observed, and even in life there are some demented parents who are permitted to retain little ones.

It might have been worse. This Max knew the idea of love, and the arts of the body: Look at von Stroheim's mournfully romantic eyes and you may be sure of it. He worked as an extra, as a wine waiter, as a magician at children's parties, and as a debt collector in a city where owing is belonging. And Julian was looked after. He had the company of a much older man who himself knew considerably younger women. He was taken to the movies, and he learned the proper care and delicacy that he might bring to the clitorises of the city. Max died when Julian was thirteen. No one noticed the boy's predicament. He lived on alone and became the gigolo for America. Sometime we'll make the movie of those years—Julian of Arc—the story of a boy and his stepfather.

Julian knows better than Joe. He should be disabused by the examples of his father and mother, and by the rueful stories that Max would have told him. He grew up amid the disintegration of Hollywood certainties that is signaled in *Sunset Boulevard*. He is, too, a creature of the age of Lee Harvey Oswald, Nixon, and OPEC, of sexual revolution, the feminist movement, and violence in the streets. Julian could see movies like *Taxi Driver* which depict the whoring of children, films that Joe Gillis and his Paramount dared not contemplate. Joe's sense of the sordid was limited to neorealist pathos. And yet, *American Gigolo* remains a far more romantic movie than *Sunset Boulevard.*

It has color, which luxuriates in the array of shirts Julian chooses from and freshens the water-bed lawns he must cross. It beholds the exquisite suede suntan of Lauren Hutton's lean body with such hues of faith that we begin to detect a soul in what was once only a model's anxious chic. The color makes Palm Springs as blandly Dayglo as a Hockney painting: It stokes up hellish reds in discos and gay bars; it sanctifies the awesome Scarfiotti egg-white and ash of Julian's apartment; it notices the apricot of one flimsy sweater Hutton wears in a record store. The color is as reverent and brimful as vision must be for a sinner whose guilt is made visible. The sense of color in *American Gigolo* is the feeling of some poor, repressed kid from Grand Rapids, Michigan, hearing about the rumored rainbow of Beverly Hills. The movie is ice cream just set out in the sun, still firm but about to collapse; it is full of a moral severity that knows it will yield. The recognition of weakness or decadence has been channeled into the visuals with a rapture that transcends the mere weakness. It is the best thing that the troubled nature of Paul Schrader has achieved, and it epitomizes the flawed art of Hollywood better than most recent pictures.

Paul Schrader is a very telling portrait of the new Hollywood. He loves and respects movies because of what they meant to him growing up. Schrader did not see any films until his late teens: The ultimate movie experience will always involve a visible medium that withholds its greatest secret. That's why Paul cuts away just before Julian has to punch that supine wife. The longing to see is the vital pulse in watching and making movies, and the quest is more necessary than the resolution. Wanting to see is a plight spelled out by the great darkness and the shining light. It is the visual pattern in *Citizen Kane*, drawing us ever inward to that small core of radiance where "Rosebud" may bloom. It is the window across the way in *Rear Window*, and the "shining" that induces our imagination up into the screen.

For Schrader the energy was all the greater for being thwarted. He was the child of Dutch Calvinists, born and raised in Michigan, a harsh domestic wasteland remembered in *Hardcore*. That movie tells how the teenage daughter of a widower father runs away—during a Sunday-school trip to Disneyland—and takes to the porno-movie business in California. The father, George C. Scott, searches for the "lost" daughter, Season Hubley, and one day sees her naked body moving to the motions of the spectator's dreams in a cheap blue movie.

Hardcore is not a good picture, but that is a riveting moment, with Scott's anguished face scourged by the light of the screen as he watches images we cannot see. Perhaps he has never felt more about his daughter: The imagination has been released from the set posture of fatherhood, and it is a fearsome beast. *Hardcore* never risks thinking that the strict Calvinist father might be erotically excited by the pictures of his daughter as well as aghast at the depravity of her life. Schrader tries to suggest that she has found a love her father could not give her. But the director does not believe in love himself, and nothing in the girl's behavior ever substantiates it. Schrader is obsessed by the tension between austerity and indulgence, transcendence and evil. Far away from Michigan now, he lives on in a religious light, believing in sin and redemption but oblivious of God or love. He is like his own character, Travis Bickle, torn between monastic self-discipline and teeming retribution.

It could be a metaphor for the young man forced to live in the snowy light of Michigan and craving the fantastical darkness of the movie house. Who will have more heightened expectations of the dark than the boy forbidden to enter it?

Movies were always the beckoning of fantasy to those who felt beleaguered in drab and irksome anonymity. Why should their escapist power be any less for filmmakers? They are most forceful as inklings of amazing metamorphosis dangled in front of those who live in secure but "ordinary" circumstances. So many movies have dealt in sex and violence just because they are the taboos most vivid and alarming to the respectable middle class. The romanticism which suffuses *American Gigolo*, and which may be the most basic ingredient of the Hollywood movie, comes from Julian Kaye having been once a very good little boy drawn to naughtiness and naked ladies. After all, he still wears ties, and he has that very middle-class tangle of feelings over love and money.

Paul Schrader was seventeen when he saw his first film; no wonder the pressure was explosive and the sense of evil so lurid. He began to see foreign-language films: If he sinned, then God help us, it was with serious movies—Bergman, Fellini, Godard, Bresson. The young heretic took film courses and tried to redeem transgression by writing furiously about the pictures. What greater admission of guilt can there be than surrounding sensational experience with sentences? Another haunted soul, torn between excitement and worth, noticed him and assisted him into UCLA, where the disease might be identified. She was Pauline Kael.

The young man strove valiantly. He edited an esoteric film magazine, and he wrote his penitential book, *Transcendental Style: Ozu, Bresson and Dreyer*. To this day, he brings scholarly references to his conversation and his movies. When the camera roams across Lauren Hutton's body, it is an instrument that recalls Godard's *Une Femme Mariée*, less loving than quoting. And at the end of *American Gigolo*, when Hutton visits Gere in jail and tells him that she has sacrificed her reputation for his freedom—she's in gunmetal blue, utterly simple—then his head sinks against her hand and he says, "It's taken me so long to come to you"—

just like the close of Bresson's *Pickpocket* when love lifts itself up to be Love.

But Schrader is every bit as knowledgeable now about Blondie and B movies, Rodeo Drive and walks on the wild side. Since UCLA, he has lived the earnestly tortured life of someone with lost time to make up, and of someone no longer sure whether he lives in reality or in a movie. There is not that much difference between a young man who grew up hoping that with effort, will, and self-denial he might be among the elect of heaven, and one who devotes himself to putting people in the picture. A kind of worship is involved in both, and neither is content with earthly actuality.

American Gigolo is full of the longing that natural solitaries feel for the idea of company and love. Julian Kaye is like Travis Bickle in that he spends time alone, honing his body and advancing on his own spirit. Both men have a burden of hope or responsibility toward the world that they need to deliver. Bickle is far less sophisticated, and he searches among women without any sense of what they see in him. Julian knows all female bodies and has become immune to their personalities until Lauren Hutton—as boyish as a Cranach virgin and as randy—manages to penetrate the very hallowed, theatrical, and romantic sense he has of himself.

In contrast, *Sunset Boulevard* is a work of self-hatred. *Taxi Driver* talks to itself, but it is a soul-searching voice filled with the idealism of cleaning the streets, halting the various forms of scum. The voice is as mad and sincere as Norma Desmond's. But the voice on the sound track of *Sunset Boulevard* is the curdled sneer of a scriptwriter aware of his own sleaziness and confined by the industry's mercenary estimate of imagination. Gillis is a storyteller whose face is twisted with the pain of seeing stories turned inside out for their market value. Norma's script may be less astute than his, far less negotiable, but it is believed in. Even his cynic's blue pencil falters when he catches the hot breath of her conviction.

Something like the affinity between Julian Kaye and Paul Schrader joins Joe Gillis and his creator, Billy Wilder, a Viennese who came to Hollywood as a writer in the 1930's. No one in the American picture business has attempted more projects that threaten the American dream, and no one has so steadily evaded the cutting edge of his own films. Wilder was a very skillful but obedient servant of the industry he worked for. But he was too intelligent not to see his own compromises, and so he became a cynic as vicious as Joe Gillis. His best movies are gestures of hopeless contempt, and *Sunset Boulevard* is a satire in which the satirist knows righteousness is useless and dishonest.

No one in Hollywood had anything to fear from *Sunset Boulevard*. Its scorn is reserved for outsiders and lampoons; nothing seriously detracts from the greatest myth, that "honest show biz" is a proper cultural diet. So Norma Desmond is crazy, but the young screenwriter played by Nancy Olson is sane and wholesome as well as a cliché so far beyond saving or Wilder's interest that she is only a plot convenience. The movie is a lamentation from Gillis, who would as soon perish as live with failure. Self-pity inspires the corpse to tell its own story of demise while floating like garbage on top of Norma's pool. The movie is full of confessions of humiliation in which Wilder's scabrous and gloating style is aligned with Gillis's tell-all nausea.

Manny Farber fixed on the duplicity of the film in what is one of its cruelest details, when Norma has Max drive her and Gillis down to Wilshire in order to buy her gigolo some decent clothes:

> *Up to a certain point, this scene was unfolded in a straight narrative line, and then Director Billy Wilder pulled his Gimp-string. The camera moved in for a very*

close close-up, the atmosphere became molecular and as though diseased—and there was a sleek clerk whispering to the slightly ill gigolo: "After all, if the lady is paying . . ." Thus Wilder registered spiritual sickness and business-world corruption in an ad-libbed shot that had all the freshness of an old tire-patch, consisting as it did, under the circumstances, of naive moral gibberish that no adult in his right mind would mouth. This indirect shot, with its leaden overpantomiming going back to and beyond Theda Bara, offers a classic example of what the Gimp can do for a director, helping him avoid monotony (by switching from storytelling to symbolic "pseudoaction"), explaining hidden content, and ensuring his position in movies as a brave, intransigent artist.[1]

That little gimmick is the key to Wilder's way of making films, and its very smartness demonstrates the half-baked but unrestrained romanticism of *American Gigolo. Sunset* need not pounce in on that close-up if it really has a visual sensibility. It's an underlining, complacent and literary, unaware that the faces and the pit of desperation could be seen in the long shot. What Farber calls the "Gimp" is like the title in a silent film, telling us how to respond to what we are seeing.

That happens throughout *Sunset Boulevard.* Gillis's narrative is forever telling us something that we ought to be free to see and feel for ourselves. There is no better instance of this crowding of the audience than when Joe looks at Norma's profuse, intense screenplay. The voice tells us about the funny, childish handwriting—yet surely a filmmaker would show us that in passing? Spelling it out is dumb, mean-minded superiority, and part of the beating-up on Norma that makes her such a caricature. The carping, captioned narrative lets us know that pictures are not enough, that meaning and judgment rely on a verbal overlay, pretending to be wisdom but actually closer to superciliousness.

Finally, *Sunset Boulevard* is a homage to the defeat of intelligence and verbal supremacy by the reckless fantasy of Hollywood.

Which is why it is not good to look at. The thing that keeps Wilder from passion, grace, and wildness is his timidity toward the visual. I do not mean that he made films with his eyes shut or that he willfully fostered ugliness. It is more a matter of insensitivity to, or placidity toward, visual texture: He could conceive of a situation so much more richly than he could realize it. That is how writers were expected to think and behave in Wilder's era. Even the set pieces of *Sunset Boulevard*—the house, the shooting, and Norma's final descent of the staircase—are strangely controlled and rational. At best, they show a wordsmith going through the motions of picture-making. There is never the shock or delight of a discovery that could only be visual, like the way the camera slides round the smooth shell of Julian's car as he drives to Palm Springs.

In recent years, rather stranded by the changes in American filmmaking, Wilder has confessed dismay and worse at the loss of construction and the excess of visual indulgence in American movies. The complaint is far from groundless. With his various screenwriting collaborators, Wilder was a master of construction. The majority of films made today would benefit from that skill. They are not better, or freer, without it; they are only lazier, less taut entertainments. But Wilder is misled if he thinks that that skill was somehow a guarantee of being close to the marrow of existence. It was always a contrivance: The most articulated films—his and Hitchcock's, say—the ones that work as plot machines, are often the most artificial and fanciful. What betrayed Wilder was that his creativity always lay in the writing, while the industry made scripts rather than movies. Thus, they trimmed and tamed scripts, and gave them positive endings in the way publishers give books indexes. The persistent source of compromise in Wilder's films is that he was not

capable of visual genius or excited by the chance of it. Yet
that was the only part of the process that Hollywood could
not tame.

Schrader began as a writer, and he has still written several
more pictures than he has directed. *American Gigolo* is the
first of his films in which the visual sensibility seems natural
or characteristic. On both *Blue Collar* and *Hardcore*, his
previous works as a director, the script dynamics were let
down by cinematic deficiencies. We should give credit on
Gigolo to photographer John Bailey and "visual consultant"
Ferdinando Scarfiotti. And I suspect that the film's quality
owes a great deal to being conceived and set in Los Angeles,
the city of ultimate iniquity in the mind of a lapsed Calvinist cineast. The film owes much, too, to the way the deadpan portrait of the gigolo sums up so many of the hopes and
the fears that attend the young as they pause on the brink
of the picture business—always the most fiendish and de-
generate establishment in the town.

We define a "gigolo" as a man who lives off the money
or gifts of a woman, generally an older woman, in return
for sexual favors. Sometimes we are as coy about it as in
Sunset Boulevard. Nothing in that picture positively deters
you from believing that Norma Desmond has given Gillis
free board, food, and clothes in return for his work on her
script, his availability as a companion, and his willingness
to empty the ashtrays. But it was a great, arousing virtue of
American films made with that reticence that the imagination goes several steps farther into the dark. It was also the
most crushing restriction put upon Norma's character. In
1950 a younger woman in a movie could be titillating and
lewd: She could be stretched out for sex, in a dress that was
only a clinging sheet, like Marilyn Monroe in *The Asphalt
Jungle.* Wilder can make Norma all the more absurd and
irrational because he is not allowed to show her in bed or
explore her lucid sexual appetite.

But in *American Gigolo* Lauren Hutton's character can

quietly tell Julian Kaye she wonders what it would be like to fuck him. Audiences gasped and giggled at that line, like children whose parents start to address them about the strong words that kids toss around like Frisbees. Lauren Hutton must have worried over mouthing it. But in the instant that she did, with a shyness that was becoming to her character's great need, she moved from being only a photographer's model to an actress. The film's perilous scheme of character begins to work because her bravery extracts Richard Gere from his narcissism.

The gigolo of the title is a male prostitute. We are in little doubt about what he does. Julian learns languages, he wears clothes, and he has studied antiques so that he may be versatile. He is a fashion plate who can be taken anywhere by women who might be the wives of doctors, realty agents, or studio bosses. He may not sleep with them all: Rest is expunged from his dedicated and blind careerism. But he is good at delivering orgasm to those for whom it may be rare, difficult, or forgotten. The orgasm has a price, to be sure, but it also bears no responsibility.

I do not believe pleasure or boastfulness are strong enough in Paul Schrader for Julian to be the spokesman for the director's own sexuality. Julian is so eloquent a romantic figure because he is a surrogate for Schrader's commercial lust. Never forget that a gigolo trades his body for money. We are so inflamed by the idea of the body that we hurry past the resonant cash. But for the listlessly attractive stud, it may be the most arousing commodity. *American Gigolo* is a work of perversity in that it gives its greatest erotic charge to money and money's power.

Schrader's film is a parable about making it in L.A., and you don't have to look too far to see the references to filmmaking. Hollywood likes to be regarded as an impenetrable, wicked kingdom—a pit of dragons. It tells every newcomer that it will break his heart and warp his soul. Gossip is cocky about starlets who flung themselves from the HOLLY-

WOODLAND sign. Despite the hardness of his manner now, Schrader would have grown up as horrified as any hero who knows one day he must enter the ogre's castle and subdue the beast.

Hollywood offers less a job than an ordeal for prowess and integrity. Its product has always been a metaphor for sex, not just in subject matter and iconography, but from the need for darkness and the hope of overpowering joy and fantastic redemption. The film director must give us all the thrills that Julian's expertise can provide, and whatever Julian guarantees his ladies is laid in our laps, too. But the system whispers in a director's ear: Can you make it in L.A. without selling out or one day watching your own balls roll foul at Chavez Ravine? Can you be rich and proud, successful and content? And so the artist or adventurer takes on the loneliness of someone who must never let the *Reporter* know that Bel-Air is not enough. Whether he succeeds or fails, or remembers the difference all his life, the pilgrim in L.A. must be good-looking, and this is the most hysterical alienation our game knows.

That is crucial to Julian's isolation. He is a paid professional who comes to the house in the mood of a plumber, prepared for what may be a messy business of clearing clogged pipes. The lady of the house has no need to care or think about her plumber once he has been paid. You do not grant him a full or an equal share of reality; he is a stooge, like a star, a figure in your dream of happiness. This is intimate plumbing, but in Los Angeles ladies have tucks taken out of their faces and resolution pumped into their breasts. We see Julian bent over one young woman, his hand in her groin. She lies still and mute, apparently ashamed of her shortcoming. The husband watches, and Julian is like a surgeon ignoring the gallery of students as he tells her he is just going to make her wet and that she is a very lovely lady. Then the husband, in a matter-of-fact way, tells him to hurt her. This is the woman whose murder will be laid at Julian's

Gucci feet. The hired hand does hurt her—the cutaway vouchsafes that. Schrader went further in shooting and then backed off in editing:

> *This picture portrays an entirely debased currency of society, a sort of society without any fix, an amoral society. He has risen to the top of it because he makes it look good. He's there [at the Rheimans], and it's not really quite what he had in mind, but he doesn't get up and leave. The way it was shot he goes to the point where he hits her. He goes one more step and really smashes her, and this was so unpleasant when we were watching the film that it just threw them out of the film. I couldn't recover from it, so I trimmed it short.*[2]

That is the romantic confessing, as well as another kind of cutting technician at work. It also points to a system in which there is a significant gulf between an "R" and an "X" rating. What people do with one another sexually is still out of bounds in feature movies unless they have decided to imitate the movies. But the suggestions are rougher and far more candid than they were in 1950. Around the corner, of course, there exists a large alternative genre—the pornographic movie in which everything that can be seen is shown, only proving the ultimate inaccessibility of some sensations of love and sex. Just as movies dealing with violence have separated spectacle and pain, so those treating sex have dislocated performance from pleasure. Nothing is more revealing of Julian, and of the film, than Schrader's throwaway line that "he makes it look good."

The supreme romanticism in *American Gigolo*—as old as Lillian Gish—is that to be good-looking is to confirm the equation of virtue and appearance. More than most movies, it attests to the notion that to be in a film is to be admirable. This is the very dementia that Joe Gillis and the apparatus of *Sunset Boulevard* believe ruined Norma Desmond. She has fallen prey to her own legend, and she sees herself as if she were always up there on the screen, more illuminated than ordinary. That is the significance of the moment when she stands up and is caught in the beam of light projecting one of her own old movies. She is, if you like, the victim of egomania. This is the heretical discontent that underlies *Sunset Boulevard* but never speaks out directly.

The argument becomes more ominous the more you pursue it toward the point that movies may have helped eclipse real experiences with fantasy and image. Susan Sontag has made the case at the fundamental level of photography:

> *Photography, which has so many narcissistic uses, is also a powerful instrument for depersonalizing our relation to the world; and the two uses are complementary. Like a pair of binoculars with no right or wrong end, the camera makes exotic things near, intimate; and familiar things small, abstract, strange, much farther away. It offers, in one easy, habit-forming activity, both participation and alienation in our own lives and those of others— allowing us to participate, while confirming alienation.*[3]

In a climate in which the majority of movies seem to be made by and for adolescents, in which the knack of packaging and the gloss of money exceed imaginative passion, and in which movies aspire to the ambiance of the theater lobby, that is a terrible warning. It is as if movies offered a way of simplifying or nullifying experience through vivid imagery. It is the most demanding question to be asked by anyone dissatisfied with the way most films match up to life. It may be why so many pictures are unsatisfying, and it is a worry that lies behind the belief that most American films of the seventies were accomplices in the aura of a great game. I remain unsure how good or pretentious *American Gigolo* is. But I know that it moved, disturbed, and fascinated me more than most American films of the last ten years. That could be because, like Paul Schrader, I suffer from a conflicting rage for the visual and the puritanically literate.

American Gigolo is better and more challenging than *Sunset Boulevard* because it is more conscious of that flux. I feel with the earlier film that Wilder never understood his own compromised feelings about Hollywood, his weakness for cruel mockery, or his dislike of people when those sharp little "Gimps" can dispatch them. He trashed Swanson and von Stroheim, and he used William Holden as the smooth, sly, handsome liar he was as a young man. It's interesting to recall that Montgomery Clift turned down the Joe Gillis part, maybe because, as Wilder charges, he was fearful of being seen on screen with an older woman; or maybe, as Patricia Bosworth suggests, Clift was worried that some might see the film as a reflection on his real relationship with Libby Holman.

Who knows what lurks in the heart of a star? They are very credulous about what it is to be good-looking. Clift could not have been quite as unflinchingly beautiful if he did not believe in an emotional, or spiritual, corollary in himself. So many stars have declined to play people who would look or behave badly on screen. They are not just professional actors, but people venturing themselves. Humphrey Bogart played villains for years and looked disagreeable, superficial, or hurried. Then he drifted into playing a different kind of role—the fatalistic, tough loner for whom audiences could feel sympathy. He slowed immediately; he took pleasure, because at last his parts overlapped with the way he wanted to think of himself; he made a fine stylishness out of being laconic, watchful, and withdrawn; he found the grace and gravity of letting the camera come to him; and he became a star.

William Holden never quite reached that peak. He never surpassed the specter in Walker Percy's *The Moviegoer*, who "turned down Toulouse shedding light as he goes. An aura of heightened reality moves with him and all who fall within it feel it." [4] The older Holden, especially the veteran in

Network, is the Marlboro man lured into *Days of Our Lives*. And in *Sunset Boulevard* he was a handsome, blank facade deserted by voice, integrity, and intelligence; he was halfway to the lovely zombie that Richard Gere has become.

Gere, too, was a replacement. Yet if John Travolta had played that part, think of the extra pathos, the sorrowful vulnerability, which would have becalmed the picture. Gere is grown up, so his blankness is that much more nihilistic and so much less sentimentally pliable. The second-choice casting was astute in both cases, for it reminded us how far movie actors are always gigolos of fashion, mere clotheshorses on parade for our whimsical fancies and for their inflated life-style. The subservience bred in film actors—the thing that most alarms stoic Gore Vidal about Ronald Reagan—is the clue to Julian Kaye's moral apathy.

There is no humor or love in *American Gigolo*. There is only one performance. There is a breathtaking fusion of picture and sound. There is a horror of sex—infantlike fear and loathing—which can be found in so many of Schrader's contemporaries, but is tempered here by the cool tone of the film. Nevertheless, this gigolo is someone who puts money and its purchases above sex or love. The film is like its surfaces—steel, glass, celluloid—hard and cold and so amenable to the slide of the camera's eye. It sees the gigolo as the heartless front of style we may aspire to, the figure that has overcome all the ordeal of feeling with the aphrodisiac of money and motion. This gigolo wants to be like a star in life, cut off, glamorous, immaculate. As such, he is the essence of the movies.

And yet there is that nostalgia for conscience and the soul, that imploring gaze which wants love and company, and can settle its plot with the benediction of some perfect marriage. But only if the film ends then and there. The happy ending is the myth that can never be inhabited; it is the state of grace that you can only have if you are in a photograph with someone. *Sunset Boulevard* despaired of Hollywood, but

American Gigolo has a more shocking dilemma—it cannot imagine the highest thing in which it believes, and so its people swoon and embrace instead of being there—in love, happy or married. The swift shadow of necessary death wish ends the film. Yet it is a film in which the quality or nerve of expression at least matches the abjectness of its thought. Its texture and tone are all imagined. This is a world seen in a dream of which Schrader can say:

> *Something always kept me back from getting into explicit sex. Maybe because the whole world is all such fantasy, such make-believe, that I felt the moment you start to smell the bodies, you move into another area.*[5]

The gigolo, therefore, is the human figure who has given up experience for looking good. He would prefer to be in the picture than to be here. He has become, through that process, a member of a society that has abandoned humanism. He is photographed man, neither dead nor alive. He would be beautiful if we knew or used that word any longer.

11

Halloween

I have sat next to a child so distressed by one moment in *Jaws* that he cried out, as if he had dreamed the death of his father. He sobbed, his body writhed away from the dreadful picture, and he seemed about to give up the ghost. Looking at him, I believed that some violent spasm had possessed his inner being.

Does that make me more imaginative than he is? He was not my child, but he was at the theater in my care, and I asked him if he would prefer to leave. In the moment of asking him, I wondered if I should even wait for his reply. Then he mastered his agitated body and treated the film as something he should not be seen to yield to. There were friends in the audience who might note his departure and never let him forget it. He said he wanted to stay with whatever else the film had in store. The incident that had appalled him occurs before the halfway point in *Jaws*. He had another seventy minutes of ordeal to face.

Jaws became, in the year of its release, the most successful motion picture of all time. It is a fantasy, a credible impossibility, a grand grosser, and this boy leaped and protested as if visceral damage or imaginative convulsions were affecting him. What we are talking about here is the existence of the human spirit, terrified by this vivid impossibility. It is what makes the dark of Halloween so vibrant, and the light of the movies luminous.

How seriously should we take Halloween? On the surface it seems like one more confusion of magic or holy days with the bluster of commercialism. Ghoulish face masks, spectral costumes, pumpkins, and candy are purchased during the second half of October. Children still go trick-or-treating. A threat they hardly understand is bought off with sugary confections, the harm in which they do not notice. Their costumes are admired. Jocular adult remarks about evil spirits are loyally rewarded with infant shudders. The next day it is over, as suddenly as Christ's anniversary is trampled in the market rush to exchange unsuitable presents.

But no other country makes as much of Halloween as America, where immense belief is still a desperate duty. In 1938 no invasion could have reached America, but the Orson Welles trick or treat, *The War of the Worlds*, made some people take flight in alarm. Not very many perhaps. But even those who stayed in the warm regarded the radio program as a wicked play upon righteous credulity. You could point to the New England witch trials only three hundred years ago as a link with the age of unqualified sorcery. But the term "witch-hunt" has been active much more recently —and seldom with more recrimination than when used against movie people. No one in the 1940's and 1950's believed that Communists or fellow travelers were creatures of the Devil—did they? Yet the popular language of the period used a metaphor that draws upon the aura of Halloween. Despite, or because of, its being the most rational and empirical of societies, America is a country of hysterical faiths and cults. Minority churches hurtle away from the dull center of religion, all brandishing their private apocalypses and perverse salvations.

Even in the more placid stretches of the country, there is remarkable adherence to the older churches that were invented in Europe. Patriotism is still as furiously possessive of God as a sports team is of its coach. Happiness is proposed like the safe stronghold in a Manichaean nightmare. Until very recently, white moral rectitude or superstition had its special bogey. The Indian and the black were themselves often warped or maddened by the totemic resonance imposed upon them. The abuse that both suffered brought the dubious recompense of respect. The white man detected a wilder, more impassioned, voodoo-like instinct that he had himself given up in the frenzy of mechanical and civic progress. Both races became the object of irrational apprehension that mixed unequivocal fear and loathing with the delicious thrill that hears an outlandish beast coming closer. They are the terror figures for guilty sophistication, Kongs that may rampage through the flimsy city where clever men have thought to rid themselves of jungle habits. When Kong seizes a New York subway train, everyone who has ever been a downcast passenger trundling through the dead-end night soars free with wanton destructiveness. There is an instant when our chained energy wants to rip sweet Fay Wray limb from limb: Peeping Tom is a murderer, closeted by dark.

The precious place of horror fantasies in America may be the fear of so much redeeming but uncertain achievement being abruptly wiped away. It could be the dark menace felt by the pale homogeneous mass. Or it could be the throb of unreason lingering in the bloodstream of an apparently enlightened constitution that was also a gesture of willful, violent liberty. Whether in *Dracula* or disaster epics, the anxiety felt by the audience may be the release of unspoken dread about an end to the world. But the readiness to believe in such a drastic transition shows us another reason for faith in spirits and one that is shared with a need for movies. Metaphor is a transitional force that has to be believed in before particular metaphors can be accepted or attempted. Transition is the beckoning call of America, the new light that might fall on lowly lives. It is the notion that a pauper, a criminal, or a fanatic could become a pillar of the establishment. Or that a man is already his own ghost if his identity is so fluid. That state of mind created and marketed the movies, where the split-second cut can tempt and guide the unstable imagination and in which the voyeuristic role of the audience allows it to pretend to be somewhere else.

Americans do not like to believe that they have pioneered and been victimized by fantastical hope. Prove it, they say, and who can? The merit of the idea is no more than that of rumor. If it clings, that alone can testify to American vulnerability. I can only sketch in the history of anxious fancy, but I can be much more precise about the way film assists it. At the very least, it is striking that a country so preoccupied with GNP, with the interlocking machinery of capitalism, research, science, social statistics, and measurable alteration in the state of man, should believe in a large rubber shark and the ominous musical theme current in the waters off Amity Island.

The incident in *Jaws* that so alarmed the child does not involve the shark. Of course, it comes in a context where we are dreading further attacks from that sublime underwater monster which is already everywhere and anywhere, a malevolence in the water. Richard Dreyfuss puts on diving gear to investigate a sunken fishing boat. This is a folly we cringe from. We urge him not to go, but he cannot hear us, and we cannot prevent ourselves going with him. Like all such films, *Jaws* sets up a pattern of safe and unsafe places, and then makes the bravery or ignorance of its characters venture from one to the other. As a model for the dynamics of terror, this repeats the violent confrontation of auditorium and screen, the safe domain of reality and the dangerous flatness of spiritual ordeal.

There is a small hole in the hull of the boat. The camera peers in over Dreyfuss's shoulder as he feels in that cavity. The audience flinches from the film's inward motion—the shark's mouth might be waiting inside the hole. Who cares that a shark could not fit inside the boat, or that sharks do not prey in that manner? We know we are not just dealing with sharks. The film is the threat that waits with such torturing skill. Our nervousness begins to subside, and then a severed head rolls into view in the hole.

I have seen the movie several times, but I still could not describe that head reliably. The panic in one's reaction scatters the observation that might allow accuracy. Emotional vehemence has triumphed over objectivity. It "is" the head of a fisherman killed at some time by the shark; it "is" a creation of the makeup department (I hope)—a kind of Halloween mask; it "is" the trick/treat that the whole sequence builds to, a prop moved into the vacant slot, a gorgeous "boo" in *our* faces, the manifestation of lurking devils that the medium is always hinting at.

But that is too many things for us to be comfortable with just trick or treat. In watching any film, the viewer is asked to join the separated elements of the screened image—actor and part—with his or her own commitment. In horror films, or in any films dealing in suspense, that commitment is regularly abused and tormented. No one making *Jaws* believed in sharks terrorizing resort communities. The social conservatism of the filmmakers, as I judge it, is such that any genuine fears would have prevented the film being made. Hollywood has a shameful record of not treating the subjects Americans have reason to be afraid of. Hollywood is far less inhibited about remote fears that can be given a spurious but shocking reality on the screen. Steven Spielberg, the director of *Jaws*, gives every sign of a kindly, simple view of human nature. In all his pictures, the ordinary man does prevail, and in *Close Encounters*, a quite remarkable optimism about all our futures suffuses special effects that are normally employed to unsettle us. Nevertheless, Spielberg's interest in the minds of the audience bears out the film industry's ruthless plan to subject the public to an ordeal that they may "enjoy." Alfred Hitchcock called it putting the audience through it.

The manner of that abuse is often lighthearted. Enormous effort and thought are devoted to the effects, and they are such cold-blooded contrivances that the filmmakers are probably too familiar or too bored with the technicalities to feel the charge of the screen themselves. But in the last twenty years it has become increasingly evident that this artful priming of fear is one of the most likely ways of making a lot of money. If ever a filmmaker felt reservations about the deliberate infliction of fanciful pain on the audience, then he can take refuge in the thought that it is only a very sensible and moderately easy way of making a profit. "I can do those things in my sleep," a world-weary Brian De Palma told me about the pyrotechnics of *Carrie*.

That kind of professionalism sees *Jaws* in these terms: The purpose of the film is to secure, or trap, an audience with a project that is incredible but so attuned to more basic anxieties and so backed up with a circumstantial reality that the audience will be gripped by it. Notice that the purpose of the venture is not to move the audience, to change its mind, to delight or console it, to do any of the enriching things that one hopes for in art, but to hold it—as one holds a kitten and thinks of drowning it. The grip is domineering and extortionate. To that end, the "story" is constructed as a series of hooks that will drag on the viewer's feelings. It is a cruelty that the canopy of "entertainment" struggles to contain.

Thus, *Jaws* opens with a sequence that teaches us the danger of relaxation: A summer night beach idyll is shattered by a force that means more to the viewer than it does to the characters in the film. We see and feel the approach of that first slaughter. We hear the music that announces the shark. We see the very sexual invitation of the girl spread-eagled on the surface from the shark's point of view. We understand the implication of those teeth plunged between her fluttering legs, and note the casual malice toward women in even so benign a director as Spielberg. The opening sequence of *Jaws* is one of the most captivating rapes ever filmed, and since the girl is only a nameless figure, no one we know, there is a part of us that exults in the rapturous power of the attack. No girl in any American love scene cries out with such honest amazement.

After that, *Jaws* is a brilliant series of shocks, spaced rhythmically so that the viewer adjusts to the neurotic rise and fall of lull and whammy. I have no doubt that the script and story were made to fit that roller-coaster structure. The movie's epic of confrontation with spiritual enormity—a pop *Moby Dick*—cut out much of Peter Benchley's novel and concentrated its deployment of characters. The *Indianapolis* speech, added for the film, tells us that the Robert Shaw character is fatalistic and self-destructive. In contrast, Roy Scheider and Richard Dreyfuss represent ordinary nobility and perseverance. The shark becomes a sardonic, omniscient devil, and that very command of knowledge is what places it at the center of the film. This cannot be overstressed. The shark knows what the personality of the film knows—the shark is the deft tease that makes the film; the shark is the system we are subjecting ourselves to.

But *Jaws* does have traces of warmth and humor as well as Spielberg's confidence in the least apparently equipped of the men to fight back best. A nastier example of the same genre is De Palma's *Carrie*, a movie closer to the lurid torchlight chill of Halloween. It is to the creative credit of *Jaws* that so much of it takes place in high sunlight—though the severed head sequence is nocturnal. Very little of *Carrie* could live in daylight, and several of its daytime scenes are shrouded by filters. *Carrie* is a night movie lit up by garish colors. It is also a picture about blood, or the scarlet suffusion that represents blood on film. The blood shines with potency and magic, daring our rational disbelief to reject or explain it, then turning into flame. Not the least interesting thing about *Carrie* is that it shows a school (the honored seat of enlightenment) being destroyed by the powers of insane spiritualism, clan hostility, and persecuted sexuality. *Carrie* is mindlessly barbaric in the way it is ready to tear up the fabric of civilization.

Carrie White should not be in high school. She is an example of a character seen often in horror pictures today, a demure demon, the horrid mix of screen grotesque and prim audience member—the manifestation of our imaginings. At first, she seems too vulnerable for the world, but in ninety minutes she will reduce all around her to tatters. She is kin to *Psycho*'s very polite Norman Bates and disturbing support for the possibility that movie theaters are the haven for people as lonely, timid, and inept as Carrie White.* *Carrie* is a fantasy of revenge for anyone bullied or teased, and an insane promise that such vengeance is heady and lovely. The wallflower ravages society because the vision of the artist seeks no more than the box-office gross of destruction.

The first shock in *Carrie* is the steamy grotto of menstruation in the locker-room shower, and a barrage of tampons from horrid schoolmates. De Palma's own distaste for people readily fuels the paranoia in his central figures, yet he can't resist lip-smacking malice. His own wife, Nancy Allen, plays the unkindest girl in *Carrie* like Eve obsessed with the succulence of fruit. What follows is a grisly commentary on the shock mechanism in such films. Plot development and the loading and aiming of the movie booby trap become one and the same. A considerate but clumsy teacher tries to rehabilitate Carrie at the school. But we know how unlikely that hope is because we have seen the Gothic home Carrie re-

---

* I am reminded of Paul Schrader's confessional delight over Michael Powell's *Peeping Tom*: "Through the maze of Powell's gamesmanship emerges a true character: Mark Lewis (Carl Boehm), a secretive, lonely, passionate young man for whom voyeurism, cinema, and violence are the same. *Peeping Tom* is a cinéaste's secret treasure. Every pale, overweight, lonely film student who has spent hours in dark rooms watching old movies cannot help but identify with this film." [1]

turns to every day and the spiritualistic mother ecstatic with the memory of sexual guilt. This mother is viewed from a distance. She is crazy and ridiculous. But her exaggerated puritanism is actually not far from De Palma's own revulsion from sexuality in favor of fire-and-brimstone retribution. The mother loathes the exploitation of herself that brought Carrie into the world and will not speak of such things—like Norman Bates's mother. Yet as much as she strives for spiritual exultation, it is her catatonic daughter who has picked up the telekinetic power that can hurl cars off the road or slip knives from closed drawers. Stupid power, it never thinks to have Mum trip downstairs. Not when it can crucify her if it only waits for a stormy night.

This household is shameless Grand Guignol. But there is enough simple-minded ordinariness in Carrie and the Bates High School to distract us. Everything in the film aims at mythology: Its most devastating failure is the absence of commonplace behavior. Carrie will be elected queen at the prom dance to make her happy. But the furies have a bucket of blood waiting to fall on her—in slow, repeated, luxuriating motion, of course. The dance *is* a set piece, and no one would quibble over De Palma's delicious stylishness with it. The film crosscuts from Carrie's radiance, so painfully coaxed out, to the terrible clot of blood hanging over her. Our own position of helpless spectator is leered at by the plot manipulation, and De Palma knows that a part of us dreads and a part of us wants that surreal menstrual flow to cascade over her.

What surprises us is Carrie's recovery, quick as temper, and the way the force in her reduces her body to an oblivious vehicle from which imprisoned eyes and thoughts beam out the energy of death and revenge. The gym is magically locked and barred; the nightmare works just as well on all of us confined in that most claustrophobic of places, the movie theater. Then she turns it into an inferno with a wish. Carrie alone walks away from the furnace like a serene sleepwalker or a saint of black magic. One cannot miss the feeling here that flame, like blood, is a fun permitted by film's splitting apart of spectacle and pain. The breathtaking punishment is an extravaganza, consuming the vicious and the innocent. It is a display of a wit and bravura in the film-maker that is supposed to condone or decorate flesh burning like lard. Is it too nagging to say that Auschwitz relied on the same kind of dislocation? Is De Palma justified in his defense that no one should take this too seriously?

It is far easier to argue the merits of *Jaws* as a healthy catharsis. That movie believes in people and likes them at an adolescent level. The melodrama ends in action where our nervous energy goes to the aid of a resolute stand against the shark. The monster is blown to pieces, and the sea immediately resumes its natural force and gravity. Two tiny men swim back to the land exhausted but proved in hardship. In *Carrie* there is no such contact with nature. The girl's trauma is beyond healing; it reaches out for the frenzy of holocaust. Her mother's madness is a comic-book mockery of belief—the very response demanded by the picture. But these are the human figures that attract De Palma's creative pessimism.

The malevolence of *Carrie* is proved in the last masterly sequence. The one girl who did not attend the dance dreams of visiting the charred site of Carrie White's house and grave. So many subtle things alert us to the macabre in this scene. The daylight is very odd and stilted—in fact, it is night for day. A glimpse of the sky behind Amy Irving is like mourning. Vehicles in the distance move in reverse. And as the girl puts flowers on the black ground, the camera lunges in, the music soars in panic, and a bone-white hand grabs out from the grave. "A sad little scene," said the perpetually sarcastic De Palma. "And all of a sudden, we're never going to let you go."

Audiences rise vertically with fear at this moment. It comes so near the end that we are relaxing—the shock goes against our trained response, just as the dispatch of Janet Leigh so early in *Psycho* contravened an assumption of the star system and suckered anyone unable to think beyond it. *Carrie* ends with Amy Irving being wrecked by her dream—somewhat like the reaction of the little boy at *Jaws.* The established authority of film itself has been overthrown, and we are left acutely vulnerable to nightmare in a medium that has always resembled dreaming. Don't trust authority, De Palma could say—his early films were full of sixties anarchism. He might even hope to pick up that respectability for his picture. But that is callous hypocrisy when the story is such poppycock and the gross so concrete. Film is at the end of its tether if it takes such risks with the imagination of its audience out of technical and monetary delight. The banality of evil is easily tolerated, but it is a condition so difficult to reverse.

Carrie, like *The Exorcist,* is complacently unconcerned with what anyone of questionable mental stability might make of it. More than *The Exorcist* even, it provides no basis of normalcy within the film's world, so the stylish phantasmagoria becomes a permit for madness. It is as if the furtive superstitions that exist within Halloween were eagerly conjured into being and fears converted into violent action —the burning of heretics, the torture of witches, the browbeaten huddle of the terrified faithful.

Halloween is only one night, but it is a rich analogy for the atmosphere of these pictures, and there is a movie itself called *Halloween* which is the most concentrated work in the genre. It was made by John Carpenter, Hitchcock's true heir in that he seems to have reduced his creative personality to Hitchcock's bleak creed of "How do we do it?" *Halloween* was very modestly and flawlessly made: By its own standards it could hardly be corrected. It has taken in more money than any other B picture—over $50 million—and it can reckon on being revived all over America at least one week every year.

Carpenter's film has another psychopath as its dynamic force. Society in these films is mean and torpid, waiting to be ravaged by the shark's attack. This psycho is confined in an asylum, but he escapes and comes back to his old territory.* Psychos, like Dorothy in *The Wizard of Oz*, know home is best. In a liberal climate, moreover, they lead charmed lives and are free to escape from one home to pillage another. The film secretly supports the psychopath's longing to be heard. It fosters the Lee Harvey Oswalds with the indulgence and the spiritual mystique given to the Travis Bickles. The psycho is also the force of pure uninhibited rampage. The character in *Halloween* is over the brink, beyond moral recall or clinical cure, and way past the parlor puns and tongue twisters that still amuse Norman Bates. He wears a mask here, for he is an untouchable, a witch doctor. Even when he is "dead" at the end, he melts away. The interests of a possible sequel merge with the immortality of the monster. Equally, our society's allowance that even Mansons can be paroled ensures that Cielo Drive stays tense. Concessions to the tempest of witchcraft always conflict with our most liberal attempts to be progressive. The era of McCarthyism was in part a wish to keep the old America isolated and uninvolved. The horror film invariably placates that reactionary mood with reasons to be severe with the mentally ill and the criminally deviant.

Halloween's charm lies in the way the brooding, watchful executioner comes to docile suburbia—a kingdom of babysitters, the bravest of whom is played by Jamie Lee Curtis, the daughter of Janet Leigh. The house is infiltrated in *Halloween*. Domesticity is not safe, and when violated it becomes a scene of especially intimate devastation. For much of the time, Carpenter plays an honored game in suspense pictures—that an unseen threat is always more tormenting

* Incidentally, psychos escape so easily in these films that the case for capital punishment is subtly emphasized.

than the greatest revealed horror. This killer lurks in darkness, often between us and the other characters. Their dread of being cut off is something we appreciate from the manner of filming.

The young woman in *Halloween* survives. She is like Roy Scheider in *Jaws* in that, finally, she reacts to the indignity of being frightened and, no matter how she is harassed, fights back. But only after she has found the corpses of most of her neighborhood friends, all of whom have been killed in the sexual act. Ostensibly *Halloween* is a simple roller coaster, but its scenery is obsessive. The killings all interrupt and repudiate sexual activities. That leaves us with the implication that Jamie Lee Curtis's most besieged state is the reward for her own sexual restraint. It is made clear that she is not as permissive as her friends. Is that why she has the courage and the strength to endure? Does it mean that the real threat is to her virginity? Why is there such an undercurrent of sex in *Carrie* and *Halloween*, and why do the films favor abstention?

As soon as one tries to answer that, one has to recognize the general hostility to sex in all these films. In *Psycho* Norman's attack is preceded by a Peeping Tom episode. The film's explosive slaughter serves to relieve the sexual tension aroused in us. Jaws signals himself by an attack on a young woman that is given explicit sexual connotations. Carrie's horror of the world around her stems from the blood that breaks from her body and the impossibility of being reconciled to what it means.

There is no need to put all the stress on these elements of plot design. The horror movie only emphasizes the sexual message contained in all ardent looking, especially when granted the privilege and security of moviegoing. Things filmed lean helplessly toward symbolism. A knife becomes a phallus because in photography all shapes are formalized. Watching from the dark is a discreet version of rape. The horror film is often a retaliation by the medium against our furtiveness. In *Rear Window* Alfred Hitchcock rebuked ir-responsible watching, and he may have needed to make that diagnosis before he could lash back at us with the manipu-lativeness of *Psycho*. The relish that goes with putting the audience through it, whether felt by Hitchcock or De Palma, is part of the realization that we are compromised by our voyeur status in the theater. This most recent flourish in the horror genre is filled with the contempt of artists for their audiences.

But they only belittle themselves with vengeance and burden the art form by insisting that it be cruel. Further, the American movie has surpassed sexual innuendo and titillation with a thinly veiled loathing of human sexuality. Paul Schrader's *Hardcore* is a disastrous confession of fri-gidity, for the more closely it looks at the night world of pornography, the less able it is to believe in the strength of love that its story claims. Again *Psycho* is the milestone picture in that progression, for there in the space of a couple of hours we go from lusting after Janet Leigh to a kind of numbed distaste that wants to abandon sex altogether. The undercurrent in these films is part of a more general hostility toward women and an inability to show sex as a relationship between mature adults.

Yet many would claim that there is more sex, or skin, than ever in American films. That is true in the sense that censorship is now far less intrusive. But the rise of skin has been accompanied by the eclipse of love as a subject or a destiny in American pictures. There could be a reason in that Hollywood's concept of love was once so bogus and evasive. But less love and more sex has only driven artists farther away from profound and familiar material—the com-mon experience of people. No matter how much it is gloated over, the approach to love and sex is like that of a repressed adolescent—a Carrie White.

The great artists in all narrative fiction describe the joys, the failures, and the compromises of love. The young directors in America today, the children of Halloween, are fatally handicapped by their reluctance to deal with love on the screen. And it is from that failure that they turn in agony toward these horrendous allegories of rape.

12

Alfred Hitchcock
and the Prison of Mastery

His age and his illness deserved decent acknowledgment. His physical condition aroused tenderness, but it was not easy to think of embracing him. We owe him our sense of intricacy in film, but we must still wonder whether crowded detail fulfills or smothers the medium. His list of movies is guaranteed recognition if only because it has labored so narrowly to ensure that no one else could have filmed a foot of it. But we settled too quickly for that authoritarian version of authorship. Signature is not enough. Without an enriching contribution to experience, it can be merely an insignia, like his own brief appearance in every film, a cute and ghostly trademark.

It is salutary, though, to notice that a recurring signature can overawe the study of film. In no other art is it possible to think of a career's work stamped with such remorseless personality and effectiveness yet still so uncertain in achievement; so exact and nerve-racking but so inimical to life. Hitchcock protested that his films were for his audience, and his commercial reputation survives despite several aberrations when self-imposed riddles left him with his back to the crowd. But the deference to audiences never conceals the gloating that they are prisoners, and his mastery is that of a jailer. His textbook precision often aspires toward the comprehensive locking up of people; better still if they are *The Wrong Man*, for then the locksmith is a black humorist, too.

The problem with Hitchcock has always been to find an approach consistent with the variety of appeal in his films.

You can regard that range as being true to the deliberate layers of meaning in his films that are unpeeled with all the expert provocation of a stripper (he is the supreme clerk-poet of the withheld as erotic, of mystery as hard-on).* Or it could be a sign of inner betrayal, whereby character discloses more than consciousness knows. The most interviewed of directors remained cryptic because of an elusiveness fearful of candid exchange with a questioner. It was his way to agree crushingly or to ignore the subtle points put to him. Metaphysical questions got shopkeeper answers; matters of trade or technique made him garrulous and avuncular, and freed that unnerving Alfred, the poker-faced tease who liked to pinch our nipples.

In times past that was attributed to his solemn wit. He was allegedly the inscrutable prick for inflated questions. But so many interviewers were more idealistic than he could appreciate. Careful reading suggests that Hitchcock frequently did not understand the drift of his questioners. But he was too wary of losing face to admit it. Time and again, the point of misunderstanding turned on his small-minded piety about "pure cinema." It was the faith of austere inexperience. God knows what pure literature or pure painting might be. Surely we require the impurity of human intransigence to temper the harsh sublimity of unhindered formalism? I cannot imagine pure cinema, yet I suppose that Leni Riefenstahl's thunder of style obliterating individualism is our most ominous approximation to it. Still, Hitchcock has been praised by men as humane as Robin Wood and Truffaut for the witless naïveté that films can be cut off from feelings, ideas, and consequences. How often he professed his own

---

* As with D. W. Griffith, we feel a greater sexual tension because of the repressive self-control. Hitchcock is a voyeur who enjoys his own guilt. He can contrive an erotic stealth in scenes that seem to have no sexual content—Janet Leigh driving in *Psycho*. A kind of innuendo is at work, and how much more pleasing it is than the grotesque and miscalculated nudity of the very uncomfortable but characteristic *Frenzy*.

shriveled purpose; and how persistently we have insisted on merciful ambiguities, no matter that this self-satisfied man declined to speak about them.

Look at a passage from Truffaut's forlorn attempt to furnish a room for the supercilious hero. It concerns *Rear Window*, a film we have not seen in years and which looms out of its devisualized zone as a supposed testament on filmmaking, voyeurism, marriage, and the drastic responsibilities of seeing and being seen. I once chose a clever image from it as cover for a book, because I felt it was a cogent nutshell of significance, a key to cinema. And if I try to crack the shell now, it is not just because the film has faded with forgetfulness. My attitude toward Hitchcock has grown more alarmed over the years, yet I'm confident *Rear Window* is still a compulsive, nihilistic diagram. But I doubt if it is a key or a good enough answer, for Hitchcock did not sense the most demanding questions film can ask. Nutshell answers are always convenient and tidy—attitudes of mind that restricted Hitchcock and protected his startling ignorance of how people actually think and behave. The master did not film the world; he armored himself against it with bitter homilies and rat-community models. The determinist survey is so foreboding that it does not need to reach a conclusion. The methodology projects its own dismal end game.

Truffaut claimed *Rear Window* as one of his favorite Hitchcock films. Yet his first question contains an indulgence that he would never have permitted to Autant-Lara * or Duvivier: "I imagine that the story appealed to you primarily because it represented a technical challenge: a whole film from the viewpoint of one man, and embodied in a single, large set." [2] We shall see in a moment that Truffaut was not really content with that stultifying challenge. But he was ready to tolerate it in Hitchcock, even if the nearly contem-

---

* "Cinematographic failure generally occurs because there is too wide a disparity between a film-maker's temperament and his ambition," Truffaut in 1956, writing about Autant-Lara.[1]

porary diary on the making of *Fahrenheit 451* shows his own excitement at moments when technique is buried by personality, chance, and life's gestures. That movie may not be very good, but it is the effort of a man who, in 1967, praised Renoir because "his work unfolds as if he had devoted his most brilliant moments to fleeing from the masterpiece, to escape any notion of the definite and the fixed, so as to create a semi-improvisation, a deliberately unfinished 'open' work that each viewer can complete for himself, comment on it as it suits him, approach from any side."

Is it senseless to chastise Hitchcock for not being Renoir? To rebuke a closed film because it is not open? I have to say that it seems not only sensible but necessary. How else can one pierce the bravura of technical completeness or purity behind which Alfred hid? It is necessary because of Hitchcock's abject answer to Truffaut's leading question: "Absolutely. It was the possibility of doing a purely cinematic film. You have an immobilized man looking out. That's one part of the film. The second part shows how he reacts. This is actually the purest expression of a cinematic idea."[3]

No, it is not the purest, and it is not even an idea. It is only the glib exposition of crosscutting which, if cherished above all else, will leave the film cold and oppressive from lack of human mystery and doubt. Talking to Truffaut, Hitchcock traced this preoccupation to Pudovkin and to Kuleshov's hallowed experiments with Mosjoukine. He never indicated the least interest in any intention behind those Russian experiments in editing or in Kuleshov's films. It is as if a social scientist had appropriated a spasm of the brain first identified by a poet; it is B. F. Skinner tidying up after Coleridge. But an idea is something that transcends mechanism. If the editing connection is neatly equated with neurological spark and the segue of information theory, then it is the possibility of resonant and transforming art that is being forgotten.

And *Rear Window* is a scheme that falls short of wisdom.

The notion contained in so many appraisals of the film, that the photographer is callous and the killer worthy, is treated with the utmost cynicism by Hitchcock himself. He never exceeded the implacable but mindless safeguard that the Law is the immaculate object of our obedience, and that obedience *is* judgment. It is not that Hitchcock himself had a reverence for life or was touched by the lives lost. On the contrary, he despised or miniaturized most of his people, and had an intense imaginative obsession with methods of killing and the attractive fantasy of wiping out opponents and problems. But he could not entertain the possibility of reason, kindness, and weary grace being driven to kill someone. Raymond Burr's murderer stays trapped at the far end of a telescope, and his reasons are as unfelt as any policeman's would be if he were to do his job without qualms.

It is seldom discussed, but Hitchcock's sensibility was one of voluntary and neurotic enslavement. He regarded the Law without a mature appreciation for its ethical or pragmatic basis, but in paranoid awe of its authority. Yet Hitchcock's mechanistic imagination was all triggers, blades, and lethal traps: It was an eloquent example of the oppressed mind being driven in against itself, of dictatorship generating self-loathing. I cannot forget that this putative great artist admitted ceaseless anxiety about a policeman's knock at his door. Whatever the childhood trauma, to go through life so overshadowed is to suffer a huge burden upon the spirit. It seems to me that it has helped sever technique from meaning, that it has provided for a ministry of fear,* and that it suggests a degree of depression in Hitchcock which emerged occasionally—in *The Wrong Man* and *Vertigo*; and, fleetingly, in *Under Capricorn* (Bergman's drunken self-destructiveness); and in *Psycho*, *The Birds* (Jessica Tandy's in-

---

* The obvious comparisons with Fritz Lang have rarely been tried despite Hitchcock's frequent borrowing from Mabusiana in the 1930's. As and when they are made, I think Lang's style and pessimism will seem more severe, more mature, and less gratuitous than Hitchcock's.

growing doubts about her ability to cope), and in *Rebecca* and *Suspicion* (where the identification with Joan Fontaine's dowdy panic is remarkably acute).

But Hitchcock was not an honest companion for his own neurosis, in the way that Nicholas Ray was. He was often churlish or superior to it. Yet his films are also heavy with self-pity. He was less of an artist because he so often disguised pessimism with a commercial smartness and a belligerent contempt for weakness. Thus, when Truffaut raised the question of voyeurism and *Rear Window*, he got this grim answer:

> *I'll bet you that nine out of ten people, if they see a woman across the courtyard undressing for bed, or even a man puttering around in his room, will stay and look; no one turns away and says, "It's none of my business." They could pull down their blinds, but they never do; they stand there and look out.*[4]

Young admirers' brave despair with the world may have tolerated that, but the duller endurance acquired later rejects it as trite and brutal. Nine out of ten would not spy on a woman undressing, and they would not shirk the spectacle because it was none of their business. They would decline to look because it would be less than human to take the sight without the other kinds of relationship we still believe should accompany it, and because we do live according to the myth that identity is dominated by appearance. We would look away because our presence was undeclared, because it would amount to a kind of rape—not just of the woman across the way, but of our own feelings for relationship. The depth of voyeurism's sadness is its self-abuse. To look at something is to aspire to have a bond with it: photography has fixed seeing as the most vibrant state of desire. That is why *Vertigo* is a tragedy and *Rear Window* a board game.

The Truffaut interview is a fascinating text. It shows how

the movie industry has promoted impact without substance, and has ordained the lowered gaze of the craftsman as opposed to the outward alertness of a novelist. So often Truffaut's teeming questions were countered with terse answers:

> TRUFFAUT: *I was still a working critic the first time I saw* Rear Window, *and I remember writing that the picture was very gloomy, rather pessimistic, and quite evil. But now I don't see it in that light at all; in fact, I feel it has a rather compassionate approach. What Stewart sees from his window is not horrible but simply a display of human weaknesses and people in pursuit of happiness. Is that the way you look at it?*
> HITCHCOCK: *Definitely.*[5]

And so they moved on to the next film, the questioner ardent and generous, the answers flat and mean. I wish Truffaut had not shelved his intuition of cruelty in *Rear Window*. The original review is very perceptive. It revels in the skills of the picture but sees "moral solitude" and "a vision of the world that verges on misanthropy." It concludes by calling Hitchcock "the man we love to be hated by,"[6] a very shrewd description of what it is to subject oneself to the Hitchcock roller coaster. There is hostility exuding from the film. What Stewart sees across the way is not horrible, it is only manipulated. It is the anticipatory spying that is loathsome, and its philosophical weighing on the action that is so claustrophobic. *Rear Window* does not address this insight, but a critic should not spare it: that Hitchcock's nervousness of people induced his flinching warning that they are menacing and nasty. His style was tyrannical, premeditated, and icily framed because the initial disposition was alarmed by human liberty.

This has made Hitchcock the victim and flagbearer of American film's vicarious violence, melodramatic fear, and fantasticated reality. We know the legend that Hitchcock expanded in Hollywood because of its greater technical resources and the more polished pursuit of craft. But I think he also flourished because the American climate was so indifferent to daily realities—indeed, worked with the marketing policy of distracting audiences from them. Not only was the dream more persuasively fabricated in America, its cultural role was more established than it has ever been in Britain, where common sense has always impeded movies.

But that is only another way of measuring Hitchcock's cautious ambition as an artist. Neither the Statue of Liberty here nor the lucky allusion to the atom bomb there suggests that Hitchcock knew or cared about what was going on in the world.* Despite the London *Times,* he seemed as estranged as Norman Bates. His sense of place was rooted in tourist postcards, back projection, and storyboard sketches. His characters are uncritically indebted to clichés, with this one reservation—he took creative pleasure in undermining certain glossy or comfortable images: Stewart in *Vertigo,* Grant in *Notorious* and *North by Northwest.* The use of Freud in *Marnie* is as half-baked as the ecological dismay in *The Birds.* In every case but *Vertigo,* his use of mental disturbance has been sensationalist and ill-informed. Of course, *Psycho* works as a roller coaster. But who can miss its bland wish to make a box-office shocker out of exploited psychological material?

There is one character in a Hitchcock film who models the director's own alienation from reality: Robert Walker's Bruno Anthony in *Strangers on a Train.* Historically this film has been used in the critical approach that believes in Hitchcock's concern with moral ambiguity and shared culpability. This interpretation says that Bruno and Guy need one another, that Guy's dilemma benefits from Bruno's irresponsible energy just as Bruno's outcast state yearns for Guy's respectable achievement.

---

* One exception to that is *The Lady Vanishes,* a thriller which depicts the range of British attitudes toward European involvement around the time of Munich, and which is robustly scornful of appeasement.

But even if you allow for the superb moment in which Guy moves behind the railings beside Bruno, any metaphysical association of the strangers is made tenuous by Hitchcock's reluctance to give them an equal reality in our minds. Casting has something to do with this. Farley Granger resists attention as much as Robert Walker is on the wing with scandalous, campy zest. We all know Hitchcock's caustic definition of actors, but we seldom wonder if that was a sign of his being so uneasy with them that he tried to intimidate them. I suspect that *Strangers* benefits from the resentful spite of Robert Walker, just as *Psycho* gained some of its poignancy from Anthony Perkins's dainty self-pity. There is no proof of that, and no sure way of arguing that any performances are outside a director's control. But Robert Walker has an instinct for Bruno's unstable caprice that seems stronger than Hitchcock's wish to understand.

It produces a special tension and amorality in the finished picture between action and imagination. The meeting on the train has no semblance of chance * because the manner of the film is so grindingly fateful that it sees criss-cross wherever it looks. Bruno could be directing the movie, confident that his schemes can dominate the world of reason and action that he claims to admire in Guy, the tennis player. Any pattern of order or purpose in a film wins adherence from the audience: We want it to be about something as much as Kane hoped "Rosebud" would explain his life. Thus, the underlying affinity of the film's wicked drive and Bruno's demented vision easily turns Guy into a stooge. It is not just Farley Granger's effete petulance, but Hitchcock's arrangement of the trap, that puts us on the unwholesome side of Bruno. More than a reversal of moral order, it makes us believe in secret design at the expense of external reality.

* If one compares it with the sudden appearance of Dennis Hopper during the clumsy murder in *An American Friend*, then Wim Wenders' handling seems truer to life and more graceful in its balancing of the unexpected and the inevitable.

By the time the train sequence is over, we see crosses, too, and have no difficulty in finding the "hidden" cross at the Medford depot, and no regret at having surrendered reality in the process. We are enlisted: Our vicarious adventurousness has been separated from conscience or responsibility—we have become Bruno and, like him, we regard the world as a backdrop and other people as instruments in our dream.

I don't believe Hitchcock was aware of the alliance, but the film assists Bruno's madness. Something like this occurs in *Psycho,* but there the victimization of Janet Leigh does provide a focus for outrage. In *Strangers* only the deserving are killed. The future of love and happiness that Guy is being denied is a hollow sham. Hitchcock never made us believe in or want it, and in none of his films is "happily ever after" more than a perfunctory, sour way of ending. The dignity of ordinary lives—the heart and soul of Renoir, Ozu, Mizoguchi, and Rossellini—was a closed book to Hitchcock. Domesticity horrified him and provoked macabre comedy or secret viciousness. That is why Bruno is so good and unwitting a portrait of the director. Bruno has no real life: Even the parents we see could be figments of his mania. He is a man of ideas, envious of doers and blithely unconscious that his elegant plans inflict a monstrous, prettified destruction on others.

He puts people through it, just as Hitchcock once confessed he did audiences. Bruno is the motor for the film. Its own delight in fastidious precision can never rise above his childish sense of perfection. His plan becomes our way of watching. Miriam, Guy's wife, is a viper egging on her own death, and just one example of Hitchcock's tight-lipped disapproval of women. We sneer at her vain flirtations as Bruno follows her. He comes up on her blind side but always holds the most advantageous ground as far as the camera is concerned. It knows where he is because it is under his psychic orders. When Bruno bursts the little boy's balloon, our cheers free him from any moral restraint. We expect him to kill; we have digested the destiny of the film's style. A boat called *Pluto,* the shadows on the wall in the tunnel of love, and the delicious delay are private jokes between the film and its audience. That is why when Bruno throttles Miriam, he tenderly hands the body down to us as our prize. We are as convinced by derangement as he is; we share in the act and the loss of reality that allows it. The real complicity in *Strangers on a Train* is not between Guy and Bruno. Guy is a minor item in a satanic plot. The true passion of identity and understanding is between the film's form and our willing support.

The eventual shower slaughter in *Psycho* is also a rape to satisfy the repeatedly frustrated sexual longing that the film aims at Janet Leigh. She is so often alone the movie accumulates a mood of paranoid horniness. She dresses and undresses so often, she commits a crime that permits us to treat her as a kind of surrogate whore—she earns our lust and provokes the knife. The cunning of the process is unquestionable. But it disregards any real life for Janet Leigh's character, and it only embroils us in the lunging attack of a sex maniac, sacrificing its own potential subject of one personality overwhelmed by another. We are the accomplices of Norman Bates, but the movie recklessly confuses voyeurist sensationalism and its panorama of health and madness. In the end *Psycho* is just the cocky leer of evil genius flaunting tragic material but never brave enough to explore it.

If you can contemplate this interpretation of *Strangers* and *Psycho,* it does demand a very serious question of Hitchcock's self-awareness. What I am suggesting is a heartless or pusillanimous endorsement of evil, *if* the trick is thoroughly understood. But Hitchcock's face stayed starched, and I do not give him credit for Bruno as an intended example of film's separation of the world from fantastic thought. That is where *Rear Window* is so crucial. It is a testament to film's insidious force only in the minds of some critics. Hitchcock himself was too prim, too complacent, or too unambitious to grasp the meaning that a few people have felt. He was too professional to insist on our noticing the ugliness in our response to film. So he concentrated on box office and purity and the smirking condescension that despises people. An adolescent tidiness settled over most of his films—notably not *The Wrong Man*—to save any risk of exposure.

Rear Window cannot begin to probe the James Stewart character because it has no interest in Raymond Burr's. It cannot handle motive or responsibility because its view of the world is so timid. Hitchcock was committed to withdrawal: He made the bomb, but abdicated from its use; he put the audience through it as a torturer, not a moral scientist or a teacher. His endings warn against participation: *Strangers on a Train* has an innocent inquiry cut off; *Psycho* says never drive off alone, never stop at the motel, never take a shower; *North by Northwest* is a screwball horror story about the perils of mistaken identity—the light obverse of *The Wrong Man; Vertigo* shows how disastrous love and dedication are; *Rear Window* tells you to keep the drapes pulled—a very English reticence; *The Birds* advises frozen sobriety lest the balance of nature be upset; *Marnie* is about a numb woman who clings to her childhood damage lest she have to behave like a grown-up. It is the terrible isolation that trusts no one but believes superstitiously in a rigged fate, bad seed, and malign nature. It is the gloomy nervousness that allows police states, and that stays at home, tends the garden, and goes to bed early.

Such men have sometimes worked in concentration camps and fretted over the efficiency of the plumbing. I am not accusing Hitchcock of that indifference, but the separation of spheres that assists it is present in his work and in the conscientious methodology which told Truffaut, "My love of film is far more important to me than any consideration of morality." [7]

That stance encourages many teachers to use Hitchcock as a way of showing students how film works. His detailed gathering together of films is intimately tied to the nature and devices of the medium—what Hitchcock would have called pure film. But he is the worst example to take because he proposes the irrelevance of theme or content. It ought to be a matter of doctrinal basis that film needs the ragged flux of reasons and actions which Renoir tries to keep in one fraught shot. The most baleful aspect of Hitchcock is the dogged discipline that everything must be fitted together and that any detail can be isolated. It needs a slave to watch all those ordained movements and oblique angles without detecting a fear of life, spontaneity, and the viewer's free mind.

Hitchcock deplored the withering tedium of shooting. We know how meticulously preconceived his pictures are. I am not just asserting that is the "wrong" way to make films—it is akin to the way of Bresson, Ophüls, and Lang. But I am arguing that Hitchcock's defects as an artist—omissions of intelligence, doubt, and humanity—were the direct consequence of his way of working. We may feel that Hitchcock was a graphic artist with as great an instinct for anxiety as Edvard Munch had. But such a comparison only exposes the lack of pity in the films. Tragedy is so protected against in Hitchcock that the anxiety becomes a fetish. *Vertigo* does possess an authentic depth of pain. Yet sadly, the director was unwilling to re-release during his lifetime one of his largest "flops" without a substantial guarantee. *The Wrong Man* does have that mysterious extra pathos of the lawyer's ineptness and the wife's breakdown. It is the one Hitchcock film that admits a level of life above and beyond the master's design. But the bulk of his work only illustrates the smallness of mastery. The movies can be more than the whiplash of superiority and domineering mistrust. When we appraise the overall achievement, we should remember the alarming taste for cinema that totalitarians have displayed. This last verdict from Hitchcock is the more disconcerting if one thinks of the enthusiasm that Lenin, Mussolini, and Goebbels had for mass emotion and moving pictures:

TRUFFAUT: *Would you say that* Psycho *is an experimental film?*

HITCHCOCK: *Possibly. My main satisfaction is that the film had an effect on the audiences, and I consider that very important. I don't care about the subject-matter; I don't care about the acting; but I do care about the pieces of film and the photography and the sound-track and all the technical ingredients that made the audience scream. I feel it's tremendously satisfying for us to be able to use the cinematic art to achieve something of a mass emotion. And with* Psycho *we most definitely achieved this. It wasn't a message that stirred the audiences, nor was it a great performance or their enjoyment of the novel. They were aroused by pure film.*[8]

13

Psycho *and the* Roller Coaster

Psycho was released in 1960—a savage assault in an age that looks idealistic and tender twenty years later. But the grip of its ordeal has not relaxed. As times have worsened, so *Psycho* has come into its own. Its cynicism was avant-garde, its paranoia epoch-making. Motels and shower cubicles took on suggestiveness from the film. We believe in madmen more readily, especially those who live in polite, brittle shells, with mothers and hobbies. The portrait of family in *Psycho* fulfilled every Laingian intuition about loving oppression and damage. The movie crystallized the threat of bad luck on strange highways, and, because of the way it was constructed, it made chance seem like a fatal surety. The fear it encouraged helped us make a habit of anxiety, and *Psycho* is the landmark achievement in marketing the fear of fear itself.

The movie is so pointed, cruel, and expert that it trained a generation in how to compose pictures and how to watch them. Revivals regularly attract and frighten people who were not born when it was made, but who hear the half-warning, half-glee of the one-word title as a deadpan promise that covers a broad range of current movie apprehension. *Psycho* is a key experiment with disturbed personality and premeditated distress presented as what Hitchcock himself called a "roller-coaster" entertainment.

The audience may not be conscious of it, but *Psycho* is a turning point in modern movie merchandising. Its startling success in 1960 initiated an attitude of exploitation on the part of the medium toward its customers. The most active commercial trends of the sixties and seventies were inspired by it. Attention to the detail of filmmaking made the medium that much more elegant and gloating a trap than it had ever been before. *Psycho* is a scourge that we purchase to inflict on ourselves. It is heavy with our duplicity and guilt, and it frees a self-hatred that is a recognizable if genteel form of the mania in the Bates family, itself expressed in so many perversions of gentility.

Alfred Hitchcock's tortured timidity never liked to admit that anything ever caught him off guard. Such monumental, droll aplomb depended on being above mistake. No director was as chilly with his own failures, or as attracted to the authority conferred by being in charge of this medium. As a result, Hitchcock talked about the profitability of *Psycho* as if it had been as predestined as the remorseless tracking shots sucking Vera Miles toward the appalling dark house. In 1966 he told François Truffaut that he had deliberately set himself the test of "Could I make a feature film under the same conditions as television shows?" [1] He worked quickly with a TV unit, forsaking color and his regular cameraman, Robert Burks, for black-and-white and a photographer, John L. Russell, who had never been entrusted with a major project. The picture cost only $800,000, and it has a harsh, drab look to it that Manny Farber called "as bare, stringent, minimal as a Jack Benny half hour on old TV." [2]

Hitchcock could tell Truffaut with quiet satisfaction that *Psycho* had already grossed $15 million (nearer $20 million today), and he always assured himself that between the pinpoint engineering of impact on an audience and those impressive gross figures there was nothing else of significance. Nevertheless, I think that the modesty with which *Psycho* was made had to do with commercial doubts. The scale minimized the risk of material so violent and grotesque, in which the taste of the project was so precarious or indifferent.

A TV crew and schedule does not alter the fact that to this day *Psycho* is more disturbing than any venture American TV would undertake. Commercially *Psycho* has lessons still not fully digested. It was a major advance in the movement of theatrical films toward material that alarms television. This is not just violence—all those stabbings in which it is a decorous insanity, and a chronic repression of orgiastic destruction, to boast that a knife never pierces the skin—but the taxidermy, the psychological oppressiveness, the treatment of Janet Leigh as sexual bait, the ultimate severity in which no one survives intact or unaltered, and the baleful view of money wads, rat poison, and used-car salesmen. *Psycho* could not comfortably contain advertisements for our consumer trash. It is a shriek of misanthropy in which the personality of the film somehow stays tight-lipped, but the cry echoes in our heads afterward. Without too much subtlety, it says that its own audience deserves such torture. Hitchcock was too narrow-minded to recognize political, social, or moral distress. That is why the film stays so odiously thorough and complacent. But it is the work of a spirit alienated from mankind. This is not television's policy, and even today on the small screen, *Psycho* seems unhealed or infectious. No one seeing it has ever come away believing it was just "a good scare." The film's pain grows slowly in the viewer like a tumor.

But *Psycho* does resemble a good deal of automatic television, if one overlooks the virtuoso editing and camera movement. It was made at the height of movie attempts to combat TV with effects of color, size, spectacle, and expense. That battle goes on, but there is no longer any doctrinal hostility involved. A budgetary scale has set in for both media. In 1960 movies were valiantly ostentatious. Yet nothing made in that year is as spectacular as the grim simplicity of *Psycho*. No audience complained of its modesty, even if very few realized how much economy added to the spiritual sparseness it conveyed. The audience was transfixed by its force. You can interpret this as encouraging evidence of the virtues of skill and imagination; or you can point to the unqualified power of moving imagery in domineering hands. *Psycho* does not demonstrate spectacle so much as submission in the viewer. Just as, historically, in the early sixties film faced the prospect of dealing with a more discriminating audience, so *Psycho* reverted to the primitive pleasure and panic in riding trapped on a roller coaster. Its deepest significance is the way it held to the Hollywood sense of what an audience is, even if it began to replace comfort with stress as the customer's allotted due.

I am not suggesting that before 1960 films had spared their audiences the rigors of suspense. The horror movie dates from 1930 in America; audiences had trembled much earlier for Pauline or the Gish sisters, just as they did for Gary Cooper in *High Noon* or James Stewart and Grace Kelly in Hitchcock's *Rear Window*. We have always wanted to know what would happen next and have paid the price for our curiosity. The B-picture producer, Val Lewton, appreciated the device of withholding any fearful threat for as long as possible so that the spectator's imagination is inflamed with speculation in what is, finally, a revealing, assertive medium.

There was the quality of a game in that suspense. The ordeal was artificial and contained. The equation between audience peace of mind and business buoyancy went unquestioned. Suspense was always an ordeal repaid with virtue triumphant, demons extinguished, and wholesome order resumed. Commercialization could bring monsters back from the dead. But every new life found them less scary, and they degenerated from fulsome terror to the playthings of Abbott and Costello. Horror movies were no more than a middle-class Halloween party. A good thrill was participated in with the same kind of conscientious effort that took "decent" people to an unfamiliar church at Christmas. The inner, irrational violence of the medium—such as Buñuel had always been able to find—was being restrained. Censorship and production codes were part of that caution, but the industry had no wish to alarm customers. People watched from the dark and had their small fears personified and then exorcised as Karloff and Lugosi strutted their brief hour and then faced the withering common sense of heroes who had the force of the End at their backs.

The end of *Psycho* is fiendish. It has a revolutionary particularity, so unlike the generalized confidence that usually wraps up endings. The dynamic of watching the movie remains unsettled to the very end, but with the mincing sense of decay that makes *Psycho* like an autopsy we are forced to conduct in a dream. The trauma of the picture is never resolved. At the end, any hope for moral balance sinks into a pretty whirlpool of iniquity. The mystery of the Bates house is explained. Norman is extracted like an angry baby from his mother's rotten sheath. The madman is confined. The sister and the original victim's curt lover preside over the garrulous account of what befell the lovable sinner who died—so long ago, it seems.

But that explanation is a grim excess of the claptrap glibness allowed to "experts" in Hollywood pictures, especially those called in to explain events that baffle the screenwriter. It may serve those viewers who expect an answer, however exotic. But the stupidity of it is a tribute to the irrationality that had propelled the film. It dawns on us that this movie is not coming back to base even before we accompany the blanket into the white cell and the confrontation with Norman. He sits very still, but his mind has conquered decor: The room is unearthly and so vacant that it is unlike any other interior in the film. It is his head, and he sits at the far end of it like a dictator. Most wonderful and terrible, this is a calm Norman, no longer the wretchedly embarrassed figure we have suffered for. He is as settled as a monument, waiting to face us; he gives us an audience. He has possessed the film itself. That's how his voice speaks on the sound track without his having to move his lips. The imprisoned Norman radiates a huge force of malice. The psychopath has been vindicated. There is no longer reason to hide, or kill. He is himself. "The mother has won," as the trick cyclist says (you can almost see his wheels whirling). The mother left in ghastly excelsis has justified misogynist dread and utterly subjugated malehood. The film worships this awesome transition: It is a moment of submission, the most religious passage in Hitchcock's work. Then, as the face dissolves to the car being hauled out of the cloacal swamp, there is that wicked subliminal—a few frames—of the mother's dead head. Of course, it is another of Hitchcock's jokes, a knife in the groin as you start to get up. But it is also a sneer at happy endings and the idiots who still collect them. That face is the ultimate leer for anyone who will sit there and take such abuse.

Psycho is a story about possession and the possibility of one personality stifling another. It is told in terms that defy sensible acceptance. But we have only to feel our pulse to know how thoroughly *Psycho* has bypassed that polite level. In which case, its motif is secretly confirmed by an ending that leaves us with the death's head still as vivid as a Halloween mask, and the gesture toward the resumption of ordinary life so feeble and broken. For forty minutes Hitchcock asks us to feel for the everyday plight of Marion Crane and the ripeness repeatedly withheld in Janet Leigh's screen presence. It is only when she has seen through her dilemma—thanks to the weird compassion in Norman—that the film's lurking design strikes her down and reveals a quite different purpose intended all along. We see in an instant that Marion was a sacrificial victim, that we have been drawn into the movie by feint, and that the power of the picture is suddenly identified with the malignance in the Bates house.

Against that, *Psycho* provides a sister and a lover who are curiously cold stooges only trusted with the action, never treated with even the hollow respect Hitchcock shows Marion. The sister, Leila, is edgy, suspicious, and abrasive, never more than an instrument for seeking out the fearful. As a sister, she is the shrewish, embittered opposite of the warm, pained Marion who is such a seeker of satisfaction: Very few characters in Hitchcock are as sensual. As for Sam Loomis, the lover, he seems like a gigolo in that first love scene, a smug beefcake stiff whose head is full of lewd thoughts and the cramps of poverty. The frustration and lust make a good cameo of self-mocking nastiness. Sam is so much less sensitive toward Marion than Norman will be. Yet Sam looks like Norman; he is an underground hint of what Norman could have been without the ruinous mother: a faceless, callous jerk, one in the gallery of self-interested, conniving people who fill the picture with dishonesty, spite, and aggressive intentions. At the motel office, we get clear signs of Sam being someone who enjoys tricking and torturing Norman. The composition rhymes the two gaunt men and makes Norman seem like the victim of manipulation just as Marion was always laid out, poked, and prodded by the woman she works with, her boss, the man with the $40,000, the traffic cop, the car dealer, and the camera making the picture.

The mean world of *Psycho* is a consequence of the film's inhuman style. It seems to be arranged by someone so disillusioned by human behavior that he feels free to goad, imprison, and dissect others. The movie could be looking through a two-way mirror in a police station. The agony, the shiftiness, and the sleaziness of other people are rammed up against our faces. We can see the sweat of worry. Only at the end does one of these faces penetrate the mirror, know we are there and greet us with that macabre grin. The style of the film—its heartless resourcefulness—is known only to the final specter of the fully possessed Norman. It is the same ladylike murderer who has been playing all those word games with the dialogue.

Hitchcock's admirers say they are tickled by this "black comedy." But this only tolerates the alienation that can apply such refined style to such harrowing material. What makes *Psycho* so violent is not the killings but the neurotic fastidiousness of the style that needs to make that perverse dance with the savagery. It is part of the fallacy that the pain inflicted in the film is secondary to the skill which keeps the hook in the audience's fish mouth, especially when *Psycho* has so many ingredients to destroy faith and attention. *Psycho* is an intensification of advertising technique. The intricacy is calculated to keep the audience in its place. As part of the selling of *Psycho*, Hitchcock declared that no one should be allowed in after it had started, for that sows the seed of difficulty anyone would have in leaving. Rather than giving the audience greater freedom than it had had in the halcyon years of Hollywood, *Psycho* celebrates the jailer's skill that can keep people confined and alert at the expense of material which really demands the most sensitive and unforced participation of audience and artist. Part of the joke is the devilry that keeps us there. But the joke is so virulent that it bars the film from the gravity it seems to be reaching out for. Style is as hostile to content here as the medium is scornful of its audience. The artfulness of so many red herrings and so much withheld information trivializes the tormented world view in *Psycho* and dumps the nervous aggression of unresolved distress on the audience. The greatest giveaway is that Hitchcock believed he had made the picture without "cheating." If he could swallow that, we have to recognize that the mechanism by which he stifled his own feelings was not so far from Norman's way of coping. The most disconcerting thing in *Psycho* is the hint of what such strenuously clever self-denial is doing to the personality of the film and the potential of the medium.

That is why it is so important to see how *Psycho* is made *at* the audience. It is not an experience *for* it, a mirror to life that might enrich and engage the viewer. It is an ordeal which has guessed our weakness for dares and which mines the lack of self-respect in that helpless readiness. The aspiration and capacity of the audience have been reduced to the raw appetite for fear as a way of being kept in line. The viewer is treated like a paying masochist without the power of protest, a fish begging to be hooked.

Hitchcock never disguised how little content interested him compared with the subterfuges of the medium. But *Psycho* is a supreme performance by that self-willed blindness to everything except contrived spectacle. So many subsequent films have been influenced by it because it excuses the eye that looks through the camera and sees only composition, plot, and excruciating traps for all those fools who may be persuaded to surrender the price of admission. Commercial dynamism has become cheerfully allied with film's voyeuristic thrill. The result is a setup.

That is how the camera slips into the hotel room in Phoenix at 2:43 P.M. without being noticed by the clandestine lovers. Their hope for secrecy is precisely confounded by the camera's knowing maneuver. Janet Leigh in her bra is fondled by inspection so that John Gavin's frustration must be all the greater. Looking through the hard eye of the camera seems so much more ecstatic than the lovemaking could be. Think of the different tone for the film if we had come upon them making love. Suppose the film began with orgasm, and peace. Instead it invents a postcoital lull that feels like lovers poised and tense on the brink of an impossible sexual situation. The most sensual thing in the scene is the camera's sweet penetration of the room. The film disrupts intimacy so that its own form speaks for the alienation and disquiet of the characters.

Janet Leigh is pursued in this way for forty minutes. She gets back to her office, and money is flaunted under her nose. She goes back to her room—a featureless place, so like a motel room—and changes her clothes once more while the money lies on the bed. Bernard Herrmann's music woos the camera and implants the idea of theft as easy rapture. It works so well as a suggestion because the scene, too, is "stolen"—Leigh is alone, she feels secure enough to undress and to let her mind play with the thought of the money. Again the presentation of the film, the implication of its unnoticed witness, embodies the possibilities that are being indulged.

In her case, too, Leigh is not just on display but on the rack, seeing and being seen by her boss, and then gazing fiercely into the windshield as she hears the drama of what she has done. The interlude with the cop and the used-car salesman is just as enclosing and just as humiliating. People in the movie are staring at her, stripping her, furnishing her paranoia; and we are like those people. But because we are unseen, our spying is that much greater an exploitation. Because we are with Janet Leigh and with the mob that gossips about her at the same time, we, the audience, manifest the greater alienation of our society.

When Marion Crane is cut to pieces, she is part of us, dying. But she is also the target for energies aroused in us and fulfilled by the furious "cutting" of the film. Those energies are the sentimental, dirty-minded, moral self-righteousness of any voyeuristic process, of any power-based privilege that has no responsibility. It makes watching movies rather like being part of the anonymous throng of gossip. When we wince at the lascivious hypocrisy in the voice of the man whose money Marion steals, we should hear our own confusion:

> *Well, I ain't about to kiss off forty thousand dollars! I'll get it back, and if any of it's missing I'll replace it with her fine, soft flesh! I'll track her, never you doubt it!*

There is a grim smile on Janet Leigh's face when she hears that, a wicked understanding, the closest she ever comes to knowing what is being done to her. She smiles with the realization of the sexual power in moral superiority. She nearly yields to the victimization and is on the verge of accepting the whoredom we urge on her. As for that fine, soft flesh, the film is full of it. *Psycho* sneaked up on any censor reading the script for warning signs. Before she is killed, naked in the shower, Janet Leigh is stripped to her underwear three times in forty minutes. Once the bra is removed, but the film delicately cuts away before we can see her breasts. Wait for the knife. A tumescence builds with this repeated offering, and it is given justification in the way Leigh's "sin" finds massive salvation in the shower.

Less apparent than the sexual symbolism is our complicity. Time and again, our sexual energy rises, only to be cheated. Rain falls to dissolve Leigh's quivering tension. But she is kept inside the car, cut off from it by the glass that pervades *Psycho*. The climax of the shower begins before the killer looms up. The rush of water overpowers the crystalline hairset Leigh has maintained all along. She luxuriates in the shower in a way that was not permitted with her lover. But even in the shower, a sober black mask fills the bottom of the frame, preventing us from seeing her breasts. In the *tour de force* of the knife attack, the cutting evades the breaking of the flesh and the erogenous zones of the stand-in who was actually hired for seven days and seventy setups—such studious massacre. Even in the orgy of killing, water, and sound, a certain prudery makes the sexual thwarting more desperate.

The process of sexual excitement realizes that photography is itself erotic. To see and not to touch is to detach the erotic from the total texture of human communication. Movies do it always, but Hitchcock was unique in his instinct for points of views as vectors of social intrusion. The "kick" in *Psycho* is very complicated. But it is inseparable from the unchallenged scrutiny that we do not have or deserve in life. It allows us to indulge our fantasies for "real" creatures on the screen. Watching can no longer evade its own incipient hostility. *Psycho*'s various cages and enclosures—so often seen through glass—are referred to with uncommon explicatory directness when Norman gives vent to his haunted isolation. Violence here is an alarmingly apt concomitant of a way of life so affected by watching from the dark:

> *You know what I think? I think that we're all in our private traps—clamped in them. And none of us can ever get out. We—we scratch and claw, but—only at the air—only at each other.*

There is a horror latent in *Psycho* that exceeds any of the marketable aims of the horror genre. It is more than Hitchcock could deal with. He was as much its victim as we are. His great prowess,, his filmic imagination, only illustrates the inadequacy of his skill and the way film flatters unprincipled cleverness. The horror is more than the obscure darkness that beckoned Francis Ford Coppola in *Apocalypse Now*. The predicament of alienation could not be more dramatically demonstrated.

I said that *Psycho* was a landmark, and that needs some explanation. The film ushered in a vogue for mental violence that is now taken for granted. The sexual suggestiveness of the first third of the movie uncovered the pornographic potential of the medium for respectable filmmakers. And *Psycho* licensed the disturbed psyche as a field of play for the suspense movie. A cold, unrelenting grip had been found enjoyable and, like any fresh trick, it was copied.

I will limit the family tree of *Psycho* to films directly in its line. But the list must include *What Ever Happened to Baby Jane?, The Servant, The Collector, Repulsion, The Exorcist, Night of the Living Dead, Jaws*, disaster films, *Carrie, The Fury, Halloween, Alien, Texas Chainsaw Massacre, When a Stranger Calls*. Enlisting the genre of disaster films allows one to allude to several others if one accepts that the apprehension of destruction comes from *Psycho*. Visceral fear is the function of the dark and of cunning hints about what waits there. Some may argue that to exploit it is a healthy unwinding of anxiety. I disagree, and I feel surer year by year that by dwelling on the momentous dark, the American movie has turned its back on human richness and enlightment. The more films credit the horrors of the dark, the more tragic and strained the affinity between seeing and desire becomes. We might go mad from the belief that we are looking at torturing illusions.

14

"If It's Going to Be Chaos, I'd Sooner It Was Chaos in Ohio."

"Just follow the dotted blue line," said the gatekeeper at the Twentieth Century-Fox lot on Pico Boulevard. Did he remember that cadence from *The Wizard of Oz,* or do rhythms of speech always hang in the jaded air of Los Angeles—as if lines of dialogue had overwhelmed spontaneous talk? Perhaps smog is just scenario clichés piling on top of the city—wisecracks, blurted confessions, and laconic utterances that need no answer: L.A.—Lines Above.

At ground level the broken blue tracer staggered through a similar collage of architectural mementoes. No studio today keeps the variety of standing sets that once impressed novelist-scriptwriters as the epitome of Hollywood's dementia. But as you walk through the Fox lot, you negotiate the *Hello, Dolly!* street set—the exclamation mark drooping now from the weather and time's attrition. There is a western street, too, where for three decades shootouts occurred. Years later the sets look as naked and humiliated as liars frozen in their deceit. Of course, sets themselves are out of fashion now: The real is taken for granted in pictures romantically attuned to actual places. But those flat facades, crowded with surface authenticity, are expressive of the great age of imperial make-believe and classical composition when the world was remade in this Rome.

The line led me through the ghost city—still given grisly life for TV—toward a nursery. There were rows of glass houses filled with plants and infant palm trees all on the

215

scale of King Tut. It wasn't clear whether this nursery was just another part of the studio props department or a commercial sideline to hedge against the possible failure of films. Beyond the nursery I saw a row of bungalows, a kind of motel area where films in pre-production serve their time. There was nothing to confirm that this was the place, except for a man sitting on the steps, his eyes closed, a script on his knee as he muttered the lines he would read in an audition.

Bungalow 3 was where *Brubaker* was getting ready to go in the spring of 1979, under the direction of Bob Rafelson. I got in to see Rafelson at this delicate and exhausting stage of any project by pestering his office with calls, by promising to be discreet, and, I guess, because long before I thought of meeting Rafelson, I once wrote that his *Five Easy Pieces* and *The King of Marvin Gardens* were as good as anything made in America in their time. That still seems just. Coppola, Scorsese, Spielberg, and Altman are better known to the ordinary filmgoer. They work more often, and they have a flashier energy than Rafelson. But I hold to the opinion that those two pictures from the early seventies are the richest portraits of dreams, kindness, and failure in modern American film. Before I met Rafelson, I suspected that he was the most mature directorial personality of his generation. His films are so full of doubt.

To make a movie is to live on the run—as Bungalow 3 revealed. There was a front office with an alcove kitchen and, in the back, a bathroom and a smaller office. It was all like a motel, with the occupant's possessions never denting the anonymous flatness of the place. One assistant, Michael Barlow, was in the front, and another, Jolene Woolf, was in the alcove, filling the place with the smell of frying and making a late lunch for the boss: a vegetable omelette and strips of bacon. Jolene was the enterprising heroine of this story, and she had been close enough to the movies and long enough to play-act nearly everything she did as a matter of show-biz habit. But cooking in these circumstances was a problematic act. "In terms of this kitchen," she sighed, "it's a good thing we're getting ready to go."

Brubaker was shot in Ohio in an abandoned prison at Junction City, twenty miles from Columbus. The Fox front office didn't know the unit was leaving until it had left, but production was scheduled to start in April, 1979, with one week of rehearsal at the prison before then. Michael Barlow was still absorbing rewrites in the script, making sure they were typed and numbered accurately and waiting for the word from on high that the script could go to mimeograph: the effective okay. But this was March 21, and the script was still in Xerox form, and Jolene had been on the phone all day to Ohio arranging the office setup there. It was a strange mixture of waiting and panic that presided—a sense that the real work was only ten days away and that the mess of detail, gambling, and studio bureaucracy was sapping energy that the true task of filmmaking requires.

Rafelson had never made a film for a major studio before, and the strain showed. He got into movies in the late sixties as the brains behind the Monkees pop group and as the creative dynamo in BBS Productions, the company that made *Easy Rider* and *The Last Picture Show* as well as his own films. But, as he said himself, only *Five Easy Pieces* of his own projects worked at the box office. *Stay Hungry*, his most recent picture until then, had earned respect, but it was too offbeat to prosper. Since then, Rafelson had spent the best part of two years trying to set up a movie from Peter Matthiessen's *At Play in the Fields of the Lord*. That meant research in remote parts of South America, encounters with tribes scarcely aware of the outside world, and the present hold-off because the *Fields* budget came out so large as to make a major star obligatory. Yet none of the biggies who were available or interested appealed to Rafelson, who has always preferred to work with close friends—notably Jack Nicholson and Bruce Dern.

But *Brubaker* came along, and Rafelson felt the need to

keep in work. It was derived from a scandal of the sixties when Governor Winthrop Rockefeller and a reform warden, Thomas Merton, discovered that the yard of a state prison in Arkansas was the unofficial burial ground for a prison system that had become a vicious law unto itself. Merton and Joe Hyams wrote a book, *Accomplices to the Crime*, and Ron Silverman (who worked for Mann Theatres) bought the rights. He hired W. D. Richter to do the screenplay in 1971, and only at the end of the decade did the project catch fire—thanks to Silverman's persistence, the corporate will of Fox, and the easeful extra of Robert Redford agreeing to play the warden. Rafelson came in on the picture when it was designed for fall 1978 shooting as a quick, small movie. But Redford had been held up by delays on *The Electric Horseman*, and *Brubaker* was a spring 1979 shoot with a bigger budget and a great deal of studio nervousness.

It was now the time during production when Rafelson adopts his welder's glasses, spectacles more like goggles with metal sidepieces to guard the eyes and save him from distraction. The quotation at the beginning of this piece is his, said with the deadpan flourish of a fatalistic general not sure whether he faces advance or retreat, but knowing that his present ground is no longer tenable and longing for a confrontation.

Rafelson is in his mid-forties, with a face worked over by being so unremittingly thrust out into pain and experience. He doesn't smile very much while he's working, and you can feel in him a power that might tear at the various spiders' webs of administration that surround him every day. Once, much earlier in his career, he overturned the desk of Lew Wasserman, head of Universal, during an argument over a script. Older now, he directed his fury into the project at hand; he was so brusque, you could miss how vulnerable he is, too. He is never loud or rhetorical, but his uninhibited dedication wins the devotion of those around him. When you talk to him, he never bothers with gossip or vanity. There are moments when he seems just like a welder, impatient and perplexed with questions that delay the heat of his work.

His day was a series of interruptions through which he had to try to sustain an idea. It was impossible, but it was a mild version of what the shooting would be like. As he demolished his lunch—no time for digestion or pleasure— and lit another True, his production manager, Gordon Webb, arrived with the issues of the hour. When were they leaving for Ohio? Did Bob want to show the dailies in the prison after work or back in the hotel? Rafelson wondered if it would be possible for everyone to spend one night in the prison during rehearsal—"with regular showers, no heating, and shit food"? He was worried about Redford having had only one week's rest between *Electric Horseman* and *Brubaker*. There was a speculative hope that in coming late to a united cast, Redford might find himself as isolated as a new warden. But "I'm afraid of knowing Redford so little," Rafelson admitted. "We talked about the film on top of a mountain in Colorado for a day. But he's a very private man, with a disdain for Hollywood." Drawings of Redford looked down on this conversation along with exteriors and interiors of the prison buildings. The office felt like a cell with such a grim storyboard on the wall. Rafelson intended to make a study of a lonely warden, an outsider who must uncover the prison's terrible secret. He had faith in Redford's shyness working well, an aloof, mordant humor that would pierce the corruption of a world of good ol' boys.

He and Webb parted with the latter's weary guarantee that the Fox lot would have union picketing next week because of the hiring of Belgian director of photography, Bruno Nytten. Hopes of Vilmos Zsigmond and Haskell Wexler fell through, so Rafelson looked overseas and the brilliant Nytten was added to the foreign competition represented by Nestor Almendros, Sven Nykvist, and Vit-

torio Storaro. The picketing would be just one more interference out of sight and mind in Ohio. There they would
be on their own in a gaunt red-brick prison that was in use
up to ten years ago and then served another five as an
asylum.

Meanwhile, in the outer office Barlow went through the
Fox catalog for a movie that could play on the TV in one
scene. He wanted a Fox picture without copyright problems—even if that meant removing the music track—and one
that was not too obviously about a prison or too slick a
movie homage. *Demetrius and the Gladiators* might be
right.

At the other desk, Jolene nursed a beer while she tried to
find out whether there was a TV in the house Rafelson
rented in Ohio; and if there was a radio, did it play tapes;
and if reception was bad, was there cable? "Magnavox
thirty-eight? What's that, screen size or bust size?" Then
she inquired if the Fox truck which would carry equipment
east had room for some cases of Coors, a beer unobtainable
in Ohio. Her job involved anything and everything that
Bob shouldn't have to bother with—a list of horrors she knew
from seven years' working for him. Trying to set up a household long distance is a small but vital part of going on location. And it innocently reflects the life-style of even so
unpretentious and socially conscious a director as Rafelson.

Jolene called the Ohio house, talking to the advance
man. L.A. thinks of the Midwest as not much closer than
the fields of the Lord. One minute she was budget conscious: "We'd like to limit purchases as much as possible;
we're only there for three months." But not quite roughing
it. They would want mattress covers and headboards for the
beds: "Are there sheets for the beds? . . . God, no, Bob
needs down pillows like he needs syphilis." But then she got
into a complicated discussion of how long the leads on the
phones were—for movie people use a phone the way others
walk the dog. And while she made faces at me over the

confusion in Ohio, she tossed a tennis ball for Sheba, the Rafelson dog, who eventually curled up on the couch next to a cushion embroidered with the text: "O Lord, Give Me a Bastard With Talent."

Rafelson was in and out. He was casting in the adjoining bungalow, still trying to fill significant supporting parts. He worked with an assistant who used a Sony video camera, putting the hopefuls on tape and running them at night to come to a decision. This day he was working on two parts: one of the few female roles and the warden who preceded Brubaker.

The actors read under a flat light, while a Fox casting assistant fed them lines. The classic screen test, on film with elaborate lighting, is a thing of the past. Rafelson ran some of the tapes and studied one actress—"She's okay, but she's picked up every New York twitch in the book." He wanted rural faces, unfamiliar if possible, and people who would fit in with Redford. There was a great tryout for Brubaker's predecessor, a glum, droll face with grand timing, a man who has seen everything but never lets on. But was he just too much of a "character" and too visibly used to taking orders instead of giving them?

It went on and on. At six, visiting French director Jean-François Stevenin invited Rafelson to a screening in the administration building, but he had to run more tapes, had to attack Fox again to see if enough had been trimmed from the budget and whether the script had been given final approval. He had spent the previous weekend at solid work on it, and it was nerve-racking to know a faceless company might ignore it or trash it. The BBS operation was close, friendly, and kind to independent risk. Rafelson had no fight with Fox, but he fretted at the inefficiency and fatigue of so much waiting. He looked already like someone who has to visit a very sick relative every day, uncertain as to whether the loved one will be smiling or the bed empty. When you work for a big studio, now just as in 1935, you must adjust to uncertainty and paranoia. But in 1935 the system at least handled all the arrangements.

"Studios don't fit in with my personality," he admitted. But this pre-production ordeal was also training for a man who had not actually filmed for three years. He talked about the coming test in Ohio, and you saw his genuine curiosity about the questions that would be answered, as well as the huge strain it would be if the film were to be worthwhile. He wasn't sleeping much. He doubted himself all the time. He was making a studio film to see if he could do it. If his personal touch vanished in the process, then he would never risk another one. *Brubaker* might not be the final title, and Redford would be the selling focus. But if it worked out, it would be because Rafelson found himself in it—just as *Marvin Gardens* is a sad reflection on whether the American genius is a soulful, introverted storyteller or a crazy, extravagant con man.

Jolene was still on the phone, sometimes fielding multiple calls, then dismayed by the evening silence as the rest of the world went home for the day. "Everything in my life is pending. Phone, ring—something happen." It did, and she was off again on the necessary provisions for the Ohio house— salad stuffs, a selection of breads, macaroni, cole slaw, fresh fruit, ham, some chickens, condiments, cheese, coffee, a range of liquor. It was like going to the South Pole in a luxury Winnebago. Sheba gave the tennis ball another beating, and her owner slouched by in the furious tiredness that was inescapable before he could once more have the chance to find out if he could still do it.

But in any case, Rafelson would have to wait longer. The muddled ship made its way to Ohio, and filming did begin. Then, ten days or so into shooting, a Fox representative visited the prison to complain that *Brubaker* was dropping behind schedule. Who knows exactly what happened next? The trade press says there was an angry scuffle between the on-site director of operations and the L.A. executive. It would not be the first time a bustling, goggled Rafelson—whose films are full of kindness and sudden helpless surrender to temper and confusion—lashed out. He was fired. The film went on hold, and then Stuart Rosenberg was flown in to pick up the pieces. There was loud talk of litigation, still unsettled a year later. Rafelson went back to L.A. or Aspen, and several months later another project was announced: a remake of *The Postman Always Rings Twice* with Nicholson in the John Garfield part. But it would be another year before Bob Rafelson could start and finish that film—his fifth in fifteen years. A movie director works as rarely as a good hired killer.

15

The Runner

Bruce Dern gives the best interviews of any actor I've met—he is as lucid and as delirious as Captain Queeg. He yarns away for hours on end. You wonder why someone hasn't just made a film of Bruce talking—the bony finger wagging, the wronged eyes rolling in alarm, and that grieving, twangy voice veering from little lost whine to querulous outrage, as unstable as a marble rolling on a hard floor. "It drives me nuts," he confides, "being the resident Hollywood psychotic." The voice grinds against its own self-pity, and the haunted confession is close to a part he might play, the outcast or the reject, soft-spoken at first about his bad luck. But then you hear the nagging discontent, you notice the unruly hair and the narrow face held tight by forlorn spaniel eyes, and you wonder if you might be in the presence of a gentle man ready to explode, like the blimp pilot in *Black Sunday*. "I don't want to sound pissed off, even though I am . . . I don't mean to sing a sad song, but I get down on myself."

He runs to feel strong again. In *Coming Home* you see him jogging in training for combat; and at the end of the film he trots naked into the sea, the apotheosis of lonely ordeal. At school he was not academically outstanding, but he was a remarkable athlete. At the age of twelve he was under two minutes for the half mile—in 1949 that was not too many seconds away from the world record. In the 1974 Senior Olympics, he set American records for the half and the mile; and in his time he has held national records for sixty- and seventy-mile runs. He runs every day, eight or ten miles. And it's not just something he's good at. He is spurred by the relentless honesty of the stopwatch, and he enjoys the sense of endured pain. For Dern, running is the perfect physical expression of masochism and guilt. He has the face of a man who hears a competitor at his back; he has the face of a man who wonders whether he is being followed by someone else with a killer finish.

That quality is hypnotic on the screen; he is like someone talking quietly to himself to still the howl of rage and envy. He is like that in *The Cowboys*, a strange western in which John Wayne drives a herd of cattle with young kids as his help. Bruce plays Long Hair, an unwashed, unlovely vagrant who preys upon the boys' journey. At first, he's sly and polite. But you can smell his deceit, and you get the idea that Long Hair's going to kill John Wayne. *Kill the Duke!* Dern's eyes flare up. Now he's complaining—to a room full of press—about film fans all over America who only remember him as the man who "killed their buddy, John Wayne." He playacts helplessness. Then he leans forward and reproach looms in his eyes. "They don't ever recall that Wayne killed *me* in *The War Wagon*. But no one goes up to him and says, 'Hey, you killed my buddy!' " He reels off a catalog of slights and affronts, but as the stories accumulate, you feel uncomfortable and notice how far his power on screen—and power is often the word—draws on the same banks of resentment that feed him in life.

The Driver isn't going to help. It's an experimental, stylized thriller; it's also a pretentious, tedious dog. I can hear Dern adding it to the list of offbeat things he's done without joy or glory at the box office. "*Black Sunday* . . . that was a big loser. I was very good in *Black Sunday*—I was *too* good in one scene. Some people were rooting for *me*— just a poor little guy who wanted his one day at the Super Bowl. But that was no good for word of mouth, because nobody wanted to like a terrorist." He made *The Twist* in

France for Claude Chabrol, but it was never released here. *Won Ton Ton, The Dog Who Saved Hollywood* was a funny idea, but not in Michael Winner's hands. *Smile* was the greatest disappointment Dern had. He liked it, expected a hit; he played an amiable jerk, his most ordinary part— it was a sleeper that never woke up. *The Great Gatsby* was a major flop of recent years, and his Tom Buchanan, strutting with the arrogance of wealth, was the best thing in it. *The King of Marvin Gardens* was the part that meant the most to him; it's also one of the best American pictures in years, but the public has never heard of it. *Silent Running* was a space movie caught in the lull between *2001* and *Star Wars*. Douglas Trumbull directed it personally, and Dern was in his melancholy element as a solitary traveler grumbling to robots and making querulous love to the plants growing on his huge spaceship. Nobody appreciated its odd mood; it was written off as a kid's picture. For *Drive, He Said*, Dern won prizes—the National Society of Film Critics award for Best Supporting Actor—but what happened? Bruce sighs in an agony of long suffering: "I don't want to bore you to death with the names of movies you haven't been to see." In part, it's an act, of course. Bruce has made more movies than most actors his age, and he has a cult following. He is one of the most neglected or underrated actors in America. But there would have been fewer pictures if more had been hits. He wants to be a big star who gets the girl and the bucks. He wants to be liked, rich, and happy.

The dread of failure must be much greater because of his background. He is not the country boy he sometimes plays, not the roadie or the redneck, but the real-life version of Tom Buchanan. Bruce Dern is from the Illinois aristocracy. His father was the law partner of Adlai Stevenson. Poet Archibald MacLeish is an uncle. One grandfather was governor of Utah and Secretary of War for FDR; the other was chairman of one of Chicago's largest department stores, Carson Pirie & Scott. Bruce was sent to New Trier High School and given a couple of years at Choate. But it was at New Trier that Bruce found the first grid for his tortured soul—the running track. He went on to the University of Pennsylvania as a journalism major, and it was there that reporting assignments faded into anecdotes. "I found I could tell stories. I invented them, but people enjoyed the lies because they were so fucking entertaining."

He elected to act, and his family stopped his allowance. If he had to act, then the Derns could see no farther than the New York theater. Bruce disappointed them, and undoubtedly lived in a great personal shadow because his mother wouldn't even see some of his films. But he didn't make family pictures. He beat up the sensitive Montgomery Clift in *Wild River*. He had his hands chopped off in *Hush, Hush . . . Sweet Charlotte*. And in *Marnie* he was the uncouth sailor who comes tapping at the window for Marnie's mum and ends up with an amazed look on a face that was substantially pulped by a poker. You can see how the early parts taught his anxious gaze to expect the worst.

Then he slipped further away from respectability. Just to keep alive he became a member of Roger Corman's stock company: There he formed a close if wary friendship with Jack Nicholson. He played druggies and bug-eyed monsters —*The Wild Angels, The Trip, Rebel Rousers, Cycle Savages, Bloody Mama,* and *The Incredible Two-Headed Transplant*. He was in a few westerns and action pictures but usually as a punching bag for the hero. He did 120 TV shows, and in 100 of them he played what he now calls "a rather demented person." He felt that things were stacked against him. His agent warned him to lay off villain roles, so he backed away from the Corman circle. He was out of work for eighteen months but was determined to break new ground. He did: He got into the distinguished ambitious failures category. Meanwhile, his old friend Nicholson grew into one of the most famous and successful actors in the world. "Was I jealous?" The huge eyes seem about to claim innocence.

Then the bitter face bites back. "Terribly." He leans back, fulfilled by resentment.

Nicholson directed *Drive, He Said*, in which Dern was the basketball coach infuriated by a star player who doesn't take the game seriously. It was a counterculture film, and Dern was superb as the hysterically rigid exponent of fitness and team spirit. He and Nicholson played brothers in Bob Rafelson's *The King of Marvin Gardens*. Dern wore a moustache and a camel-hair coat, and was swept along on artistic self-hype, dreaming of a business kingdom in Hawaii that awaited the next throw of the dice. Nicholson played the depressive brother who is sucked into the absurd venture against all reason and foreboding. Maybe only friends so suspicious of one another could have made far-flung brothers so touching. The part stayed with Method actor Dern five months after the shooting finished, and he tells how some inhibition in Jack couldn't handle Dern's improvising in his on-screen confession, "I really love you," and its sweeping, perilous merger of actor and part.

Dern believes in total immersion and acting without safety nets or restraint. He has to become his parts—no wonder some of the roles are affected by his neuroses. "The last two years have been tough," he admitted. "It's very hard to play guys who're so unhappy when you're an internal actor." At a crowded press conference I heard him assert that he had had to be in love with Marthe Keller when they played one scene in *Black Sunday*. "And she *knows*," he added with the sublime instinct that fires all paranoids and mystics. But he has never even been alone with her, and he watched her go off into *People* magazine with Al Pacino without saying a word.

His most prestigious film yet was one of the most painful to make: *Coming Home*. Bruce was the odd man out in that picture. Jane Fonda and Jon Voight had always spoken out against the war, but Dern had never been identified as a protester. "I was so busy hustling, trying to stay alive, the war of me staying alive was of more importance than the war over there." He reckons it was a bad war, but he respects the men who fought and did their duty. So he appointed himself to look after their cause, and he invested the Marine captain with the pride of a trained athlete. By his own account, he battled with Jane Fonda for his character to be treated honorably. "I wanted people in the audience to put their arms around him and say 'You don't have to go.' " Along the way there were scripts in which his character ran amok at the end on a killing rampage prompted by the madness of war. "I have to tell you, it was not an easy thing to get the final ending past Jane—but, to her credit, when she saw it she cried and accepted it." The showdown scene was not in the script, and its eventual form came out of a daylong "behavioral rehearsal" that sounds more gripping than anything in the film. The actors started talking out their own feelings. Jane described what *Julia* had meant to her, and how long she had labored over *Coming Home*. Then Bruce started: "I talked about what she ought to feel sorry for. Like, *They Shoot Horses, Don't They?* Yeah, *Horses*. I was in that, but who remembers me? I told her how unhappy I'd been getting a bit part while she had the lead. I reminded her about the Actors Studio and our shared background. And she's a super dame but filled with as many frailties as anyone. And I got to her. I scared her."

That scene in *Coming Home* grew out of his traumatic soul-searching. It is both his strength and his limitation as an actor that he can be so scary: He gets high putting on the frighteners, as if this power eased all his hurts. He will continue to play character parts only, I think, with more freaks and comics as he gets older. But he may be our most motivated actor in a time and place of insecure people frightened of being beaten in the race. Sometimes his eyes go blank as if he were acting catatonic, and he says, "You can only have 'no' said to you so many times before it takes its toll." The pathology of self-pity has its poet in Bruce Dern, and in a country that loves winners, someone must heed the huge crowd of losers.

16

The King of Marvin Gardens

By Hollywood standards, Bob Rafelson has a perverse need
for difficulty. Perhaps it comes from being born rich and
working out his politics in dismay at the discovery that he
had been given advantage. Comfortable is a better word
than rich. But comfort could be more disturbing to a young
man who wants to test himself against experience without
any unfair benefits. Money you might put aside, but comfort
will have seeped into your body and your attitudes. Something in Rafelson would like to be Rimbaud, Kerouac, or
Dostoyevsky. Instead, he is Ivy League and Aspen, Colorado,
tense and irritated about it but still well provided for.

The irritation flares up in his bouts of creative energy—
some of America's most complex studies of success and
failure, extravagant journeys of personal exploration, and
the sardonic, absurdist coup that invented the Monkees.
He is at odds with his own heritage; it makes him look
angry when he is really desperate to wait and hear the other
person. His famous outbursts of anger may only occur when
craziness has washed up to his feet. Even the tragic murder
in *Marvin Gardens* comes when heartbreak has gone beyond
itself and reached the dreadful clarity of nihilism. Rafelson
knows too many easy ways have been adopted in movies.
That may be one reason why this most eloquent study of
the moods of Hollywood is set as far away from L.A. as is
possible in the U.S.A.—in Atlantic City as winter approaches.

This film is a dream without benefit of music, a comedy
that stills laughter, but a comedy nonetheless in that it is

231

about our shortcomings. So many American films are crippled by their determination to ignore or compensate for failure. *Taxi Driver* is about a failure so great that Travis Bickle must become a legend of destruction. *The King of Marvin Gardens* is Monopoly minus the reassurance of toy money. Even its tragedy omits the well-shaped finale of pathos, as upholstered as the seats we sit in. The movie conjures with the prospect of Hawaii, but delivers nothing more tangible than maps and an airmail-blue shirt that will be stained with blood. Atlantic City is a resort of burnished winter, where the beach provides no other festivities except the fevered burning of chiffon and satin, the burial of sweet Maybelline, and the despondent last confrontation of buddies from a western. The fun house is empty, and our intruders rattle around in its dead cavern. Storytelling's graceful shapes are adrift from life's fits and starts, and this film makes a habit —perverse again but one reason why it was a flop—of shrugging off its viewers' attempts at attachment.

David Staebler is mocked by the pun in his surname and the Biblical hero he was named after. He is the best-observed depressive in American film. Dowdiness, short sight, and flat intonation are the ways in which he advises other people to leave him alone. He has also vowed with himself not to become involved because that has always been the prelude to agony. In his case it has meant an asylum somewhere in the past. He is walking slowly through his own life now, giving off every signal of emotional blindness so that others will walk around him. But he wants happiness, lyrical moments of community, and the chance of imaginations reaching out to one another. He is an artist, or an artist type. He will be acknowledged as such in the middle of one disturbed night, sitting in the john, confiding in his sole companion, a cassette recorder. The girl who interrupts him there goes away, ready to knot her bladder or pee out the window so that serious art may have the quiet it deserves. Yet he would dearly love to make love with her, were it not for the dulling fact that she would as happily screw with him as have muffins for breakfast. She might give him more than that, even if she is not touched by his depressed ideals. There is warmth and kindness in her, and a dull, unaccented stoicism. But David wants nothing to do with survivors.

The originality of this character study owes so much to the playing of Jack Nicholson, a longtime friend of Rafelson's. But the concept is as strong as it is because Rafelson has used David to explore his own disillusionment with the idea of the great and lonely artist. David Staebler is a wreck, but he has the dignity still that goes with the possibility of such a man existing. Moreover, the concept can see the extent to which David's art depends upon him being removed from life.

The very arresting opening to the film should be viewed in that light. In a film that will gradually dismantle David's life, he is given a prolonged passage of magnificent authority at the outset. It is the command of the artist, the serenity of a storyteller who cannot be interrupted. The camera very slowly draws back from David's face, surrounded by darkness. The image lets us feel his psychological dilemma, but the situation explains how he survives. He has pursued loneliness and found a version of it that lets him be himself. In the early hours of the morning, he has a radio show in Philadelphia, "Etcetera," in which he beguiles the mike and the darkness with talk. No call-ins; not too much music; and ads? Let it be public radio.

He tells a long story about his childhood as the film opens. Even the people who dislike the film as a whole respond to this beginning. There is no fuss at the film's start, no establishing shots, no overture or clue. We are suddenly presented with a creative face, speaking to us as intimately as a voice in bed that doesn't want to wake the household. And there's no escape. Most films work up to their greatest intensity. *Marvin Gardens* begins with it and never actually regains it. The impact of later scenes is always more diffused. We feel the ecstasy of children being told a story by a narrator we trust—he knows the story and we abide by his pauses, his choice of words, his sense of human value. We are in the palm of his hand, Lois Lane clinging to his flight. This is David's glory: to tell a story and be attended to in a way that transcends belief or interest. His face never shows satisfaction, but this is as telling a picture of creative fulfillment as any film has given us.

He is interrupted. A red light starts flashing on his face. He looks away from the runway of his story and has to compress its ending a little. It is a story about a day when he and his brother let their grandfather choke to death on a fishbone. He is dragged away from his story because the brother is on the phone. Then he trudges home and finds his grandfather still up. The old man mimics choking in derision. The story was a lie, and the masterful storyteller actually spends his life looking after the old man. It is a startling disclosure of the oddity of family life, and a very unglamorous transition. I daresay the film lost the crowd then because they preferred the fantasy of a Nicholson who would let tedious elderly relatives wither, and then go easy-riding. Rafelson's films, though, are willfully loyal to the ties and burdens that link the old and the young. *Five Easy Pieces* does show Nicholson abandoning everyone in his life, but only with our uncomfortable awareness of his immaturity.

David Staebler is not a self-portrait, but I think he stands for Rafelson's wish to do work of seriousness, sincerity, and quality—a label that could scarcely fail to raise eyebrows in L.A., so anyone with those interests would need to keep them to himself. Rafelson was the son of a merchant, and he has always known people close to the movie business. There is another side to him, Jason Staebler, David's brother, who relishes deals and the great scams that will put the operator in Bel-Air, where the pools are Hawaiian copper sulfate.

Rafelson was Dartmouth, class of 1954. He had run away from his father's New York textile company when he was fourteen, and roamed the Southwest and Mexico. He played jazz, tried being a rodeo rider, and landed in jail a few weekends for rowdiness. You may recall the character Nicholson plays in *Five Easy Pieces*: Texas oil rigger who turns out to be a lapsed concert pianist. The yearning to contain those diverse urges is what motivates Rafelson. While he hoboed in Arizona, he occasionally thought of entering the priesthood. He resolved that uncertainty by going to Dartmouth: "It was one of the few colleges that didn't require any entrance exams."

He was a philosophy major, active in college plays, and an editor of the literary magazine. But in later years he recalled feeling at ease only with one or two faculty members and a close group of friends. In 1970 (two years before the release of *Marvin Gardens*) he told Rex Reed another story about college days that viewers of the film will want to sniff thoroughly before swallowing:

> *When I was a child, I remember watching the demise of my grandfather choking to death on a fishbone. Every Friday night I had to ram a piece of bread down his throat to keep him from choking. But when I got into English class, I wrote a paper about that and the teacher sent me to remedial reading class.*[1]

He went on to the University of Benares and let a prowl of the East take him into U.S. Army service in Japan. The Army was compelled to court-martial him twice:

> *I had gotten out of one court-martial for hitting an officer by persuading them I could do a valuable job broadcasting so they gave me the "Hawaiian Hour" playing Hawaiian music, which I hated, so I went to sleep on the board one night and when I woke up they court-martialed me again and threw me out of the Army as a saboteur.*[2]

Hawaii? I hear you murmur. And could you also believe

that he told stories on the radio in the small hours and got through a couple dozen grandfathers? Would *you* believe that *your* kingdom had come and was called "Staeblarabia"? Here's the tallest story of all. Rafelson returned to New York for a while and worked for Channel 13. He was doing very well until he got into an argument over one program and overturned a desk on the lap of Lew Wasserman, the fabled potentate of Universal. Fired again, he met Bert Schneider, son of an executive at Columbia, and they took a stroll through Central Park shooting the breeze. It was the time of Beatlemania—the Plaza was besieged—and they thought of finding four Americans who could be transformed into a sensational singing group. The four they picked (and one of them wasn't even American) were called Tork, Jones, Nesmith, and Dolenz, and their creators called them, for the purposes of residuals and other business considerations, the Monkees.

Would you swallow that? The world did, for a while. Long enough for Rafelson, Schneider, and another friend, Steve Blauner, to make a film about their protégés—*Head*, in 1968, which included the lads being sucked up by a vacuum cleaner and ending as specks of dandruff in Victor Mature's oceanic hair. The picture also starred Sonny Liston, Frank Zappa, and Annette Funicello—it was a cast that only Jason Staebler could believe in.

Jason is the zealot Bruce Dern has always been searching for. He may be as effective as he is on screen because Dern is not quite aware how misguided or reckless Jason seems to us. Dern has a self-belief that suddenly comes into focus when Lewis, the long-suffering mobster boss in Atlantic City, says there's no accounting for Jason because, after all, he's an artist. Jason has a tottering scheme for running an Hawaiian island. There could be casinos, tourists, loot. But his spasms of jazzy hype need no detail. They leap from one cliché to another with the vitality of hope: "We're goddam Hawaii, babe. Pineapples."

Jason's panache draws the gloomy David into the plan and keeps two women in tow. But does he ever intend going to Hawaii? The only sea in sight is the cold Atlantic. This seems the wrong point of departure. The frenzy of preparation is always too eager to go off on dreams of what it will be like. The plans come no nearer fruition. But Jason is able to have a ball in the nearly empty hotel—one among many birthday-cake structures gutted of the cream of confidence and customers. David might have enough grudging, inept practicality to get to Hawaii and be a beachcomber there. But Jason is no more, and no less, than a rabid dreamer. Dern's burning eyes look past everyone. He can only bear to be alive by living in the future—it is the reverse of this actor's customary self-pity. This loneliness has a different thrust and a contrary mood, but Jason is as disabled by hope as David is by seriousness.

Neither man is an artist in the sense of Rembrandt or Flaubert. They are both neurotic, spasmodic, and unnoticed by everyone except the few who meet them. Neither of them believes in art. But perhaps that is characteristic of America's need for art. Unable to support, or endure, the dedication and industry of the committed creative artist, it wants its most inventive people to be an exciting blur of fraud, somewhere between bullshitter and prophet. Orson Welles is so piercingly American an artist because we cannot separate his genius from those two conflicting strains. On this wintry Atlantic seaboard, Rafelson has woven together two strands in the wish to make major motion pictures—the visionary and the promoter.

The context is twofold: the parody of a Monopoly game, and the actual fate of the Staeblers and anyone associated with them. Duller routines creep forward—the radio station in Philadelphia, Atlantic City waiting for another summer, Lewis's humdrum rackets, and Jessica's willingness to make the best of whatever comes along. The brothers are extremists, outsiders, and private disasters. But Rafelson persuades us of their exemplary roles in the American dream. They might still move or inspire us if the country could be roused from somnolence and restored to the level between sleep and waking where dreaming occurs.

David is the man pushed back on his own destructive integrity, deemed odd or inaccessible by others, and prepared to live out that reputation. But he is absolutely stubborn about working in the way he thinks proper. His diffidence should not conceal the self-righteousness that he opposes to the world's demeaning compromises. In movie terms Rafelson has been David, walking angrily away from setups that were betraying his vision. But Nicholas Ray is a more complete example of the artist who stopped working rather than knuckle under.

As for Jason, he could be the unit publicist on one recent film that was written so that it would have sequences in a South American country. It was being made for Paramount, which has holdings in the Dominican Republic sufficient for location work. But then the project was dropped by Paramount, and, as an independent picture with a reduced budget, it had to settle for Mexican scenery. No problem, said the publicist, twisting to be where the light fell. Mex is best; tequila tops. Then another reverse, another cut in budget, and the picture went before the cameras with "a number of very Spanish-looking places carefully researched in the Valley area." At last, cried the publicist, the sublime solution. South America has been hiding all along in the outskirts of L.A., and we've found it. The old studio homily is proved—that all the world can be found in California; it is an encyclopedic zoo. In his office (which he never leaves) the publicist was sunny that everything worked out. It's going to be better this way, he yelled. In a minute he would realize that it looked more like South America than the real thing. This was a man who couldn't name the president or prime minister of one South American country.

This metaphor is the more satisfying for being indirect.

You can happily read *Marvin Gardens* as the story of a bizarre pipe dream. Only the two unexpected references to "artist" give you the clue to the larger significance. But that would be artificial if the film did not also show the havoc the two imaginative brothers bring to those around them. Sally's inarticulate helplessness is in part the confusion of anyone trying to live with an obsessive who can never argue about his poetic monologues without going into fury. She is also a woman who knows her youth is gone forever. It remains a great insight from Rafelson that when Sally is usurped by her own stepdaughter, the two women continue to feel kinship despite the competitive situation forced on them.

Sally's murderous outburst—the shooting of Jason in full speculative spate—is desperate and shocking. We do not expect it, but we appreciate it exactly. Very few recent movie killings share its impact or its emotional authenticity. You know that Sally will be found mentally unbalanced by her trial, provoked beyond reason, but you know that it is her sanest act, reclaiming dignity and merciful action from the haze of dreaming. Instead of romanticizing murder, Jason's death makes killing understandable as a practice for consenting adults in their hotel rooms.

One brother dead, the other goes back to Philadelphia and the grandfather who is watching home movies of the boys on another, long-ago beach. The dying fall is so resolutely set against melodrama or alienation. Rafelson's compassion insists on something like the complexity of human nature that surprises us in life. We feel loss after the film, not the stirring aberration of becoming Travis Bickle. *The King of Marvin Gardens* sends us home more aware of ourselves. So astute about the romance of success in America, it was always likely to be a commercial failure. But it will survive that.

17

Angel Face

He came on the scene when James Dean was dead. Montgomery Clift's face and nerve were shot. Marlon Brando was finding it harder to believe in or negotiate an honorable career as a movie actor. Warren Beatty was straightaway identified as a beauty, no easy status in a society dedicated to rugged male virility. In hindsight, one may notice that the actual homosexual—Clift—had to disguise his disposition on film. On the other hand, Beatty could let his glow reach out toward a new sense of gay loveliness without anyone doubting his own heterosexual nature.

In his first film, Elia Kazan's *Splendor in the Grass* with Natalie Wood, he produced a heat-haze atmosphere of erotic frustration. No film had been so infused with the adolescent's thwarted urgency about sex. Beatty had a desperate smile fixed on some faraway bliss or orgasm he could not yet feel, but which accounted for the wild dark hair, the luster in his narrowed eyes, and the perpetually gaping mouth. *Splendor* was like a wet dream; you came out of it in a stupor of rapture and guilt. With one film, Beatty was established as a male sex symbol.

Kazan was the most prestigious American director of the fifties, the man who had given Dean and Brando their film starts, and a guru of the Method. Kazan always dug into his actors' real selves, and he put the fresh kid from summer stock and TV in with Natalie Wood, Dean's girl from *Rebel Without a Cause*. Beatty's hairstyle was like Dean's. He had the same hunched stance, and he brooded physically over an inner torment that could not be expressed. He seemed like another rebel.

But *Splendor in the Grass* was a turning point. It was Kazan's last Hollywood film for years; the studio system had already begun to crumble. And the movie's portrait of adolescence was not just tumescent, it was a portrait of midwestern puritanism, money, and stability cramping vitality. The film was a harbinger of issues that would disrupt the sixties—no longer "Can I stay out late?" but "I can't get no satisfaction." Intuitively Beatty picked up that message and studied the business for more control of his projects. No crackup or crash for him. He has stayed lean and ambitious.

Heaven Can Wait opened in 1978 after five months of intense post-production work. Beatty worked eighteen-hour days, but he was his own slave driver, for he was the producer of the film, its codirector (with Buck Henry), and coauthor of the screenplay as well as its star. It was a landmark in the development of Beatty as a tycoon-packager of products. He had forsaken sex and violence, tried to find a gentler screen persona, and fashioned a romance that only showed how well he understood the mood of the public. *Heaven Can Wait* didn't get or deserve great reviews. Its second part was unduly muddled. But the public made it one of the hits of the year, and thereby ensured that Beatty would be richer still. When you are producer, star, cowriter, and codirector, the points do mount up.

The picture disappointed several people. *Heaven Can Wait* was so much milder and less urgent than other Beatty films. Something suspiciously like soft-focus charm was being sold, and the beseeching wistfulness with which Warren photographed himself gave generous house room to some lazy thinking. It was a remake of the 1941 picture, *Here Comes Mr. Jordan*, starring Robert Montgomery. The script still felt as if it needed more discipline and old-fashioned structure. The quarterback of the Los Angeles Rams is prematurely whisked off to heaven after an accident. He protests to two heavenly bureaucrats—James Mason and Buck Henry—and they give him extra time. But the quarterback's body has been cremated too soon, and, as an alternative, they put him in the still-warm corpse of an eccentric corporation magnate just murdered by his wife and her lover (Dyan Cannon and Charles Grodin).

Yes, of course it's whimsy and wilder still when the movie seems to forget or throw out its own rules. But the script needed a kind of care that was not in fashion, and Beatty never grasped a style or an atmosphere as a director. This fanciful situation required a Vincente Minnelli or a Michael Powell to do it justice—the story is so very close to Powell's *A Matter of Life and Death* (1946). What worked best, and carried the movie, was Beatty's own performance. As never before, he played a simple, naïve man. Without being cute or sentimental, he let his own face and wit run slower while putting a lot of athletic gusto into the part. As the millionaire, he was always running upstairs and along corridors, giving "Hi" greetings to the bewildered servants. With more stringent direction and a better sense of visual humor, this conception could have been funnier and a lot more touching. But the fantasy had too little point; the "reborn" tycoon's new approach to company policy (dropping any scheme that might conceivably hurt anyone) seemed only a fatuous part of Beatty's absentminded political awareness—the Hollywood liberalism that wants to be liked and sees the sharing of amiability as a way of improving society.

Beatty on the screen looks too mercurial or self-indulgent to be a producer, until you feel the very watchful force of his eyes. He was not well educated; a football scholarship took him from Arlington, Virginia, to Northwestern. But he was bored in a year and dropped out to try New York. His hard times there were brief: the Stella Adler acting school, attic living, hepatitis, and work as a sandhog on the Lincoln Tunnel. Then, in New Jersey summer stock, he met playwright William Inge and got the lead in his play, *A Loss of Roses*.

He did a screen test with Jane Fonda as his partner. Whatever he learned came from private accumulation, hard reading, and native instinct. One of his acquaintances, director James Toback, says he has "a steel-trap memory . . . he's as intelligent as anyone I've met . . . ten times as smart as any other actor."

Beatty's expressions are as quick as ticker tape. Rerun that superb opening to *Bonnie and Clyde* in your mind's eye. Beatty is a glaringly smart guy in a country town, flashy and alert but limping around on a leg stiff as a hard-on. It was Faye Dunaway's first movie, and as Clyde sums up Bonnie as a possible accomplice and offers her his pistol to touch, so Warren Beatty, producer of the film, seems to be scrutinizing his actress and muttering between the matches clamped in Clyde's teeth—the mouth is so often the focus—"Oh, yes, she'll do."

Bonnie and Clyde was his first production, only ten years after his start. It was an overwhelming hit, and it identified a new range of subjects, a young, passionate audience, and the opportunity for independent productions by creative filmmakers. His second venture waited eight years: *Shampoo* was another sensation. When his cowriter on it, Robert Towne, was asked, "What is behind the moment in the party scene when Julie Christie goes under the table?" he replied quickly, "Probably thirty million dollars of film rentals." [1] The sexual daring was as much of a box-office coup as the exhilarating violence in *Bonnie and Clyde*. *Shampoo* tickled audiences, even though feminists deplored the way Beatty seemed to condone the hairdresser George's restless screwing around. There was the vague intimation that the film was its producer's confessional; it thrived on the glamour of rumor.

Towne wrote a first draft for *Shampoo* in 1970. Then he and Beatty argued over the treatment of women. The actor who played George wanted them to be tougher. Towne remembers: "He was very angry about it, and I was very angry about him being angry about it." [2] They stopped talking for a while, and the project was shelved for several years. When it was revived, George had become a man harassed by an arena of demanding women, and Beatty responded to the changed political consciousness of America by staging the action on Election Day, 1968, something not conceived by Towne but part of the final suggestiveness of *Shampoo*.

It would be going too far to call Beatty politically sophisticated, though he did work for McGovern in 1972. Speaking for the candidate on TV and across the country, Beatty regretted appearing so earnest—without that captivating grin, his eyes recede and he can look perplexed. Besides, McGovern lost, and Beatty doesn't like to back losers. But he has been a part of the chic Hollywood Left, and he does show an idiosyncratic interest in the nature of power and control in America. He signed petitions against the Vietnam War in *Variety*; he once listened to the Black Panther case, and thought he should hear the L.A. Police Department point of view before committing himself; and he was around in the early hours of the morning when Hunter Thompson considered dragging Chuck Colson down Pennsylvania Avenue. This political interest of Beatty's is not distinguished, but it's not dull—which separates it from real politics.

Yet on several occasions, he has lent himself to adventurous projects with a philosophical undertone. *Bonnie and Clyde* owed some of its impact to the way a thirties genre was invested with the search for self-determination of sixties youth. Arthur Penn, the director Beatty chose after several others had turned the job down, said, "We were trying to distinguish between the rigid morality which could very well render somebody impotent at the interior, private level while at the same time he could exceed all limits of external morality and still feel at one with himself." [3] That's where Beatty's belief in energy expressing itself comes close to the incoherent, emotional politics of the sixties.

The Parallax View, in which Beatty acted for Alan J. Pakula, is a paranoid vision of a corporation conspiring toward a totalitarian America, assassinating presidents, and using Beatty's investigative journalist as a fall guy. Time, I think, will prove it a more profoundly disturbing work than Pakula's *All the President's Men*, in part because Beatty identifies a more acute sense of danger than will ever trouble Robert Redford. (Uncredited, he worked on the script for *Parallax*, and today he would never act without involving himself in rewrites and the script concept.)

The Parallax View is a coherent expression of the alarm underlying one of Beatty's most audacious films: *Mickey One*, directed by Penn in 1964. The latter is a somber, abstract movie about a nightclub comedian who believes the Mob is after him and who hides away in an urban wasteland, intent on vanishing. Mickey is as flawed as most of Beatty's heroes.

In fact, Beatty rarely glamorizes himself. As early as 1961, for *The Roman Spring of Mrs. Stone*, he begged Tennessee Williams to let him play the sleazy Italian gigolo opposite Vivien Leigh. The following year, he was prepared to be the dissipated shell of a handsome American hero in John Frankenheimer's *All Fall Down*. Then in 1964 he played the male nurse in Robert Rossen's last film, *Lilith*, an unhappy man trying to help others but so infatuated with a nymphomaniac patient (Jean Seberg) that he becomes the instrument of her passionate madness. "The most exciting American male in movies" regularly denied himself confidence or triumph in his films. But he was always thinking of the picture. Beatty urged Seberg on Rossen after Yvette Mimieux had been the favorite for the part. *Lilith* was not a popular film, but most people saw it as a revelation of Seberg no matter that the actress was in constant conflict with her costar.

The lip-smacking picture of Beatty in the press was of an adventurer involved with many women and several of the actresses he played opposite. But on screen he played fakes, misfits, and neurotics; his sensual face was twisted with worry and self-doubt. At best, he faced up to a threat—like Mickey going through with his club act, daring the mysterious forces behind the merciless spotlights—or lived as cheerfully as he could against the odds. Beatty has a sublime moment in *Bonnie and Clyde* when he tells his brother how he shot off two toes to get out of the penitentiary, unaware that a pardon was on its way. "Ain't life grand?" he sighs with the laidback amusement of a fatalist. And in that same scene, after the gusto of fraternal reunion and the boasts about the times they're going to have, the two men fall silent and wonder just what in hell they can do. Beatty is then a romantic disappointed by the confining world; his angel's face darkens with the shadow of negation, and his character strikes out in a frenzy of action to defy the threats to human worth and vitality.

The most convincing work Beatty has done in this vein is in Robert Altman's *McCabe and Mrs. Miller*. It is a winter western about solitaries unable to forge the personal links that will prevent them from being destroyed by archaic codes of honor. He plays a gambler and a businessman, a mixture that must have appealed to the actor. McCabe is not articulate or especially capable. He cannot voice his feelings for Mrs. Miller or escape the trap of having to fight the syndicate that wants to buy him out. In his clumsy independence, he tries to play with their offers, and he dies alone in the snow while Mrs. Miller, his impossible love—Julie Christie, Warren's steadiest girl friend—consoles herself with an opium pipe. Altman seldom allows emotional effects without the safety net of irony and mockery. But Beatty brought a tempering dignity to the film; it is a wistful tragedy about a man who dies rather than lose face.

McCabe and Mrs. Miller is far more poignant than *Shampoo*. Beatty's most personal undertaking so far was a failure, or at least the sign of creative immaturity. George's suffering is claimed by the film but not felt by the audience. Beatty never said that *he* was the hairdresser. But by 1975 he had been one of the beautiful people for more than a decade. His looks were still exceptional, and he was a perennially eligible bachelor "seen with" Joan Collins, Natalie Wood, Leslie Caron, Michelle Phillips, Julie Christie, and several others. Over the years, Carly Simon has neither confirmed nor denied that Beatty was the model of sexual arrogance for her song "You're So Vain." Equally, the promotion for *Shampoo* let us think that the central character was a version of Beatty himself.

The idea for the film came from a seventeenth-century play, Wycherley's *The Country Wife*, in which a beau, Horner, screws around the more freely after spreading a rumor that he is impotent. *Bonnie and Clyde* had already used the theme of impotence: One of its more banal elements is the idea that Clyde robs banks because he and Bonnie can't get it on. On screen, that textbook cliché was animated by Beatty's yearning and by the emotionalism of his scenes with Faye Dunaway. But it's worth underlining his repeated interest in sexual failure. He is the actor who seems most conscious of the absurdity of sex.

When he and Towne wondered about the modern equivalent of Horner, Towne suggested an actor, and Beatty topped that with a Beverly Hills hairdresser. As a plot device, it was brilliant, and Beatty unerringly caught the feverish, tacky art that George is dedicated to: He transforms Julie Christie in one scene and nearly loses sight of her in the process. Hair is his music, even if *Shampoo* skirts the most prevalent axiom of that trade—that hairdressers turn queer because they weary of women. The movie saw George (or Beatty) as the insubstantial lay lusted after by Julie Christie, Lee Grant, Goldie Hawn, Carrie Fisher, and Jaye P. Morgan. At the conclusion, George is left alone with a woeful moral that betrays Beatty's superficiality.

Shampoo is too picaresque, too hopeful that "dirty" flourishes and the political subtext give it significance. The film doesn't criticize George's blow-dry morality, it only shares it. Joan Mellen, in her book, *Big Bad Wolves*, dismissed the half-hearted candor of the picture:

Nor do the self-serving announcements by the film-
makers that Shampoo *is really critical of stud Beatty*
carry any conviction. Beatty *plays the sexual gymnast*
who, like body builders and weightlifters, calls such at-
tention to his body that it is reasonable to wonder what
fuels his need of such display. Compulsive and exhibi-
tionist heterosexuality finally appears to be a mask for
the distaste of women.[4]

Mellen's disapproval is directed at most of Hollywood, not
just Beatty. Yet *Shampoo* is a confession entranced with its
own escapades. George screws endlessly but never luxuriates
in the pleasure or restfulness of sex. There may be many
women who could speak for Beatty's appreciative company.
But he is unattached, and the sum of his films presents a
picture of devout, even suspicious, self-sufficiency. He is not
isolated, but he prefers a one-man operation. No one who has
worked with him complains of ego or arrogance; he is an
astute listener, usually receptive to ideas. He can be very
amusing; as Buck Henry says, "He makes the best Warren
Beatty jokes himself." *Shampoo* may be limited by being
only the most elaborate of those jokes.

James Toback calls Beatty "a chameleon." Toback is the
director of the brilliant *Fingers*, on the strength of which he
sold a movie project to Beatty—*Love and Money*. Beatty was
expected once to produce and play the part of an invest-
ments analyst who falls in love with the young wife of an
elderly conglomerate president. It could have been the best
thing for Beatty in a long time: a movie that examines the
intricate but muscular knot of money and romance in America. It reminds us of McCabe's inept role as a brothel manager; of George's wish to open his own salon; of Clyde
Barrow longing to be known, rich, and potent; of Mickey
One's troubled attitude toward a public he needs to face and
overawe. It reminds us, too, that at forty-one Beatty is handsome, accomplished, and very rich. *Bonnie and Clyde* bank-

rolled him, and since then money has made money.

To research Beatty is to discover the ideal actor to play Jay Gatsby, for he is as caught up in business and inaccessibility as he is in sex and romance. He is a slow preparer and a furious worker. Robert Towne says, "Warren is the kind of person who, once he makes up his mind to do something, is hysterically committed to it. He's like a sergeant blowing his whistle and going over the top and leading the troops into the machine guns." Buck Henry has seen the same thing: "He likes to work under pressure, and if it's not there he'll create it. He's a demonic producer . . . he fills every minute. Nothing deters him, nothing stops him. He barely sleeps and he likes to do as much as possible himself."

But that is during times of battle. There are long intervals when Beatty goes into retreat and is reachable only by phone, living no one knows where but collecting messages at discreet hotels. His head has been full of projects for years, and he will not rush any of them. He has wanted to make a picture about John Reed, the American radical who observed the Bolshevik Revolution. After five years' research and hesitation, he had a screenplay, *Reds*, by British playwright Trevor Griffith. The script was reworked and then filmed in England during the course of a year at an estimated $40 million. Beatty's new romance, Diane Keaton, played Reed's love. Beatty was now the sole director. The Moscow of 1917 was rebuilt. A starry supporting cast was hired, and, reportedly, interviews were filmed with people who had witnessed or lived through the Revolution. *Reds* began to attract the weight of expectation that Beatty had won for all his films.

He has always known that the picture business deals in attention. As a result, he is mean with himself. He lived for years in a two-room suite at the Beverly Wilshire hotel. It was very small, with more phones than furniture and only a hot plate for cooking. There was a sun roof, and one of his assistants remembers the untidy den, a sofa collapsed from the weight of scripts, and Warren in a yellow towel wandering in from sunbathing as five phones rang. Business fulfills him. He might be tempted by the thought of producing other people's movies, without acting himself. His looks are not slipping yet, but Buck Henry reckons that "50% of him is looking forward to their going and being free from the world's superficial impression."

Is it possible that Beatty might one day go into retreat, reachable only by phone, and not always then if he goes cold on an idea or a contact? Does that remind you of anyone? It should, for the project that Beatty nurtures is a movie in which he plays Howard Hughes. Not yet, though; he will probably need to be ten years older. Hughes preoccupies Beatty, and in his own life-style you can see a pattern of business, beautiful women, and secrecy merging in the charisma of a tycoon who may one day live in a citadel penthouse, directing his affairs, receiving his ladies, and taking star glamour to its vanishing point—the alienated neglect of self that consumed Hughes.

Yet he might have more respectable designs. In the last year of the Second World War, the rather lonely child dreamed of the future. When he was six, he wanted to be President; at age seven, he fancied the governorship of Georgia; the year after, he settled on acting. But he never promised the order in which he'd take on the targets.

18

James Toback: Odds Against Success

It was late afternoon in San Fernando suburbia, outside a Spanish house at the intersection of Pico and Maclay. Actor Tom McFadden was sprawled patiently on the ground. James Toback, the director, prowled around as a makeup man drew a pattern of blood on McFadden's shattered chest. They worked at it like surgeons or painters until dark puddles surrounded the actor. A Mexican waif stopped to watch, impressed that anyone should have spilled that much blood, or that this violence was being played with in broad daylight. You might kill anyone in the Los Angeles area if you made a show of filming it.

Then a camera recorded the illusion of carnage, and Toback's second film, *Love and Money*, was wrapped. McFadden went into a trailer to extricate himself from drenched clothes. An assistant swilled away the stains on the sidewalk; the crew congratulated themselves on the end of the job—amiable, conscientious men oblivious of the towering emotions in *Love and Money*. Toback didn't consort with the team. He was just as preoccupied as he had seemed during rehearsals and shooting. He crossed the street to a drugstore, where he wolfed down junk food and played the phone while he waited for transport back to Culver City. Food in one hand, phone in the other, he scanned the sports pages while he told the operator to call a public phone booth in Bermuda where he knew a woman would be waiting. Wherever he is, those assignations drag him to the phone. His own head is full of numbers to call, numbers to leave, and the numbers he owes around town—to hotels, the IRS, and the book-makers who cater to his reckless guesses about any kind of ball game.

I'm sure he called the production office at Lorimar, too, for news. He was on another brink, needing a success to stave off creditors closing in from every corner of his life. Only a few days earlier, at the company previews in La Costa, some selected sequences from *Love and Money* had been a big hit with foreign distributors, especially the one in which the young stars, Ray Sharkey and Ornella Muti, make love, and Muti sings "The Star-Spangled Banner" to help him get a hard-on.

In *Love and Money* Ray Sharkey plays Byron Levin, a hero who lives out Toback's own search for extreme experience. Sharkey was unexpected casting. Before the film was shot, he was known chiefly as one of the thugs who tortured Michael Moriarty in *Who'll Stop the Rain*. He subsequently played Allen Ginsberg in *Heartbeat*, and had a lead in Paul Mazursky's *Willie and Phil*. It was a gamble: Sharkey is slight, reticent, and his hair is receding. He wears a discreet hairpiece in *Love and Money*, and he studied Toback for weeks in an effort to catch his lunging energy. Sharkey may become a star, but he always seems outpaced by his director. Toback never stands still or listens patiently. His presence reorganizes the shape of a room. You feel the dangerously unresolved blast of his personality, like a stove being thrown open. He interrupts with serene assurance; he clears his throat and spits out noxious fluids; he fingers his crotch to make sure that everything is still there; and he notices every passerby. He prides himself on never thinking about less than two things at once. His horror of boredom is always nudging his life toward uncertainty and away from stability.

Byron Levin in *Love and Money* feels trapped by his life: He lives with a half-senile, half-brilliant grandfather and a bookselling girl friend in a love affair that has gone stale.

He has a dispiriting job as an investment analyst. So, as he plays with other people's money, he studies other men's wives, especially Catherine (Ornella Muti), the young wife of Frederick Stockheinz, the head of Trans Allied Silver. Byron has an affair with Catherine, but does not realize that he is being set up by Stockheinz, who likes to think he owns the silver-rich Latin American kingdom of Costa Salva. That country has a new Castro-ish leader, Lorenzo (Armand Assante), who was Byron's friend at Harvard. Stockheinz offers Byron $1 million to persuade Lorenzo about the joys of multinational corporations, but Byron is drawn into violence and intrigue more by the dream of winning Catherine than by the wish to keep silver prices strong.

Love and Money was on and off for two years before suddenly, in November, 1979, it went into production. "I never thought it wasn't going to happen," says Toback, "but the more unlikely it became, the more I believed in it." He's the kind of man who gets his greatest charge the instant a hot favorite loses—it's the pressure of a dead end that inspires someone to fly up sheer walls to escape. It feeds on insecurity. That's why Toback mistrusts a happy unit: "It's dangerous to be carried away by enthusiasm for anyone's work on a film. It lets them become satisfied, and the insecurity is more useful."

Temperamentally, therefore, Toback should never make it as a safe Hollywood figure, but remain a rogue outsider. As credits before *Love and Money*, he had only the screenplay of *The Gambler*, a moderate failure, and *Fingers* (1977), so entirely *his* film that Hollywood regarded him as the man who had perpetrated an impossible picture—not just shockingly violent but obscure, indecently confessional, and viscerally sexual. "It did virtually no theatrical business," he tells you, "because Brut, the company that made it, decided that it was a diseased film."

And just as no one who saw *Fingers* can ever forget it, so some in the film business were stunned by its rawness and originality. Warren Beatty for one. That most inaccessible of actors saw the movie and, over the phone, yielded to Toback's torrential determination to read him a new script —*Love and Money*, a project that had already been turned down by several studios. Toback wanted the challenge of a direct confrontation—he wanted to assert himself by telling Beatty the story while considering which waitress to pick up. Beatty bought it over dinner for six figures, and said that he would produce it and maybe act in it.

Still, Toback's imagination can frighten people. Beatty said that he was getting his John Reed picture, *Reds*, ready, too, and wasn't sure what order he would take them in. Toback waited on the decision, though his own nervous readiness was as brimming as that of a lover about to come. Then Beatty said he would place the picture at Paramount in such a way that Toback could go ahead whenever he wanted. The director wasn't sure whether Beatty still wanted the central part or was just prevaricating with a talent as willful as his own. Paramount was happy to accommodate any Beatty whim, but less convinced about *Love and Money* without the Warren who had sold the slight charm of *Heaven Can Wait*.

Then early in 1979, to maintain his commitment and to reassure the studio, Beatty presented Toback with a producer who would help get the script into shape. Toback needs producers the way Roberto Duran needs table manners. But this helpmate was the oddest curve ball in years: Pauline Kael, nearly sixty, inexperienced in the business, on indefinite leave of absence from *The New Yorker*, and the latest member of Beatty's own company. She had actually given *Fingers* one of its more understanding notices, and she had known Toback in New York. The movie world went into frenzies of bogus indignation and malicious glee—that a critic should sell out, that a big studio might rely on her judgment, and that the otherwise enigmatic Beatty possessed such a wicked sense of humor.

No one thought the match was less than a comic disaster, except for Pauline maybe, the one with most dignity to lose. None of the skeptics had long to wait. Toback and Kael were lodged on different floors of the Beverly Wilshire hotel. They had script conferences, argumentative phone calls, and a showdown after several weeks when Beatty had to concede failure and—not surprisingly—backed a man and a filmmaker against Pauline.

Everyone now speculates about some great scandal in that breakdown, but that forgets the reasons for incredulity when the arrangement was announced. There were angry words at the Wilshire, of course, competition, and the mounting farce of two virulent egos at loggerheads. Pauline wanted a better-organized script, more coherent ideas, less extremism. Toback is nothing if not extremist, and "I felt that my story was being tidied up and diluted. Neither of us is or will ever be an easy collaborator." It's in his nature that he will admit now that he should have followed more of her suggestions. But Toback can only take advice if it's slipped under the door anonymously. He and Kael are still friends, or wary and respectful loners in the L.A. jungle, which can stretch to cover a character escaped from Dostoyevsky and a Jane Austen on speed.

If anyone behaved rashly, it was Beatty. He had managed to compromise two people who deserved better understanding. Shortly thereafter, he and Kael parted company, and Pauline was picked up by Paramount, who were impressed by her verve as a story analyst. She lingered there awhile, and then went back east to reclaim *The New Yorker* and undergo Adlerian analysis. As for Toback, Paramount now had extra reasons for believing he was unmanageable and dangerous. Show the guy a deal and he gets difficult. *Love and Money* was on hold by the summer of 1979. Minus Beatty or any big star prepared to risk it, the script had had its budget cut several times.

"Then, one day, I bumped into David Picker on his way

to a new job as production chief at Lorimar." He asked about *Love and Money,* and within a month a turnaround deal was worked out, with Paramount absorbing its considerable investment and Lorimar picking up a bargain. They set tough conditions, though: a $3 million budget—a third of the original, Beatty-based estimates; instead of Latin American locations, the fictional country of Costa Salva would have to be filmed in the L.A. area; and if Ray Sharkey was to play the lead—Toback's choice after considering nearly every actor in sight—then the female star had to be a top Continental actress. Finally, as far as Lorimar was concerned, Toback had been paid already by Paramount. He would have to go the rest of the way for love and a chance of points one day.

With Lorimar's involvement, he went to Europe looking for actresses and leaving unpaid bills at several luxury hotels. He signed Klaus Kinski, the demonic star of *Aguirre, Nosferatu,* and *Woyzeck,* to play Frederick Stockheinz, the tycoon at Trans Allied Silver. And for Stockheinz's wife, Catherine, he considered Laura Antonelli and Ornella Muti. Antonelli was interested, but when the *paparazzi* snapped her in Rome with Toback, her good and rather possessive friend, actor Jean-Paul Belmondo, had a fit of jealousy and forbade the deal. So Toback met Muti, a major box-office attraction in Italy, Spain, and South America but unknown in America. "I liked her looks and her sense of humor. She had the best English of any European actress in thirty years, and she wanted to do the picture." But she was under exclusive contract to Dino de Laurentiis, who has starred her in *Flash Gordon.* He seemed determined to block his protégée, until the resourceful Toback found L.A. pressures that could be put on the Italian. In the end, Dino released Muti on payment of $50,000, half of which had to be provided by Toback himself.

Moreover, Toback and his agent, Jeff Berg, were required

to put up a bond against completion and to sign a contract making Toback responsible for all monies if anything else went wrong. And something did. The substantial role of Sharkey's grandfather was to have been played by Harry Ritz. But only a few days before Ritz was to start shooting, the veteran comedian fell ill. On impulse, Toback asked King Vidor, the eighty-five-year-old director, who had not worked professionally since 1960. Vidor accepted, learned his part well enough to carry off four-minute takes in which he is talking most of the time, and will win a lot of attention with his rich portrait of a man drifting between confusion and insight.

So, after two years of procrastination, the picture was shot in thirty-one days. To make a movie is still one of the toughest adventures in the world. To write it, produce and direct, to insist on it in the face of all odds, is a more desperate commitment than 99 percent of the world's talented film students can imagine. It takes a single-mindedness worthy of Attila and a need that comes from holes in the spirit.

Fingers is one of the most intense American pictures of the seventies, but Toback came back to the set after lunch late on eight of its twenty-three days. This is the calculating habit of deadline that cuts everything finer and finer. Being late is like not coming early, an assertion of will, and the will may be so acute that it can waste time to get back at all the frustrations it has suffered. The imperative of authority was taught to Toback when he was fourteen. His grandfather had taken him on a trip to Israel, where he came upon the words of Chaim Weizmann: "If you will it, you will have it." Thus the unnerving mixture of tyranny and sensitivity in Toback, the composite of artist and gangster.

I was driving with him in L.A. one afternoon when we stopped at a light. He saw a woman in the car behind, got out, made a date, came back to the car, and talked about a detail in the music that had been playing all the while. Before it was dark he had screwed the woman and abandoned her: He is dismissive of women, as well as a relentless collector. Like so many members of the new Hollywood, his pursuit of sex doesn't conceal a fear of it or a contempt for women. Yet he holds on to one or two relationships that seem to depend on mutual suspicion, sometimes phoning several times in a night to make sure a woman is faithful while undertaking a casual adventure himself.

Toback chuckles if you mention these stories, half-rueful, half-proud at being so appalling. It is a black, terrifying side to him. Yet he is also generous, entertaining, informed on any subject mentioned, and so alert to human nature that it is doubly shocking to hear him recount some brazen, brutal exploits. So humane, he is driven to discredit virtue. So menacing, he insists on insight. He is his own character, and when you are with him, you wonder how abruptly his darting eyes and instinct for long odds could plunge *you* into absurd nightmare.

In his day he has been pursued by unsentimental creditors and distraught women. On the phone to me once, he was attacked physically by a woman and had to ring off in a mixture of exasperation and delight at melodrama taking over life. From time to time he is attended by the watchful representatives of others waiting for losses to be paid. Even now, he loves the excitement of making films, but faces such debts that he can never view prosperity or ease seriously.

He talks about his predicament but warns you, "No gambling and no fucking," as limits on what can be printed. Then he grins to let you know he realizes how little that would leave. He might end in prison, in exile from the law, or in the East River: He'd cheerfully give you odds on all those destinations. With admiration and amusement, he recalls a bookmaker he knew once who had a surreal business card: "There was just a flower, a rose, in the center and in the four corners four statements—'no phone,' 'no home,' 'no job,' 'no future.' " It is the underworld to which Toback aspires.

James Toback was born in 1944 in New York City. His father was vice-president of a brokerage firm, and his mother would become president of the League of Women Voters. An only child, Toback adored his mother and was dazzled by a father who was himself a sexual adventurer. A grandfather—still alive and honored in *Love and Money* by the "young" King Vidor—was a clothing-store merchant who owned a fat chunk of Columbus Circle until he sold it to Gulf & Western. Two out of four grandparents had been born in Russia, and one ancestor was trumpeter to the Tsar.

New York is home to Toback: *Love and Money* is the first of his movies set away from what he regards as a small town because he knows it so well. Despite much time spent waiting in L.A. hotels, he keeps an apartment in the East Eighties, where the blinds are always down and the rooms seem smaller than they are because of the clutter. It is less a home than the lair of a man with obsessive interests and an unstinting need to be ill at ease. Comfort has been deliberately denied; Toback fears it more than murder. "Peace of mind is the only truly false state of consciousness available to people." But it is a strange abode for a man who dreads solitary confinement and speaks of a primitive need to "punch my way out of my mother's cunt."

He knows the argument that it's indulgent for the only child of considerable wealth to sound so barbarous. But he's done a lot to detach himself from his family. He gambled away much of his money, and he presented a pair of parents in *Fingers* who were like psychic monsters attempting to consume their son. They were also people from opposite worlds: the father a mobster, the mother an intellectual. That's what makes the hero of *Fingers* (Harvey Keitel) the victim of contradictory callings: He wants to be a concert pianist, yet he collects underworld debts for his father.

There are equal amounts of fantasy and autobiography in that tormented portrait. In *Fingers,* Keitel lives alone, and so does Toback, surrounded by books, papers, records, cassettes, piles of laundry, medicines, and the gloom of claustrophobia. Telephones lurk beneath all the papers like primed traps. The walls are nearly blacked out with pictures —of Aaron Copland, Mahler, Richard Strauss, Shostakovich, Dostoyevsky, and Oscar Wilde. A grim kitchen seems never to have been used. The apartment is like a tomb of inspiration for Toback's sense of himself as artist-outlaw. He has very few friends, and a personality which requires levels of secrecy so that one woman never learns about the others. Intrigue is his most stimulating fiction. It is what allows him to think he might be anyone—concert pianist Glenn Gould or hoodlum Frank Costello—and what lets him believe that the debts and the abandoned affairs are not quite real.

He had a nanny whose family had been part of Viennese intellectual society at the turn of the century. She had met Freud and Mahler, but she ended up as a refugee from Hitler in New York, pushing young James through the park in his carriage. Nini was her name, and she revealed the world of music to him so that he yearned to be a pianist. "She died while *Fingers* was being shot, but as I came to one location I remembered a childhood fight in the same place. I had been beating another boy's head on the pavement and was only restrained by Nini's cries." *Fingers* is about a pianist not quite good or confident enough to play in public who rips out the genitals of a gangster who has killed his father.

The violence and the melodrama are the shadows thrown by Toback's own psyche. Frank Costello, a Mafia leader, was shot down in the lobby of the Majestic Apartments where the Tobacks once lived, and Toback tells the story as if it vouched for him. On and off, he has mixed with the underworld, and like Norman Mailer he is attracted to what he sees as the existential glamour of the criminal outsider. One of his favorite movies is Jean-Pierre Melville's *Le Samourai*, in which Alain Delon plays a brilliant schizophrenic criminal (named Jeff Costello) who lives alone on the brink of life and death.

Toback cultivates brinks for himself all the time. His pursuit of sex expects no ultimate satisfaction. "Suppose you were just about to come and a voice said, 'You can only come if you do this or that.' Kill, for instance. You'd do anything. There's a moment of no control whatsoever." His hectic career relies on that extreme discipline, and like all extremists he's spared the realization of how simpleminded he can sound. It is his great weakness that he might indeed kill if only to hold on to his terrible rule. He tells you about a plan that if he ever knows he is going to die, he will use the last hours to eliminate the several people he believes deserve killing. It is another movie, of course, still just within the frenzied realm of a screen. But "I have no wish to live past fifty. I would right now settle for ten more healthy years—and die at the end. How sad it is to be old, making the anguished comparison with one's body, mind, eyes, sexual organs—all the functions one has taken for granted."

This compulsive journey toward climax at all costs was trained at the Ethical Culture School, at Fieldston, and at Harvard. He was even, briefly, married to a member of the English aristocracy: The pirate Toback is actually named in *Burke's Peerage*.

He graduated from Harvard in three years and still had time for experiments with dissipation and his discovery of gambling. English was his major, showing him the mysterious pleasure possible in words on a page. But he tested out the terrors of his life through the perspectives of anthropology and astronomy, and evolved a personal philosophy of the individual who can vanquish all anxieties by a total commitment to risk and experience. That this can be damaging and fearful to others close to Toback is beyond question, but he is magically unhampered by guilt or consequences—even if that bars him from the real travail of art. Such liberty only came gradually. In his twenties there was depression, analysis, drug addiction, and "a completely irrational temper." But in recent years he has known a surging momentum in which his life is like a journey hurtling through him: "Narrative is the story of yourself, the extension of yourself, the fantasy that you will go on and that time will stop." He likes films to feel like a perilous moment drawn out over two hours, and he may want a great crisis as much as Gordon Liddy did.

While he was at Harvard, he was traveling one night with a girl in the car when they skidded off the road. "We rolled over and over in the snow. She was screaming, in tears, but I was exhilarated by the suspended danger. We struck a tree. She had a splinter of glass in her eye, but we got out and trudged through the snow to find a police station. When we got there at last, it was somehow empty: The weather had sent all the cops out or kept them all at home. So we fucked there and then on the floor in the hall of the deserted station." I never learned what happened to the girl's eye.

In 1969 he married Mimi Russell, granddaughter of the Duke of Marlborough, in Las Vegas. The marriage was annulled at once, then they remarried and divorced at leisure. Toback calls it "a strange cutoff part of my past." On the rebound, as an *Esquire* assignment, he got to know star running back Jim Brown. He lived with him in L.A. and won his trust: Brown is a sultry macho god in *Fingers* who smacks the heads of two of his women together—something based on a real incident for which Brown was arrested, but which Toback talked him into reenacting.

A book resulted, *Jim*—awful by its author's confession. But it was a time when Toback "got to the bottom of all sexual possibilities." He knows Brown reckons he's smart, insane, and manipulative, and he denies none of those charges. Toback was writing now and teaching part time at City College.

He hoped to complete a novel, but when it faltered he whipped the bits and pieces into a pornographic story, *The Substitute Gun*, published under the name of Duke Morrison, a bookmaker of his acquaintance. He also wrote articles on Norman Mailer and Susan Sontag, and a piece on Texas for *Harper's*, as well as book reviews.

Then a Harvard acquaintance, Jake Brackman, got him in on a screenwriting job for Arthur Penn. "Nothing came of it, but I had watched Jim Brown make a movie, and it looked interesting." Accordingly, in 1972 he wrote the screenplay for *The Gambler*, about a college literature teacher who is being pursued by the Mob for gambling debts: It was his own life given the glamour of fiction. Orion boss Mike Medavoy was his agent then, and he sold the script to Karel Reisz. Robert De Niro, the first casting, attended Toback's classes to study the part. But Reisz made the script more coherent and less convulsive—De Niro was replaced with James Caan. Seen now, *The Gambler* is a fascinating picture full of Toback's own delight in terror and hazard:

"The passion to gamble," he explains, "is as beyond description as sex or violence. It's essentially onanistic: The loneliness of gambling exceeds everything but that of deadbeat alcoholics. The intense uncertainty is ecstatic, nearly religious or hallucinatory." He says he never gambled to win or lose, and he often bet on sports he didn't follow or on games of blind chance. He won't say how much he ever won or lost, but at times he owed close to a million. Whatever the sensation, it's hard to think he didn't need to lose. He says that chips are like shit and that the process is sexual, excremental, and financial, straining for an answer to the question, "Are you completely out yet?"

After that, a movie is the only thing that has ever satisfied him. The huge returns and the remoteness of winning are so like gambling. He served his time as a writer. Fox encouraged him and Michael Cimino to work on a story about Vito Genovese, Albert Anastasia, and Frank Costello. They got on well, Cimino talking and Toback writing. But changes in studio control terminated that project until . . . *The Deer Hunter*, another Cimino study in male bonding that, Toback claims, bears the imprint of their Mafia script. Then George Barrie of Brut hired Toback to work on a life of Victoria Woodhull, Marxist, feminist, faith healer, writer, and free-lover. Faye Dunaway was eager to star in it, and George Cukor was slotted as director. He and Toback had an uproarious time together on the script, during which Toback lived at the Beverly Hills Hotel charging everything. But Cukor's Russian coproduction, *The Blue Bird*, was such a setback that the director developed a loss of nerve with back problems that kept postponing the movie.

It was then that Toback plunged into *Fingers*. Brut said they would do it: perfume trying to anoint savagery. Then three days before shooting, George Barrie tried to back out because he hadn't been able to make any advance foreign sales. Toback hunted Barrie by phone and found him in Singapore. He told him he would kill him if the film didn't go ahead. You can imagine the pause, long distance: "Jim, I think we have a bad connection." Barrie gave in, but the budget was cut by $700,000 (to $1 million), and Toback had to drop a handful of scenes, including a homosexual encounter. The leading players and the director took deferred payment, and Brut allowed a bare three weeks' post-production.

Worse still, they distributed *Fingers* as if it were a leper's hand. Yet it picked up some impressive reviews here, and it was a success in France, where François Truffaut adopted it as one of his favorite pictures. *Fingers* made no concessions to audience tranquillity. The story is the acting out of all the fear and loathing, juice and exultation, that gather in the bowels and the loins. Is there another American movie that features a rectal examination or that so savors blood, shit, and semen? Every gesture in the movie is part of its study of struggling maturity and threatened sexual identity. As you watch it, you feel yourself caught up in the imagination of a very intelligent psychotic.

Which brings us back to the ordeal of *Love and Money*. That script is as autobiographical as the others. Just as its hero takes a young wife away from a powerful industrialist, so Toback himself had an affair that ended the marriage of a well-known show-biz impresario. The president of Costa Salva in the movie is based on one of Toback's Harvard contemporaries. There is also a moment when the hero, on his way to a dull job, stays in his car to hear out the climax of a piece of music. In his own cars, hired and changed regularly like numbers in roulette, Toback talks, drives, and searches through all the music on the car radio. The deepest affinity with Toback's own crammed life is the way sensation is preferred to reason and routine. That attitude is romantic, but it leaves human wreckage behind him. A persistent philanderer himself, he broke the nose of one woman he thought was being unfaithful to him.

For all the fantasizing egotist in Toback, he is ruthlessly practical when he makes films. He respects both the craft and the compromises. When he came to cut *Love and Money*, he found that Sharkey was not as bold or passionate as he should have been. The original concept had called for a total resolve in Byron to remake his life. But Sharkey was wistful and a touch self-pitying; he was only dreaming of change. And so Toback abandoned his own optimistic first ending. It was a relief in a way: "I hate leaving someone with anything at the end." The gambler, like the lover, wants to be wiped out.

More drastic still: "I decided to have a love scene that was darker and nastier. So I talked Lorimar into giving me a bit more money, and we brought Sharkey and Muti back for one more night of sexual shooting."

The original love scene had been shot in a Marina del Rey hotel. But Toback wanted more space to let the camera move around the bed, so he built another room on the Culver City lot. As darkness fell, he began to talk his two stars into the improvisations that would create a scene before dawn. "Muti was immediately apprehensive of the mood I was weaving on the set. She didn't think the reshooting was necessary, and she felt threatened by this new, ugly tone." But Toback can convince any woman naked in bed, and he preyed upon her and used her fear.

The new sequence moves from conventional lovemaking to Byron's neurotic grilling of Catherine about all the rich men she let fuck her and about marrying Stockheinz for money. He hounds her with questions and demands acts of slavery from her. She sucked his toes; he fucked her from behind. Those scenes were shot but not used. However, they changed Catherine's mood and left Muti's face dark with regret. Catherine begins to cry and starts talking about the day she found her father after he killed himself. He was hanging from the ceiling, his feet blue, his penis erect. This glimpse of pathology now lines the sexual adventure with mourning and uncovers a stew of sadomasochistic undertones.

Along with some relooping of the dialogue and a twist at the end, this moment of orgasm and death facing one another in the night has shifted *Love and Money* toward the somber and morbid. There are problems: The pace feels rushed and the intrigue is confused. Sharkey never grasps the mad assurance that Byron needs if some of his lines are to sound justified. Moreover, in the attempt to make a commercial picture, Toback could have discovered things he needs to learn as a craftsman—or forsake altogether. Godard is one of his idols, and despite the headlong commitment of his own life, Toback may suffer from Godard's polarization of thought and feeling. *Love and Money* wants to be convulsively emotional, but it is often chill, watchful, and schematic. It is to Toback's credit that one wonders whether he won't end up as an underground filmmaker, deliriously inspired by minute budgets and the thrill of being outlawed.

But *Love and Money* could be successful. It is far more

accessible than *Fingers*: It still has a love story, spectacle, and an odd, bitter tone. Why not? Toback began by wanting to make a Warren Beatty picture. Even without Beatty, his stock may be secure. Which would be fine if he wanted security. But fame and opportunity would only make him more perversely unmanageable. Perhaps he will attempt the story he has been writing, *Pick-up Artist*, about a man who wants to fuck every woman but who still lives with his mother. Toback regards his own mother as "my Rock of Gibraltar," yet the mother in *Fingers* is contemptuous of the son. There are depths of mixed feeling there, and Toback might be the filmmaker to reveal how much the American male longs to screw his mother. Wouldn't that have to be an underground picture?

If that doesn't offend the industry, then there is always his own lust for chance and the telephone furies closing in on him. Like someone who has told a lie and has to live the rest of his life by it, so the death wish can never cash in its chips. It must stay at the table until nothing is left. It also insists on seeing our highest goals—love and money—as the shit that will poison the soul if it is not voided. Even orgasm, eventually, is an attempt to forget evil.

19

The Godmother

In silent movies Pauline was a desperate heroine tied to the rails by beasts and left to flutter with alarm as the locomotive whistled with glee. Today's Pauline requires no thugs. In a whirl of dextrous risk, she lashes herself to the track and prepares for the delicious vibration in the rails.

In the spring of 1979, the most famous, admired, and disliked of movie critics—the only one who has managed to matter—gave up her platform, her freedom to moralize over movies, and her bastion of domestic taste in the Berkshires to walk the Hollywood streets.

The movie community went into frenzies of gossip. Lesser critics practised their self-righteous backhands. In *New West* Jeanie Kasindorf used the incident to dispute the integrity of critics interested in making pictures. The ever-tactful *American Film* coasted in on the controversy, noting that critic John Simon had fingered James Toback as "Miss Kael's escort (an evocative phrase) around New York a couple of years earlier."

There hovered over the stories the scandal of a Jean Brodie turned Sadie Thompson. And Pauline Kael, I suspect, knew bliss in the outrage she had caused. At last, at fifty-nine, she had gone beyond intellectual respectability and returned to the California that made her. She had become a star. There has always been a willful vulnerability to Pauline Kael, a determination to be exposed. It makes her life worthy of a role for Bette Davis and Jane Fonda. I can see a biopic in three parts: *The Girl from Petaluma,* in which Jane is the vibrant radical growing up north of

San Francisco in the thirties, rehearsing a Bette Davis strut, blown along by crusades against poverty and fascism, and gradually emerging from disconsolate domesticity to be a spike of opinion, as urgent and truculent as the cries of orgasm. Then *All About Pauline,* Manhattan years, with Bette parading a mannered style in a conservative magazine, becoming a household name in *New Yorker* cartoons, falling in and out of love with the people who make movies, surveying the business with "What a dump!" The finale is still in the crucible: We may have to call it *Coming Home* or *What Ever Happened To Baby Pauline?,* or even *Jezebel* if the highly strung heroine meets a fevered end.

Her affinity with movie stars is a critical strength. She has a deepdown skepticism for all admiration, and an agonized assurance that love will wither or fool her. It is the same paranoia that keeps any movie star glamorous, apprehensive, and sexy. There is an erotic panic in the star, flinching from but grabbing at the awareness that everybody is looking at them. It provides a sediment of sex and violence—for peeping sexually is like latent assault—in all pictures. And Pauline is most aroused by the looming of sex and danger in movies.

I do not know her—though I have met her. This is not a commentary on her private life. I feel the sexuality in the thing she offers to all of us, and about which she is most proud and insecure: her writing.

Consider how the titles of her collected criticism treat movies as a surrogate lover; listen to the little girl's bold innuendo about capitulation: *I Lost It at the Movies, Kiss Kiss Bang Bang, Going Steady, Deeper into Movies,* and *Reeling.* The earlier titles are more cutely suggestive, but the older woman clings on to the hope of being Scarlett for a Rhett movie, as witness this 1961 memory of an occasion when Pauline was twenty-eight:

When Shoeshine *opened in 1947, I went to see it*

alone after one of those terrible lovers' quarrels that
leave one in a state of incomprehensible despair. I
came out of the theater, tears streaming, and overheard
the petulant voice of a college girl complaining to her
boyfriend, "Well, I don't see what was so special about
that movie." I walked up the street, crying blindly, no
longer certain whether my tears were for the tragedy
on the screen, the hopelessness I felt for myself, or the
alienation I felt from those who could not experience
the radiance of Shoeshine. *For if people cannot feel*
Shoeshine, *what* can *they feel? My identification with*
those two lost boys had become so strong that I did not
feel simply a mixture of pity and disgust toward this
dissatisfied customer but an intensified hopelessness
about everything . . . Later I learned that the man
with whom I had quarreled had gone the same night
and had also emerged in tears. Yet our tears for each
other, and for Shoeshine, *did not bring us together.*
Life, as Shoeshine *demonstrates, is too complex for*
facile endings.[1]

That could be the close of a short story or the lament
from a Bette Davis picture. It is touching but self-conscious.
Such flagrant mapping of emotion makes one suspicious of
emotionalism. But it is as good an imprint of a person as
if the page were hot wax and Kael had slapped her impul-
sive self down on it. Notice, too, how her ardor is defined
by the dullness of others. As a movie critic, Pauline Kael
has often been the vexed reporter of an audience situation
in which her lyrical intuition rose above the mass, instigat-
ing her sharpest political sensibility: that you can't trust the
crowd if you have fine feelings.

Her prose is nervously haughty, autocratic but jittery, like
Bette's stare when she's dominating a film. Kael writes in
showers and explosions—stunning openings and abrupt endings. But along the way, the process can reach radiant pin-

nacles of the thrill at flying so high. Here is a passage from 1978, on Brian De Palma's *The Fury*, where the language embodies her perception of a film, and where the fervent pace suggests the bliss of someone being seduced by a movie:

> *No other director shows such a clear-cut development in technique from film to film. In camera terms, De Palma was learning fluid romantic steps in* Obsession; *he started to move his own way in* Carrie—*swirling and figure skating, sensuously. You could still see the calculation. Now he has stopped worrying about the steps. He's caught up with his instructors—with Welles in* Touch of Evil, *with Scorsese in* Mean Streets. *What distinguished De Palma's visual style is smoothness combined with a jazzy willingness to appear crazy or campy: it could be that he's developing one of the great film styles—a style in which he stretches out suspense while grinning his notorious alligator grin. He has such a grip on technique in* The Fury *that you get the sense of a director who cares about little else; there's a frightening total purity in his fixation on the humor of horror. It makes the film seem very peaceful, even as one's knees are shaking.*[2]

Kael's style is most alive when mooning over the look and come-on of photographed skin. She may not always realize that she is conjuring with the prospect of an actor or a movie screwing us. But whenever she does, it makes her prose taut and daring. On at least one occasion, it brought a disconcerting ambivalence to a review. With *Straw Dogs* she submitted to the dark hostility Sam Peckinpah visits on Susan George. Her delight at being head over heels in the balling of a movie surpassed itself. It became vulnerability aghast at being victimized but unable to denounce the sensation:

> *The rape is one of the few truly erotic sequences on*

film, and the punches that subdue the wife have the requisite languor of slightly slowed-down motion. This same languor is present in the late slaughters; the editing is superb in these sequences, with the slowing-down never prolonged but just long enough to fit the images of violence in your imagination, to make them seem already classic and archaic—like something you remember—while they're happening. The rape has heat to it —there can be little doubt of that—but what goes into that heat is the old male barroom attitude: we can see that she's asking for it, begging for it, that her every no means yes.[3]

I am suggesting that Pauline Kael has been writing about herself, with the striving candor of any writer intent on self-expression. She admitted as much in the preface to *Deeper into Movies* when in one sentence she asserted her artistic soul, her horror of phonies, and her hope that sensation can be made lucid: "I would feel like a fake if I dedicated a book to anyone, because I know I write because I love trying to figure out what I feel and what I think about what I feel, and why." [4]

That seems to promise the methodical onion peeling of film's impact. But Kael's approach celebrates impulse. She prefers the gaiety and slipstream of hurry. Her best writing matches the rush and zoom we feel with "roller-coaster" films, movies like *The Fury* in which thematic responsibility, novelistic ideas, or "content" have been abandoned to the splurge of the medium. She loves the superstitious process of sitting in the dark and going with speed, losing it at the movies, pretending earnestness but wanting a whammy, saying no but meaning yes.

It's a mania in Kael that she can project onto others. For instance, this verdict on Jane Fonda in *Klute* is the writer possessing the star for herself: "Jane Fonda's motor runs a little fast. As an actress, she has a special kind of smartness that takes the form of speed; she's always a little ahead of everybody, and this quicker beat—this quicker responsiveness—makes her more exciting to watch." [5]

That description fits Kael, who attends the theater with the nervous expectation of an actress or of a saint fearful that her church will let her down. In the December 1977–January 1978 *American Film,* Bruce Cook recounted sitting in front of her at a special preview of Robert Altman's *Images:*

> *She talks incessantly. Well, not exactly* talks—*but exclaims, grunts, groans, and generally carries on in a manner most unbecoming to the doyenne of American film critics. We were not ten minutes into the picture when I heard behind me a sharp puff of breath between pursed lips, unmistakably an ill-suppressed laugh. And then, a little while later, at a sudden twist of* Images' *rather convoluted plot, a voice identifiably Pauline Kael's said, "Oh, no!" in a very loud whisper. And so it went on all through the screening. There were further exclamations, high whines of contempt, and most frequent of all, that sharp, sucking pop of disapproval that is usually expressed in print as "Tsk!" It was quite a performance.* [6]

Her presence belies her five feet, and quivers with concentration for a film. At another preview in New York—of *The Fury* (again)—my own disappointment with the picture made me aware of the hunched and very busy woman next to me. There were no "Tsks." She was carried along by this film. But there was another noise: her sharp pencil rasping away. As far as I could tell, she was noting more than words or reminders. She was reeling off sentences in the dark, with a momentum that never seemed to lose touch with the film. I felt she was writing *with* it—which makes her review of *The Fury* challenging, no matter how much I disagree with it.

She probably frets over every sentence, within the limits

set by weekly deadlines. But the notebook has a primitive authenticity, and I doubt if she would significantly revise its instantaneous messages. It is part of the relish for haste and sensational atmosphere that the momentary becomes a creed. It is less odd than shrewd that she was replaced at *The New Yorker* by Roger Angell, who is, among other things, a baseball writer, for Kael treats movies as packed sporting instants without the benefit of replay. You see, she only watches a movie once. Most of the pictures a critic has to see do not merit that single viewing. It is often difficult for even a Kael to make the time and the arrangements for more than one shot at a new movie. Nevertheless, most of her work reports one-night stands in the spirit of love/hate 'em and leave 'em. And Kael's virtuous immediacy has been maintained even as more and more Americans have been seeing films again to go deeper.

Thus, the idea of Kael at a Movieola, suspending a sequence, running it back and forth to explain an effect, is inconceivable. She wants to be hurtled, banged, and trampled. The analytical doldrums are a major reason for her mistrust of film academia, typified in her warning to a 1965 conference that if anything could kill the movies it would be education. Still, her faith forces her to preach instinct as a kind of methodology, and to legitimize the roller-coaster movie, a Coney Island amusement that some-how proves as indicative of profound cultural traits as a museum piece:

This collection of my reviews from The New Yorker *from September 1969 to March 1972 is also a record of the interaction of movies and our national life during a frantic time when three decades seem to have been compressed into three years and I wrote happily—like a maniac—to keep up with what I thought was going on in movies—which is to say, in our national theater.*

Right now, movie critics have an advantage over critics in other fields: responsive readers. And it can help you to concentrate your energies if you know that the subject is fresh and that your review may make a difference to some people. I suspect that my reviews gain rather than lose from the speed and urgency of making deadlines and reaching the public before the verdicts are in on a film.[7]

Despite her aversion to taking a teaching position, she does lecture occasionally at colleges. I have witnessed this once. She spoke to a class of 150, for two hours, on her feet, without a note, swaying and gesturing with conviction, not so much a planned lecture as a way of wrapping the students' questions into a racing survey of movies today, forming a brilliant portrait of her own endeavor and commitment. It was a starry performance, and she did it on this occasion for no charge.

But it was also a haphazard battery of her recent opinions, a swing through the "In Brief" section on films in *The New Yorker,* a chore she always guarded carefully for herself. She bounced off students' questions. Arguments never developed: You had to be the willing target for her brisk arrows. I think that many people would attest to the way she deals with queries in small groups by saying, "Well, I wrote about that . . . look me up." She does not enjoy mulling over those rapid estimates. There may be a titanium core of vanity in such sidestepping. But I think that dissent, and reappraisal of a picture, threaten the validity of the instantaneous scorch marks movies leave in her receptive mind— and that is how photography itself works. The light burns into the emulsion, and the scars are called beauty.

Pauline Kael was born in June, 1919. Meeting her, you might not credit that: She is so restless and animated that the facts seem wrong. But her age has heightened her vulnerability and helps explain the recent kicking away of her safety net.

She was the fifth child of Isaac Kael, a Polish Jew who owned a chicken farm in Petaluma. They lived in rural sufficiency until the Depression halted the business. They moved to San Francisco, which Pauline treats as her native city, as witnessed by her street wisdom when reviewing films like *Dirty Harry* or *Invasion of the Body Snatchers*. She finished high school when she was seventeen and majored in philosophy at Berkeley, graduating in 1940.

It was 1953 before her first movie review appeared in print: for *City Lights* magazine, on Chaplin's *Limelight*, entitled "Slimelight." Those intervening years involved marriages and divorces, life in New York and San Francisco, some work in experimental filmmaking, and an unsuccessful attempt at writing plays. The gap covers a time of turbulence, indecision, and obscurity that haunted her later fame. I suspect her hurry springs from the worry that she squandered her youth.

Throughout the fifties she developed as a freelance critic: in *Sight and Sound, Partisan Review, Kulchur, Film Culture, Moviegoer,* and *Film Quarterly*. She earned peanuts but wrote with the crush of love—on *Shoeshine*, Ophüls's *Madame de . . .* , and Renoir's *Golden Coach*. Then in 1955 she started doing volunteer radio reviews for the Pacifica station, and she became manager of the Berkeley Cinema Guild Theaters, the first twinned art house in America. She married the owner of the theaters and wrote program notes for the films she played there. Those and the radio reviews were too emphatic for many: attack-as-clarity, force-as-feeling, was already her trademark, and it did not assist relaxed viewing. In *I Lost It at the Movies*, she reprinted "Replying to Listeners," from early 1963. It shows her creative use of exasperation:

I want to say a few words about a communication

*from a woman listener. She begins with, "Miss Kael, I
assume you aren't married—one loses that nasty, sharp
bite in one's voice when one learns to care about others."
Isn't it remarkable that women, who used to pride
themselves on their chastity, are now just as complacently proud of their married status? They've read
Freud and they've not only got the idea that being
married is healthier, more "mature," they've also got
the illusion that it improves their character. This lady
is so concerned that I won't appreciate her full acceptance of femininity that she signs herself with her
husband's name preceded by a Mrs. Why, if this Mrs.
John Doe just signed herself Jane Doe, I might confuse
her with one of those nasty virgins, I might not understand the warmth and depth of connubial experience
out of which she writes.*

*I wonder, Mrs. John Doe, in your reassuring, pro-
tected marital state, if you have considered that perhaps caring about others may bring a bite to the voice?
And I wonder if you have considered how difficult it
is for a woman in this Freudianized age, which turns
out to be a new Victorian age in its attitude to women
who do anything, to show any intelligence without
being accused of unnatural aggressivity, hateful vin-
dictiveness, or lesbianism.*[8]

You can hear in her early voice the altruistic bite, know
its rationale of caring, and guess at the sexual anger mas-
querading as feminism. There is also the keening of grievance. She had made less than $2,000 from criticism in ten
years, and had worked as a seamstress, a cook, and a textbook ghostwriter before she moved to New York in 1966.
She was hired and fired by *McCall's* because she proved
too belligerent toward popular hits like *The Sound of Music*.
It was only in January, 1968, that she joined *The New
Yorker*. She was forty-eight, and she flowered under the

benevolence of editor William Shawn: "He gave me the space I needed to develop a sustained position from week to week, and, for the first time, that total independence from advertisers and from anxieties about reader response that make criticism possible." [9] I don't know whether she or Shawn recollect an earlier aside about the magazine: "*The New Yorker* carries sophisticated consumption to extremes: it is 'knowing' about everything. The reader is supposed to 'see through' what he buys—whether it's a production of *Macbeth*, a lace peignoir, a biography of Freud, or a $10 haircut." [10]

The New Yorker made Kael famous, and she became one of its leading attractions. But the years there have not been unrelieved paradise. Pauline fought editorial battles all the way, often over a strength she wanted in her language, and she felt that she was not generously paid. But the thorn in her flesh was Shawn's cleverest ploy. Kael alternated six-month stints with Penelope Gilliatt, the English novelist and story writer. Kael was bitter about this teaming and never friendly with Gilliatt. In 1971 she pinch-hit for Gilliatt when *Sunday, Bloody Sunday* opened: Gilliatt had written its screenplay, thus acquiring something Kael has never yet had, a credit. "Miss Gilliatt and I are ships that pass each other in the night every six months," Kael wrote at the end of her review. "It is a pleasure to salute her at this crossing." [11] Yet the review balked at the movie for being something "very far from my life and my temperament." From Shawn's point of view, whatever the reasons for keeping Gilliatt, there may have been the thought that partial denial would inflame Kael. (Ironically, he lost both of them within six months, Gilliatt having retreated after an embarrassing charge of plagiarism.)

Kael was an opinionmaker a few years before she settled at *The New Yorker*. But she cut against the grain of critical debate in the sixties. She is not clubbable and not disposed to cults established by others. Her dismay at wordy over-

analysis also applied to the wave of auteurism most identified
with Andrew Sarris. None of her contemporaries impressed
her. She had always scolded the older order, personified by
Dwight Macdonald. She could dissect the bogus gravity of
someone like Siegfried Kracauer: "There are men whose
concept of love is so boring and nagging that you decide if
that's what love is, you don't want it, you want something
else. That's how I feel about Kracauer's 'cinema.' I want
something else." [12]

She offered her own way instead: an elusive path between
the crass exploitation of Hollywood and the cerebral excesses of art-house cinema. She has always hoped that American films could be the best, popular but penetrating, sensational and serious. *Cahiers du Cinema* and Antonioni
alarmed her as much as *The Sound of Music*. She would
occasionally write longer pieces, identifying trends. They
are her least satisfactory work, but they reveal a higher-
mindedness, no matter how pop it tried to be. "Fantasies
of the Art-House Audience," from 1961, and "Trash, Art and
the Movies," from 1969, were testaments against smug respectability and for honest excitement.

The longer she wrote for *The New Yorker*, the clearer it
became that she wanted the value of movies to vindicate her
function as soothsayer. She often deplored the damage
Hollywood did to creative urgings, and she despaired of
the casual vacuity of audiences. She said she wanted films
with ideas. The wish that there should be a bond between
America and its movies superseded her early desire for
sensation. It was like a nymphomaniac searching for a sound
husband. But the times were barren. In *Going Steady*, for
instance, covering the years 1968–1970, it is depressing to see
how few films of lasting quality she had to discuss.

When the critic loves the medium but has to inspect its
dross, he or she may go frantic over the rare good picture,
or pontificate with undue violence when a sacred cow
wanders into the line of fire. Kael was lit up by *Last Tango*

in Paris; she descended on *Citizen Kane;* and she went out of her way to be a part of *Nashville.* *Tango* has never seemed to me the film she reviewed: I think the material moved her and maybe blinded her to its pretension and obscurity, and the weary selfhood of Brando. With *Kane* she only exposed her own sketchy research and the preset killer instinct. It was an odd attempt at demolition, for *Kane* is just the stylish magic act she likes, a movie so aglow with seductive light that it need never mention sex (it is sexier than *Last Tango*). But its ambiguities defeated her and left her longest work, "Raising Kane," a petulant, ill-judged study in resentment.

The case of *Nashville* is more problematic. She had noticed Altman earlier as an in-and-out maverick. *Nashville* was due to open during one of Gilliatt's terms on the magazine, but Kael preempted, reviewing a rough cut. She marveled at the off-hand epic, and I believe she was more right than wrong. But she had laid herself open to charges of partiality and career brokering. And if she had selected Altman as her hero, she could not have chosen more disastrously. He is blindly facetious and inconsistent, a lout when faced by admirers. He "betrayed" her trust with later, inept films, yet the example did not deter her from fixing on other masters.

Thus, she took her indefinite leave of absence from *The New Yorker* and went to Hollywood as the employee of Warren Beatty. She had given a very timely rave to *Bonnie and Clyde;* she had turned to lather over *Shampoo;* and she felt that the young actor-tycoon respected and needed her. There had been other offers over the years, all turned down in the gloomy knowledge that Hollywood was a crazy house for intractable taste.

At fifty-nine it was a dramatic but understandable act, not least because of its drama. She may have felt financially insecure; she may have been just as attracted by a last great risk. She cannot have doubted the mirth and envy it would provoke. But I think she overestimated Beatty's wisdom and consideration. He assigned her to produce and assist on *Love and Money,* a script he had bought from James Toback, and which Toback was to direct. Kael knew Toback, and presumably believed she could help shape the energies of America's most uninhibited filmmaker.

No one else believed in the match, and no one had long to wait. It was a confrontation like that of Stanley Kowalski and Blanche Dubois. In the crunch Beatty was too Hollywood to back a critic against a filmmaker, or a woman against a man for whom he feels awe. Kael and Beatty parted company, and Kael's Hollywood ticket was picked up by Paramount, which was impressed by the script tidying she had done on *Love and Money.* It could be that Beatty had originally purchased the script on Kael's recommendation, and it was a sad irony that Kael and Toback both seemed stranded by Beatty's whimsical actions.

It was a year before Kael came up for air. She kept an office at Paramount longer than she felt able to stay there. But she must have known what she risked in going back east without a credit. Perhaps it was the offer of full-time occupation as *New Yorker* film critic that made up her mind. That had always been the most provoking compromise.

But her return could not go unremarked. Andrew Sarris took her on in *The Village Voice* [13]—a rough but not unappreciative putdown—and Renata Adler published the kind of thorough demolition in *The New York Review of Books* [14] that could have been a year in the writing. It was a very acute, deadly piece, unhinged by malicious predisposition. What must have hurt Kael most was its detailed abuse of her literary style. So comprehensively founded in Kael's own texts, the piece artfully turned the excitement of Pauline's work into a dreadful record of intemperate bitchiness.

I hope Kael can recover her confidence—she is nothing without it. Her story shows the lamentable predicament of the earnest critic, especially one who loves her subject. Anyone who has been thrilled by a movie can see how good she is at catching those dragonfly moments. Her failings are real and honorable ones. She is no more profound and no less headstrong than movies themselves.

20

The Discreet Charm of the Godfather

How does one convey outrage these days without sounding pedantic or shrill? Critics, professors, and the picture community have shelved that tone in the effort to elevate films with goodwill. The role of active dislike is nearly in abeyance. Let me, therefore, attempt a discriminating attack. I will be as calm as possible with it, even if outrage is upsetting.

The public is a womb, and taste has become a pill able to reject any germination. Its individual members regularly perish, but the body maintains its stumbling, lifelike progress. The crowd has had to find an impassivity greater than the dismay of its individuals. We absorb trash, the humdrum, and masterpieces with indifference: Critical diagnoses are no more penetrating than the warnings on cigarette packs. TV, the medium that reaches so many people in an instant, mocks connections. It has suppressed the individual with its ratings. It has nullified the prospect of works of the imagination enriching the masses. We know now that the process merely impacts us, erasing the strenuous duties of personality and responsibility.

The wonderful and the abominable have collapsed together in mutual resemblance. They measure our time and permit the buying of time that sustains TV, a medium in which the chance of enlightenment has passed beyond the disappointment of half-baked information and dispiriting entertainment to become a household monotone, switched on like a light. TV is a distraction from concentration, solitude, and company. It removes burdens we hardly recall: —to be troubled or pleased, to be ourselves. TV is altering the nature of movies.

I am talking about *The Godfather*. It is no longer necessary to specify which of the two parts. TV has amalgamated them, just as it has the volumes of *The Forsyte Saga*, the tableaux of *Civilization*, and its own daily ingredients— news, drama, comedy, sports, movies, commercials—until they are all different complexions of the screen's haze. TV is a jelly in which the sediment of cell life is in perpetual motion, confounding earlier cultural expectations, such as narrative, understanding, and moral sensibility.

I am talking about the two films made by Francis Ford Coppola, which seemed to me on the larger screen a landmark of personal work in the popular industrial context. Part I had everything except the Buñuel who might have intertwined baptism and gangland *coup d'état* with barbed-wire ribbons. Instead, Coppola treated that compromise with a pained, straight-faced acceptance which now seems a fundamental shortcoming. Perhaps he hoped that his inability to take a stance at the end would be read as irony or ambiguity; perhaps he never realized his own predicament. For all his sophistication, there is something guileless in his pleasure at the grim machinery of slaughtering rivals intercut with the baptism liturgy. Francis enjoys the sardonic timing as much as Michael does, and he may be as unable to measure or feel the human consequences that it veils.

Still, *The Godfather* had the virtue of the best American films: It did not cheat its own compulsive melodramatic energy. Paramount required a wholehearted climax, and Coppola's straight face was too intent on mechanics to confuse it with disintegration. Coppola is misled by expressive perfection: He thinks it alters or places the human situation being shown. The American movie has never dealt with doubt without the feeble excuse of self-pity or madness. Its dramas work like trustworthy engines: The gravest flaw of *Citizen Kane* is that Welles cannot abandon his babyish satisfaction with neatness—everything fits, works, and hums. The director has fallen for Kane's debilitating ambition: to have the people think the way he tells them to think. American movie heroes are as convinced as scripts, schedules, and release patterns imply. They accomplish and achieve; even the alienated, dying Kane initiates an elegant riddle that has lasted to this day and become a slogan for enigmas.

Just as Michael Corleone ended that first part secure, so Coppola had a brimming hit. I doubt if anyone in America, let alone Hollywood, disapproved of him—that is a measure of his negligible risk; it also reflects the sweet poison of the product. In its brief time, *The Godfather* was the biggest grosser ever, and that easily overlooked the moral disarray of its own pusillanimous ending. *The Godfather* was filled with the superficial dynamism that *Kane* first identified, and which has been the ideal of the intelligent-pic trade ever since: It is sensational narrative powered by the hush and detail of gravity and consequence which are never really explored because the show must keep moving on.

From a full-page ad in *The New York Times*, November 11, 1977—Pacino's blank saint's face and the massive headline: "*The Godfather* as you've never seen it!" Then:

> *Starting tomorrow—and continuing for the next three nights—NBC will broadcast one of the major presentations of this or any season. It is called "Mario Puzo's* The Godfather: *The Complete Novel for Television." For the first time viewers will have the opportunity to see the Godfather story told in chronological order. The keynote of the nine-hour presentation will be the first television showing of* The Godfather, Part II *plus important film never-before-seen on any screen! . . . The entire production has been personally—and*

masterfully—reshaped for television by the man who directed . . . both "Godfather" movies, Francis Ford Coppola. He has been able in this new form to achieve a sense of continuity and scope that simply could not be realized in a theatrical presentation.

Then, in far smaller type at the foot of the page, came this grim waiver couched as solicitude: "PARENTAL DISCRETION ADVISED." Has anyone adding this phrase ever wondered about the sentiments that compromise parental judgment? Does anything else in TV help nourish it? Or is it the slick escape of the medium from the consequences of offense and distress? Did anyone pause to reflect how far *The Godfather* itself is a devout study of the efficacy of cruel parental discretion? Or is the avoidance of real parental care only part of the pessimism that supports the inhumane patriarchy of *The Godfather?*

The network hype has the language of critical judgment, no matter how inflated; but parental discretion so advised is the cowardly sidestepping of any fixed attitudes toward TV's own materials, part of the irresponsible orthodoxy: "We just carry these programs . . . you can always turn off . . . the views expressed in this program are those of the contributors, not the station." "Parental discretion" is usually invoked to excuse acts of violence, sexual scenes, and what is called "language." No one ever advises it in the total matter of watching TV, or of submitting to the systematic fragmentation of all programs with the aromatic glue of commercials: *The Godfather,* say, interrupted and sticky with pizza, spaghetti sauce, tomato paste, and olive oil—the staples that made a legitimate business for the Corleone family. Perhaps they also offered a paste that could be sold to the movies for an easy-spread and non-cancer-causing blood?

> *There is a good deal of blood in* Pierrot.—Cahiers du Cinema.

Not blood, red.—Jean-Luc Godard [1]

In other words I covered in the shooting every aspect of the killing. Actually some of it was shot in slow motion. I had the camera slow and the girl moving so that I could measure out the movements and the covering of awkward parts of the body, the arm movement, gesture and so forth. I was actually seven days on that little thing; it's only forty-five seconds really.—Alfred Hitchcock. [2]

Francis Ford Coppola is an American success story. Everyone loves him for his very rapid transit from film school, Corman quickies, and off-the-cuff nudies to the prestige, epic panorama, and box-office plenty of *The Godfather* and *Godfather II*. It was tactful of him to separate those two films with the posed paranoia of so "difficult" and "unconventional" a film as *The Conversation*, in which blood gushes back from the toilet in a traumatic plumbing malfunction. As he finished *Godfather II*, Coppola gave *Film Comment* a statement of dreamy contentment. In that interview he rejoiced in the big bucks of Part I, the freedom he had won for Part II, and the limitless vistas that confronted the movie world's new Don:

> *I'm not that rich, but I'm gettin'. I had to go through a lot of agonizing decisions because I can always say why don't I just go and make money. I could sit down and write the most commercial movie ever made. I feel I could pull it off. Just make a hundred million dollars and spend the rest of my life . . . I'm now thirty-five and that's what I thought I was doing with* The Godfather *and then with* Godfather II. *I was making a film that would appeal to an audience. At some time you've got to cut off and say, "O.K. I've made enough money."* [3]

> *This contempt for money is just a trick of the rich to keep it from the poor.*—Michael Corleone

By 1976 Coppola was no longer so relaxed. The project that he moved on to, *Apocalypse Now,* was proving as much a white man's grave as its subject, the Vietnam War. Immense difficulties of scripting, casting, finding locations and military assistance, and of violent weather were hindering the picture. *Apocalypse When?* it was called in 1977 as George Lucas and Steven Spielberg slipped past Coppola in the championship for best bankable movie-maker. Way behind schedule, the picture would not open until the autumn of 1979, when Coppola fashioned something commercially coherent out of 1.5 million feet of film.

It was in the time of *Apocalypse* that Coppola was called on to reshape *The Godfather* for TV. No other director had had an opportunity to reassess a released film.* Part I was televised in 1974, to the largest audience ever for a movie—since surpassed by *Gone With the Wind.* NBC and Paramount immediately worked out a deal (reportedly $15 million) for an eventual amalgamation of both parts that used a chronological sequence, "laundered" the violence and language, and restored some footage cut from the theatrical-release versions.

By the time the work came to be done, Coppola was marooned in the Philippines, so no one can say how "personally" he worked on the TV *Godfather.* But surely this unique opportunity would have appealed to him. No American director could be blasé about the size of the audience, the thrill of national unity—as tempting to filmmakers as to presidents—the chronological clarification, and, perhaps best of all, the originality of the venture for a man tempted by the role of young entrepreneur of new ideas and brilliant imagination. Coppola's editor, Barry Malkin, assembled all

---

* TV may offer more second chances. Scorsese made one *New York, New York* for theaters and another for the small screen. The advantage this offers is clear, but what may it do to the necessary discipline of decision making? "You should have seen what they cut" might give way as a defense to "See it on TV."

the possible material, some of which had to be retrieved from the Paramount vaults. In three months Malkin compiled a nine-and-a-half-hour version. This was put on videotape so that Coppola could examine and approve it from his jungle hideout.

Much more had still to be done: Two hours were cut from Malkin's assembly, and the whole had to be broken into well-formed episodes that would fit the four-night plan. Great care was taken to anticipate the commercial intrusions so that they would do the least damage to a structure of self-contained acts. The two men used telephone and telex, and they met on several occasions. In addition, they had to find a framework for all four nights—an aura for the "Godfather Show"—that would bind the series. The TV version testified to the ingenuity and thoroughness of the work, even if Malkin did most of it under Coppola's distracted guidance. By March, 1977, "a version edited to our ideas" was put before NBC.

All I want is your respect.—VITO CORLEONE

The golden rule with a "commercial" film is that it must never surprise the public except physically. It may draw from the audience cries of terror at the accumulation of murders and disasters, but the audience must not be confronted by any kind of problem.— JEAN RENOIR [4]

And so it rolled, stopping and starting, on the nights of November 12–15, in three two-hour episodes and a three-hour conclusion. What can be said about it in the way of sensible criticism?

There was an air of well-being in the land. The press admired the emphatic development of its new form. Ordinary viewers congratulated one another on having seen it. The ratings were good, if not extraordinary. It was an event as widely appreciated as *Roots*, the running of *Gone With the*

Wind, Star Wars, or the live coverage of a celebrity's funeral. Only a fool would endorse the extra "continuity and scope" of the TV version, yet hardly anyone complained at the wearying flaws in those very areas. Chronological sequence on TV was obtained at the cost of having to see six and a half to seven hours of film over a span of seventy-five hours, with some thirty interruptions in the filmstream for commercials, introductions, and wrap-ups. Of course, no one ever debated the merit of chronology as a structure. The original tension of two distinct approaches to the family, the second one framing and reflecting on the first, was mutely sacrificed. Yet again the orthodoxy was heeded that films should have a beginning, a middle, and an end—in that order. Eighty years old, the American movie remains pledged to the suitability of story as a way of taming time and alleviating any critical interpretation of history, society, or ourselves. What does that do to even apocalypse if there is a beginning, a middle, an end, and then a rating for the end? The screen size (on average) was reduced from about 240 square feet to one and a half square feet. An electronic patterning of lines was substituted for Gordon Willis's photography, and the film's contrast of interior gloom and exterior sunshine was more than a TV set could contain. By turns, the movie was glaring or lost; throughout it was stippled and miniature—a film on a dusty horizon. This was scarcely remarked on: One might reasonably conclude that TV is not watched, it is endured or countenanced.

The devices used to bind the film were very revealing. There were persistent voice-overs so that the film should not be interpreted as a slur upon Italians. On the first night, Talia Shire, Coppola's and Michael Corleone's sister, appeared on camera—reportedly Coppola himself had declined this chore—to say that it would be "grossly unfair" to let the Corleones represent all Italians. (It would have been wittier if the real, hard-working, and conscientious Mafia had been absolved, too.) Titles also announced that, despite the bloodiness and the latently admiring portrait of the gangsters, this was actually a study of "the self-destructive effects of crime and violence." The film was framed every night with a tragically composed close-up of the brooding Michael Corleone, sitting by the ruffled lake where his last brother had been executed, surveying the past, and embodying the lonely travails of presidential retreat—Sunset at Lake Tahoe? The TV film was shaped as Michael's testament, the family history seen through his eyes. Despite the listless decadence of Pacino's presence, it became the tragedy of a man who had become malignant trying to preserve his royal line. Every execution and betrayal is justified by his Nixonian urge to keep the thing together. We half want an Attila of principles, if he will struggle against change, breakdown, and our indistinct anxieties.

The amalgamated work is dark proof of the attractiveness of the villain in the American movie, so long as he is photographed in repose and seen to think before he destroys, and so long as sincerity persuades him to trample on principle. On TV this was accentuated by the small screen finding close-ups in what once were fuller compositions; where sheer space or another person competed with Michael's head, the TV image closed in on his pensive face and made it royal. When Michael assures Kay that he did not know, we respond to the necesssary damage our hero has had to do to honor and himself for the good reason that the film respects poker-faced deceit and is anchored in Michael's insolent look. It never mocks him—there is no humor anywhere in the film —it only shows him. And whatever such balanced filmmaking shows, it implicitly glorifies. That is why Coppola claims he has analyzed wickedness, while the audience of *The Godfather* identifies with its inner basis of noble sacrifice. The public watches in a spirit of wanting to belong to this family, wanting to share its heroic purpose and embattled unity.

If Coppola sought irony, it has been smothered by the romanticism of the American movie: unflawed melodramatic progress and undimmed prestige bestowed on the people. Together, they define our response: identification, never any sort of detachment. None of the characters has the all-around raggedness of people in Renoir or Rossellini films, for they are all slyly turned toward us for inspection—they have only that single facet. They are sensibilities aware of being seen, and calculating the effect they make upon the spectator. It is a movie tradition flanked by politicians and the aggressive charm of people in commercials. The politician has been taught by the American movie, and there is a natural association between *The Godfather* and recent political manners in America. Michael is a grasping vote-seeker; he campaigns with people instead of mixing with them. Business, the family, stability, and development are cloaks for his one ambition: maintained authority.

Al Pacino devours the opportunities offered by the role of Michael and makes him the most baleful, depleted father figure in American pictures. Nevertheless, the figure outweighs the drabness of the man. There has never been so reticent a study of iniquity. There could hardly be clearer proof of the way presentational style disarms intention in the characterization. Perhaps Coppola deplores and fears Michael, but he cannot communicate that. The process of showing and seeing a central character, without ridicule or dangerous critical rebuke, is insurmountable. Michael is Satan, but he impresses as a wounded angel; the self-destructive criminality turns into the self-abuse of a lapsed saint. The film is compromised by Michael's self-pity.

Let me mention two things in Pacino's performance, one a moment, the other a motif that lasts three hours. When Michael arrives at the hospital to visit his father, he finds the police guards gone. He smells a plot, and with the timid baker, Enzio, he mounts guard on the hospital steps to deter the coming assassins. A black car loiters and then moves away in frustration. Enzio's nerves are in tatters, and he fumbles a cigarette into his mouth. Michael's own firm hand lights it for him. The newfound Michael notices his own calm with a faraway satisfaction that promises the most cold-blooded of the Corleones. He mentions his nervelessness to no one else in the picture, but we see it: It is one of those privileged moments of communion between a lonely character and the anonymous crowd—as when Kane whispers his enticing clue, knowing that there is a link between our curiosity and his urge to explain himself.

Moments later, the fragile Pacino is beaten by Sterling Hayden's crooked cop (a character of nearly amiable viciousness who seems so much more hateful and coarse than Michael's shy Iago). Michael's face swells immediately, and the bruising stays there for months. Pacino's childlike speech lisps all the more with a broken face, and his stealthy hands are often up to guard or cushion it. The bruising never fades. It spreads through the whole face, like the fatigue of someone too suspicious to sleep. The moment of establishing himself also sets off the gradual degradation of his character: As a creative design it is beautiful, but it cannot rise above the beseeching pain that Pacino projects. Even at the end, he is a morbidly sentimentalized version of the waif, Vito, who came to America with a shipload of immigrants.

There is an undeniable pleasure with the TV version in collecting those moments reclaimed from the out-takes. Our family loyalty treasures every incident in the scrapbook: the discovery that the young Hyman Roth was once employed by Vito Corleone; a glimpse of the girl who was ruined by Johnny Fontane and cherished by the movie mogul; vengeance on the man who caused the death of Apollonia; a moment when Michael's Sicilian guards beg him to tell them marvelous stories about America; Frankie Pentangeli remembering the old ways at the first communion of Michael's son, and surreptitiously teaching the boy to drink wine; and Kay and Michael in bed together when Michael might have been with the family. This last detail lays the subtlest hint of his guilt at being associated with

Kay. She will be his wife, and the instrument he uses to provide a dynasty, but she presents a challenge to his single-minded family obsession. She is the only outsider in the film not treated with contempt, killed, or ignored—and it is a very perilous status. She is also the figure around whom a greater film might have been made; she is the only person who questions the Corleone ethics and who stands for an alternative, if sketchy, faith in people. Diane Keaton was quoted amid the fuss of *Looking for Mr. Goodbar* as saying that in *The Godfather* she had felt a helpless onlooker to all the scenes enjoyed by the men. But that only shows the career pressures on an actress of uncontrived benevolence. It also accounts for her feeling compelled to try the callous novelty of *Goodbar*. Keaton fits few American stereotypes. Her presence is alive with an uncompromising but unconscious kindness. She is capable of playing a decent person in any film committed to human values. But she is not a paragon or anyone confident of her own nature. Her virtue is the more precious for being insecure. The comparison I think of is with Ingrid Bergman in the Rossellini films.

As it is, in *The Godfather* she has moments of pain, crushed innocence, and humiliation that her dignity endures: Tom Hagen sends her away without Michael's address; the black beetle, Michael, returns from Sicily and claims her for a street walk, with a chaperoning car of bodyguards prowling behind, reminding us of the village women who attended his courting of Apollonia—a marriage he never mentions to Kay. She is excluded from the inner chamber at the end of Part I, and is heartbroken at leaving her children. This is the one act of moral courage in the film, and if illusionist realism was the only mode conceivable to Coppola, then that act should have been expanded and Kay made central.

Imagine our perception of the Corleones if it came through her eyes—not especially acute or refined but capable of being appalled, dependent on a man yet loathing his acts. Kay's dissent could be crucial, but it would have driven the audience away in the millions, for it would have opposed principle and the film's magnetic attraction to Michael. Imagine, too, a possible development of her part: Suppose that she cut across the half-hearted antagonism of police law and Mafia order and uttered a cry of abused nature—of life itself—rather than the methodical business of Murder, Inc. That might leave Keaton's Kay as vulnerable and moving as Bergman in *Europa 51*. Then it would no longer be possible to feel such reverence for the Corleones.

Could Coppola have conceived and tolerated an ending in which Kay informs and is ordered dead by Michael, or would that have infringed on the property of Puzo and Paramount, as well as on the comfort of the audience? The Corleones require a quite unexpected opponent, not rival hoodlums, for then the *film noir* claustrophobia would give way to the openness of all our lives. The Corleones are the body- and spirit-snatchers of American cinema; only impersonal style in movie-making has made them admirable. But that hypothetical film would be as disturbing as *Europa 51*, and much less "viable" than *The Godfather*:

> *It's not personal, Sonny—it's strictly business.*
> —MICHAEL CORLEONE

> *I think I'm a good director. I felt that especially in this last picture,* Godfather II. *I think it's really beautifully directed. Maybe I think that because I feel, "Jeez, I got all these nice performances and it's really fantastic looking and it works—it goes together."*—FRANCIS FORD COPPOLA[5]

> *If history's taught us anything it is that we can kill anyone.*—MICHAEL CORLEONE

> *You know, I took my kid to see a forty-five minute assembly of some of the stuff of the old* Godfather, *and I*

said what parts do you like better? He said, "I like when
the guy gets shot." Everyone is like that. Even when
you're shooting the film. The second you're going to do
a throat cutting or something, everyone including the
crew crowds around.—Francis Ford Coppola

Perhaps it is forlorn criticism to wish that Rossellini had
directed *The Godfather*—though he would have called it
The Age of the American Mafia, shifting attention and questions from the spider to the web of circumstances that form
him. Nor does the juxtaposition of things written and spoken by Coppola deny that he is a respectable ringmaster, a
Hollywood model. *The Godfather* is the work of a deft manager very skilled at putting a dreadnought together, but
someone unaware how the process of his own film works.
Paradoxically, that is only possible in a system brought up
on the simpleminded notion of pure film, detached from
consequence, life, society, and the profoundly impure personality of an author.

The Godfather is a magisterial American film, but it is
not good enough. Worse than that, it resists the potential
that makes all imaginative work hopeful: that the public
may have a more searching sense of themselves and their
lives. Coppola's film is a fantasy that lets us be less concerned with our real experience. It is part of the American
movies' mythology that experience is as private as fantasy.
The loss of individual integrity allowed by this leads to the
blurred mass of millions that registers the success and the
meaning of *The Godfather*: The reassured audience—confirmed in its dreadful nihilism—is the model for a public
resigned to its powerlessness to resist or affect authorities.
One must be brutal with Coppola because his tastefulness
is easily mistaken for worth. He is thoughtful, clean, and
pretentious; he wants to make a righteous critique of the
Mafia, not a gangster movie. If he could settle for a sim-

pler target, the film might be wilder, more personal, more touched by poetry—*White Heat*, say, or *Baby Face Nelson*, pulp works trembling with vitality and as funny as they are fearsome. *The Godfather* is as classy and socially significant as an expensive hearse. It has only entrepreneurial force and reliability. Its most prominent personality is the narcissistic and anal Satanism permitted in the moodiness of Al Pacino; not even its villainy is generous or outgoing—discretion smothers everything.

But this respectability is as much a cultural aberration as it is in the bourgeoisie that Buñuel scolds. It is the blind eye of the American film, condoning the starriness of its central figures and turning the subject into a fantasizing melodrama. We long to be with the Corleones: They are samurai or Arthurian knights standing guard over threatened values and defending them to the death, including the death of value. The blind eye is like the face of every Hollywood star who pretends to be unaware of the camera taking the close-ups that will win the hearts of the audience. The realism required for the proper treatment is not photographic or a test of art direction. It hangs upon the attitude of the filmmaker—it could be the humane scrutiny of Rossellini or the scorn of Buñuel. But it cannot be Coppola's meek, facile complicity. He does not appreciate how far the approach of a skilled mechanic perpetuates the Godfather's code.

As for the public, we have abided by *The Godfather's* Stalinist implications, without knowing if there is really a Mafia. Perhaps no one puts more faith in those sinister figures than the people who make and see the films. Movie Mafiosi are the creatures of our insecurity and paranoia—we wish for resolute fathers and comprehensive organizations in what often seems a scattered, undesigned world. To admire the Corleones, to digest their melodrama and the commercials in the same meal, is a symptom of our longing for some domineering conspiracy. It is a movie for those who prefer to live in darkness.

21

"Are You Listening to Me?"

The Conversation has the reputation of being the intense chamber work of a director otherwise employed on large movies where spectacle takes precedence over private themes. The modesty of scale, after *The Godfather*, is regarded as a token of gravity. It was made clear as the picture opened that Coppola had used some of his own profits from the big movies to make this study in intimate anxiety. In sanctioning that gloss, Coppola appeared to be grappling with the demands of the industry and the inner responsibilities of the artist. The film is therefore a parable about talent, private satisfaction, and public duty.

But it is the most despairing and horrified film Coppola has made. Harry Caul's plight is agonizing, whereas Kurtz's (in *Apocalypse Now*) is blurred by the revery that surrounds him. *The Conversation* is a more piercing warning of the dread that forces us into the dark cave of paranoia. The loneliness of the Coppola hero is the burden of the man who cannot believe in society or feel for others. If we regard *The Conversation* as a confession, then it is so overwrought and so smug that its own process masters whatever guilt the repentant once felt. There is even a confessional scene in *The Conversation*, but it is filmed with such exquisite stylistic ambition—the priest's head an enigma through the grille—that it turns into another luscious riddle, like the magical tape. There is no way the soul can stay naked in that baroque visual atmosphere. The mood of the setting has diminished the possibility of the people.

There is an unhappy comparison available between the film's soulless stylistic bravura and Harry Caul's insistence on the technology of his job at the expense of the people it involves. Caul is put through the wringer of soul-searching in order that he will regret his own indifference. Whereupon he tries to redeem himself with action. But Coppola's own superficial view of human motive betrays Caul. The narrative landscape of *The Conversation* is as lurid as Harry's efforts are clumsy. Harry hears wrongs, but only because the director has rigged what he listens to. Human ambivalence and duplicity make an idiot of his expertise. Harry backs further away from a world where no one has dignity and no gesture is valid. The alienations of the character and the director become one, and the viewer is left to suffer the film as a daunting miracle in the Church of Paranoia. A gloomy complacency at having been proved right settles on its last scenes: The artist and the bugger are left fearfully alone. A wistful tableau of madness removes Caul from society.

It is a great achievement that Caul is neither likeable nor sinister. Gene Hackman's closed face, his recessive personality, his skinlike raincoat, and his pitiless lack of appeal bravely exclude glamour. Caul is not endearing. He has several nasty habits that never gather into the sentimentality of noble defect or beguiling flaw. Michael Corleone accepts isolation with equanimity—his stillness enchants the camera. Harry Caul dwells in it as a haven where he can fidget at his nerves. What a film it would be if Caul masturbated in his privacy—that would finally erase the cinema's meek respect for any figure alone. Sexual self-abuse is hinted at in the film, but all the metaphors for it are kind and evasive. That may be because no one would be more affronted by the bleak act than Coppola himself.

Nevertheless, Caul fingers the knobs and keys of his saxophone all night long. He spurns the generosity that discovers his birthday, and yet he is ready to use the drab celebration of the day as a way into his girl friend's body that foregoes wooing. He believes in things hidden away; he loses his only friend and colleague, Stan, because he will not offer him any trust. Like any fantasist living alone, torn between the need to be anonymous and the huge dream of glory, he is ruinously prey to sentimental atmosphere. There is a mordant shot of him sinking into sad revery in the applause that greets the recorded sax solo he pretends to play. His crossed-fingers face has an ugly, timid joy—greedy but pleasure-hating—whenever a professional acclaims his bugging prowess. Despite his deliberate dullness, Caul thinks big. He would understand Michael Corleone, and he believes in tycoons high up in glass-and-steel palaces with Dobermans and sleek aides as company. The same taste for melodrama jumps at the pert defenselessness and the soulful dark-circle eyes of Cindy Williams. Harry knew she could be a hit in prime time, long before *Laverne and Shirley* was thought of. Harry has misty dream sequences out of shampoo ads in which he may rescue drugstore madonnas from the appalling blood. He is young at heart, and his anonymity is just a way of acting cold.

But business has suppressed passion for him. The self-satisfied cunning of all the innuendo about buggery is part of a distrust of heterosexuality. Harry's women are not living people, but figures from soap opera and pornography. Amy waits for him in bed in a silk robe, and Meredith is the stripper who will perform privately for him in romantic half-light as he lies in bed like a child waiting for his mother's tender services. Both women betray him in and around the bed. In Meredith's case the cheating is classically foreshadowed when, at the surveillance convention, she struts and flirts in her sales routine like a pantomime hooker. Harry never notices something the audience knows from the moment she appears—that Meredith is a flake out of *film noir*, the epitome of treachery.

There is something in this of the homosexual's misjudgment of women: giving his trust mistakenly so that the woman's deceit will justify his contempt. In *The Conversation* Coppola does let the impacted brotherhood of the Corleones relax enough for us to feel the ardor in the band of buggers. More important—and, I think, the most disturbing and original thing in the film—the hotel sequence hinges on a sense of plumbing that is a very potent, visceral metaphor for buggery, and links the sexual cold-bloodedness in Caul to an ultimate constipation. The tight ass is hanging on grimly against rape. It is a moment of archetypal anal retention when Harry proceeds to touch, count, and treasure the $15,000 laid out for him—and is told to do it in private like a dirty little boy. When the toilet overflows with submerged blood and sheets, that is the anal torrent Harry dreads. It is also a menstrual holocaust for a frigid man. (In passing, we might remember the execution scene in *The Godfather*, so dependent upon the rites of eating and the nearness of the lavatory.)

In other words, the sonata for loneliness in *The Conversation* is both fond and loathing, and is the best sign yet of a capacity for feverish psychological imagery that Coppola usually keeps under lock and key. *The Conversation* is his most romantic film, the one in which he relaxes from the unfailing linkage of narrative construction that made *The Godfather* compulsive but airless. But just as passion or something irrational breaks Coppola's austere surface, so it lets us see how naïve he is.

The Conversation is a mess as a narrative, but a mess from an author who still nurses Caul's craving for order. All through the picture that meticulousness is at work: It organizes the series of transparent or translucent barriers— windows, Perspex, frosted glass—that will culminate in the divider between two hotel balconies and the plastic bag in which "the director" is carried away. The same possessive sense of detail repeats "When the Red, Red Robin Comes Bob-bob-bobbing Along" without fruitful coincidence. It is only a gratuitous touch of the sinister in which melodrama overshadows spontaneity. The echo is heavy with the clever director's breathing. The fateful tape talks about a bum on a bench as we see Harry stretched out on his bed. The hesitation over the madonna statuette cannot dodge the film's knowing chuckle. The flash forward to the actual killing as part of Harry's anticipatory dream only suggests a gloating omniscience. There is even the point that the scenes in which Harry reconstructs his tape would not play without such extensive reprising of what we *saw* in the square. That can come from nowhere but the controlling director, for the things seen and shown again were not even witnessed by Harry. This leaves the tape laboratory scenes in *The Conversation* far less satisfactory than the sequence in *Blow-Up* in which the photographer assembles his scenario. Antonioni's Thomas is alone with his prints. But Caul's credulity relies on an extra thrust from the boss.

When a director has to help, and when his pictures are taut with care, then he looks very foolish if a larger unbelievability goes free. *The Conversation* has several fatal lapses that show casualness or an inability to imagine the characters fully. Harry Caul is a stooge if we have to believe that he would even have a girl friend; that he would tolerate the conventioneers returning to his sacrosanct workshop for their party; or that he would not know instantly that the pen Moran puts in his pocket is a plant. He would not be so inept. If Coppola wants to show error and human vulnerability, then he is obliged to go back to zero and start again with something more than a self-sufficient monument to suspicion. Worse still, Coppola's style is so pointed that it trains us to look for clues—I have never met anyone who didn't know the giveaway pen was a bug. But Coppola is victim of a scripting strategy that is so painstaking it exceeds his invention. How much richer the picture might be if it was made in a spirit less anxious to join up every dot with order.

There are larger problems of a similar kind. We may not need to understand the entire plot Harry has overheard. Yet to know so little is to settle for the oppressive certainty that everyone is out to get everyone else with a malice that is more important than reason. No one here is allowed common sense. The atmospheric pressure of kill or be killed amounts to a climate of fear and loathing which Coppola attempts to deplore even as he urges it into the body of the film.

Again, generalized anxiety distracts us from specific anomaly. The cutting of the picture suggests that Martin Stett, the director's aide, is part of the final conspiracy. If so, the original recording was only a ruse to mislead the director. But that asks us to believe that the lovers in the square planned their movements and their utterances, knowing how hard it would be to isolate the crucial line but knowing it would be possible—otherwise there is no picture and no trouble with Harry. Far from being a voyeur, Caul is the set-up victim in that scenario. Coppola cannot rid himself of such tortuous spirals, and he cannot escape the nonsensical complexity they spread through the story. The engineering of the filming is itself an irrational cult that has overshadowed the vagaries of experience, the interplay of hope and fear.

This brings us to the pregnant line, the source of Harry's dilemma. "He'd *kill* us if he had the chance" is what Harry hears, and what we hear. But at the end of the film when the line is played back again—for no other reason except to goose us—it has become *"He'd kill us if he had the chance."* Anyone who sees that pen for what it is hears the difference. Film cannot disguise it. There are two versions of the line, the clearest and most woeful proof of technology suppressing human ambiguity. In a novel the one line could support either reading. But film is so manipulative, Coppola's game has to be rigged. The fabrication of melodrama has been preferred to the way a human being can be misunderstood. And it is because Coppola cannot allow that perplexing element of doubt in his people that Caul goes into shock and isolation, and Kurtz's dead end is prefigured and made inevitable by the artist's scant interest in people, their vitality, or their ability to generate rational doubt.

22

Somewhere, Over
the Apocalypse

For years, it seemed, there was an apocalypse promised, a legendary Pynchonesque rainbow that filled hopeful moviegoers with Dorothy's longing to see its entirety. We fell silent, speculating over its clash of darkness and inferno. The youthful gravity of a lavish Ending captivated us. We crossed our fingers for the Vietnam film our debtor consciences required, and waited.

Then, after nervy postponements that began to strain hope, the bang collapsed one night in August, 1979, at the Ziegfeld Theater in New York. It was exotic, moody, and spectacular at first, to be sure, and then suddenly a feeble echo, far from the convulsion we had wanted or United Artists had gambled with. In the flares of explosion, you could see the crucified figure—never entirely un-Christlike—of Francis Ford Coppola, mortgaged and mortified if the picture failed.

Apocalypse Now went into nationwide release, but the "Now" was as stale as yesterday's hype. The movie could use a second title—*River of No Return* or *American Graffiti* —it is so much more obscure and less decisive than the shock we had anticipated. Still, the boyish energy of Coppola must feel born again to be rid of its weight. The making of the movie will always haunt him, but the film is like the disappointment of a ghost-hunter who spends the night in an allegedly possessed house and sees the dawn rise without any eloquent apparition. The "horror" of *Apocalypse Now* is only a wishful slogan, muttered out of the debris of a misbegotten movie. Coppola knew it himself at times as over a million feet of film circled his head, and his wife was noting it all in her diary:

This morning I asked Francis what his inner voices were telling him to do. He said they tell him to do nothing, don't push, don't act, just wait. The complete opposite of the way he is used to being. He said he was afraid that his voices were telling him to be alone, with no one in his life. He said, "Can't you see how scared I am, Ellie? You are saying, 'Hurry up and define our marriage, I'm not waiting much more.' United Artists is saying, 'Hurry up and finish the film, we can't hold off the banks and exhibitors much longer,' and part of me is saying, 'Just tough it out, don't make some quick resolution in order to get off the hook.'" He said the more he works on the ending, the more it seems to elude him, as if it is there, just out of view, mocking him. He said, "Working on the ending is like trying to crawl up glass by your fingernails." [1]

Coppola was born in 1939. Already he has ridden out career fluctuations and achieved so much that his failures are read in the light of success. Even if *Apocalypse* had lost a lot of money, Coppola could have reassembled his image as a fiscally potent filmmaker. His reputation for talking up a storm persists—which could also mean that offers financiers can't resist inflame him in the process. He had an armful of Oscars available to be scooped up and hurled through the window during one *Apocalypse* tantrum. He has his own company in San Francisco and L.A.—part crafts guild, part rival to Hollywood, part trainset—called Zoetrope.

He made the central American movie of the seventies, the two-part *Godfather*, a milestone box-office smash, acclaimed by critics, too, yet as compromised by the sultry glamour of money, violence, and power as every film since *The Great Train Robbery* (1903). Francis didn't know it, or couldn't bear to believe it, but he wanted to be Michael Corleone.

There were moments in his Oz/Zoetrope when he was. Thus, he spent over $30 million on *Apocalypse Now,* telling himself that the picture's journey toward the heart of darkness was a voyage into his own ambiguous soul—as if the voyage itself solved the ambiguity. Psychic superstition made him drop "Ford" from his name—either because people might not trust a man with three names or because he was intrigued by the possibility of having a blank inside.

The question of whether Coppola had a breakdown on *Apocalypse* is prime gossip material. But it only veils the grim truth that the movie director in America is rarely adult enough to lose his mind. Because the movie took so long and cost so much has nothing to do with insane arrogance: It's the extremism of the system. Coppola could not make up his mind what to do with it because he was out of his depth with a film that transcended action. Even now, there are two endings on show, out of five or six that beckoned his wavering concept. The movie is never a serious examination of the limits of civilization; it is what happens when a showman imagines he's being important and philosophical, and is editing on video so that his lazy ideas are indulged by the dissolves—instead of cuts, the drift and melt of hallucination.

The failure of the movie is in the splitting of cultural identity, as if "Francis" and "Coppola" moved away from one another without the splice; as if Dorothy came back from Oz wanting to be Virginia Woolf; or as if the protracted adolescence of the American movie glimpsed how junky its ideas are. That is the struggle to be profound and popular at the same time—the torment which has always beset Hollywood. The same conundrum pledges America to both equality and happiness; and it may be the idealistic contradiction that promoted the Vietnam War—wanting to win, be moral, and feel good all on the same day.

Yet Coppola is the pioneer of young success on the new movie scene. He was the first film student to move from kid brother, patronized by the family, to shark-eyed god-father who may order executions and new suits for his pro-tegés with the same impartial authority. The brotherhood between Coppola and Corleone shows the influence Holly-wood exerts on those trying to gain entry. You do not bring revolution to that system. You have to slip the crown from the dull head wearing it. Hollywood is a court of intrigue where you never question the rules, since you will need them as soon as you are in power. Instead, you jostle for more clout and make sure your emblem is the top hat or the road-ster. Coppola articulated the strategy himself, like an ap-prentice Borgia, too tickled by advancement to be quiet about it:

> *The way to come to power is not always to merely challenge the Establishment, but first make a place in it and then challenge and double-cross the Establish-ment.*[2]

So the path from film student to success is not just a mat-ter of talent and hard work. It requires the wit and the timing, the nerve and the guile, to forge a career. The striking aspect of Coppola's "talent" as a filmmaker has been his excitement with incidents that embody the piercing di-agonals of Machiavellian double cross. We know less about Coppola's characters than about the way his creative acumen coincides with their prowess: *His* style has the pointedness of *their* decisiveness, as witness Michael assenting to the ex-ecution of Fredo at the end of *The Godfather, Part II.* We may deduce from that a desensitized director of operations, the corrupt genius of efficiency personified by Al Pacino's Michael. But the nastiest part of Michael is the self-pity that cloaks his depravity—sitting alone so that the close-ups can console him.

Coppola was the son of an orchestral flautist. He was raised largely in New York, in Queens, but his father's itinerant and not very successful life made for upheavals. Francis was not the oldest son, and he had polio as a child. He dreamed of being a writer, and of becoming as robust as others—as a child, he may have been closer to John Cazale's Fredo than to Pacino's Michael. It helps explain a distaste in his films, never devoid of envy, for extroversion: It is there for James Caan's Sonny in *The Godfather* and for Robert Duvall's Kilgore in *Apocalypse*. These men have a sublime, stupid confidence spied on from the shadows by the more withdrawn and depressive Michael, Harry Caul (in *The Conversation*), Willard, or Kurtz.

Francis studied theater in the late fifties at Hofstra University on Long Island and then in 1960 he went to UCLA to do film. From his first ventures he was intent on getting ahead in the industry. He made *The Peeper*, a student blue movie; his screenplay, "Pilma, Pilma," would win the Goldwyn Award; and he answered the call from Roger Corman when that emperor of exploitation scouted UCLA for some kids who would work for next to nothing. By 1962, when he was only twenty-three, Coppola slung together a first feature for Corman—*Dementia 13*. It was shot in Ireland for $40,000, with crew, cast, and some sets left over from another picture. The project also discovered an Irish artist, Eleanor Neil, who was hired as set decorator and who soon married the director. They have since had three children.

Back in America, Coppola was hired as a writer by Seven Arts. He worked on *Is Paris Burning?* (1965), *This Property Is Condemned* (1966), and *Reflections in a Golden Eye* (1967), and he got to be a script clean-up man in the Warner-Seven Arts Studio corporation. Ever since, he has been proud but irked that his best skill may be as a packager of other people's movies, a godfather like Thalberg or Selznick.

It was for Warners' that he got to direct *You're a Big Boy Now* (1967), taken from an English novel that he had purchased personally. *Big Boy* is his only comedy, but it is part of the fearful vision of women that has beset his work and led to the emotional stress on male dominance. In *Apoca-lypse*, for instance, it is hard to tell whether the Bunnies sequence is a concession to so much male material, a loathing view of sex, or a half-baked explanation of the war in terms of sexual frustrations. In *The Conversation*, too, paranoia is linked to frigidity in the central character. In *The Godfather* sex is an inescapable means to dynasty, treated with a suspicion still at the adolescent stage of guilt, especially the guilt bred by Catholicism. Coppola's men are hounded by the need to redeem themselves through work and duty; all his films flinch from frivolity or pleasure.

The nearest to an exception is *The Rain People*, made in 1969 after the cold-blooded attempt to dupe conventional musical sentimentality with *Finian's Rainbow*. *The Rain People* was made by a group of associates, traveling together across America. As a portrait of a perplexed, pregnant woman (Shirley Knight) struggling to find significance in her sexuality, it is Coppola's most anguished and personal picture. Throughout the seventies it remained in his mind as the model of intimate, small movies an artist might make if he was not preoccupied with blockbusters. *The Conversation* is sometimes paired with it in scale, but that later film is altogether more melodramatic, more dazzled by movie technology and genre anxiety.

Immediately after *The Rain People*, Coppola formed American Zoetrope, which was intended to foster like-minded filmmakers and their tender thought that the kingdom to the south of San Francisco was dying. It has also provided Coppola's aura as half-Pope, half-Kane, dispensing patronage, owning radio stations, trying to run *City Maga-zine*, and buying real estate, vineyards, and some elaborate film equipment. *The Godfather*'s perverse instinct for the creativity of crime as an exemplary middle-class business is a testament to Coppola's pleasure at trading respect and favors in a network of deals. Indeed, it may miss the point to say that the delays over *Apocalypse* were all agony. Coppola has often hesitated to conclude his films, as if he dreaded to be out of the web of a project. Remember how Vito Corleone spent much of his daughter's wedding indoors doing business. Coppola, too, has a lovely country house at Napa, but often prefers smoke-filled enclaves of negotiation in Frisco or L.A.

Despite Coppola's soaring plans, Zoetrope's early days were troubled. He discovered and supported George Lucas, and set up his first film, *THX-1138* at Warners'. It proved the only failure Lucas has yet been associated with, and it put Coppola into the same relationship with Warner's that his then subject, *Patton*, suffered with the high command. That screenplay was Coppola's strongest credential before 1971, and a hint of what *Apocalypse* might be. Beneath the bravura of George C. Scott's acting and all the hardware, there is a literary adoration of the magnificence of the rogue leader who scorned the trappings of "civilized" war. It is enough to wonder whether Scott could have brought clarity and passion to Kurtz beyond Brando's fuddled dreams. The scripted Patton is somewhere between Hemingway's Colonel Cantwell in *Across the River and Into the Trees* and the bookbound mystic Kurtz, high on Eliot and Fraser, who lives in the moldering recreation of Angkor Wat.

Coppola's Patton dreams of posterity and the heroes of antiquity he is linked to in the mad communication system of reincarnation. The Corleones are less fanciful. But they believe as fiercely in continuity and honor: Frankie Pentangeli bows to the needs of a Roman suicide. Vito is a child who travels to America alone, a young man who stalks his enemy privately, a victim deserted in a hospital room, and a throned Solomon who can settle petitions. Michael, too, is beyond the Corleone group. He uses the claims of family but only because he feels superior to the others. He moves from being the one who wanted to go straight to the only one who embraced the chill of power. In *Part II* he is a solitary whose wishes are communicated without words to a waiting organization, and who sits in the sickly shadows of shuttered rooms. Kurtz lives in a cave, and Harry Caul retreats into a room stripped bare by his own mistrust. For someone commercially unproven, *The Godfather* was a breakthrough. It is an immense narrative machine in which the time inversions and parallel action never disturb a spectator brought up on the conventions of 1940's movies —the era in which Part I is set, after all. It is an intricate mosaic: the diagrammatic lighting, the care taken in accumulating authenticity, the exact dialogue, the faultless acting, and the overall enchantment despite corpses and blood. With so much tomato in the film, anyway, the various Mafia recipes for the good life blend together. But craft has eclipsed ethics, just as surely as the well-arranged assassination makes it easier to overlook the pain of murder. We have contributed to it with our allegiance since the moment when timidity came of age and shot down McCluskey and Sollozzo, betrayers of the Godfather's grasp on order, part criminal but part replacement for the control squandered by politicians. It is as conservative a film as *Birth of a Nation*.

Coppola's austere attitude toward sex leaves room for the aphrodisiac present in power. But it left him troubled at having seemed to glorify the Mafia. Still, nothing is so irrevocably immature as the futility with which he plunged into Part II, intent on correcting endorsements and identifications far deeper than his critical understanding.

The Godfather is a love story in which the ambitious American woos and marries power. There is scarcely a moment of overt sexual affection—unless it be the kissing of brothers. But the making of alliances, the application of "pressure," and the whispering of conspiracy have an erotic luster that shines out of the siesta gloom. Nor is money emphasized for its own sake. The Family are after something more spiritually satisfying: They want power. It is the ideal for people who sought the country as persecuted outcasts from Europe. *The Godfather* is a celebration of acquired possessiveness and caution in the once adventurous and intransigent. It is about keeping the unit intact—at all costs. The Corleones amount to a cult, and they would sacrifice all around them, or all among them, to guard their purity.

That is why *Apocalypse Now* was doomed to resemble the last days of the world according to Jim Jones. It didn't fail because a typhoon washed away the sets; because of Martin Sheen's heart attack (a greater crisis than anything his character faces), Brando's bulk, or Coppola's faith in the actor's unscripted wisdom; the pretensions of realizing Conrad; the cheerful hawkishness in John Milius's screenplay . . . or even because Coppola had an affair while he was making the film. On the contrary, I would guess that the affair grew out of alarm that the project's elusiveness threatened his manhood. It is an error of adolescence to think that an audience and philosophy can be reached with one sweet stroke. Coppola has no adequate sense of the horror he has claimed at the core of his movie. Once the journey is done with, we find the narrowness of Coppola's imagination exposed. He can offer only a very rhetorical, romantic image of evil, with Dennis Hopper serving as its witch doctor. Such grandiose schemes of iniquity reveal a mind insensitive to everyday compromise. As the film was being shot, Coppola overcame worries that stray peasants might be caught in the film's real explosions, and was irritated when the helicopters supplied by President Marcos had to be diverted to deal with real rebel actions. That is a blindness which is very close to the mood that fought the Vietnam War.

The limits to Coppola's philosophy can be demonstrated by comparing two of his movie situations: the role of Kay in *The Godfather*, and the "fucking helicopter battle" in *Apocalypse*. Kay is the last trace of moral awareness in the Corleone world, and potentially the most interesting woman in modern American cinema. Her principles hover uncertainly around her undemanding sense of self. She is caught up in an ordeal that exceeds her horizons and demands radical reawakening. She sees the evil of the family she has helped perpetuate, and for a long time she looks away. If the movie trusted her or properly noticed her, Kay could be the focus for a very moving process of discovery and awakening.

But Coppola cannot transcend the Corleone treatment of women. He never feels the sacrifices Kay makes in aborting one child and leaving another. He excludes her with the theatrical gesture of the closed door, whereas he might have made her a brave but humble conscientious objector, someone who takes the Family to court. It may sound irrelevant to rearrange the story. Yet in not seeing this alternative to our helpless abetting of Michael, Coppola showed how little the Corleones offend him. It indicates a willingness to share the last dark refuge of the poisoned father who still looks like an invalid child, pale from self-regard.

As for the helicopter sequence—the most unequivocal tribute to combat ever filmed—its surrealism is as daring as anything Coppola has done. The grotesque history of the war is contained in this orgy of destruction, which aims to liberate a fine surfing beach. But the dynamic is led astray by Coppola's surrender to effect. He is always best when he is "with" a sequence, giving it *his* energy. So he cherishes those approaching helicopters, the bursts of fire, the ecstasy of headlong tracking shots, the editing's command of multiple action, the thrill of Wagner, and the blissful strutting of Kilgore. There is satire in that colonel's name, just as there must have been in the choice of Wagner. But once Dolby and Duvall are given their heads, it becomes a triumph of the will. How could Coppola begin to measure a Kurtz when his heart and mind are so bowled over by this buffoon Patton? Between Michael's doleful cruelty and Kilgore's boisterous indifference, Coppola is armed against thorough despair.

When Coppola attended the New York press conference to mark the opening of *Apocalypse,* he declined to speak about the book his wife published on the years of his film: *Notes*, by Eleanor Coppola. Eleanor Coppola would probably not align herself with Kay Corleone, though *Notes* is the diary of a wife and mother beginning to emerge from the shadow of a husband. She is desperate or bereft most of the time, having to cook amid cockroaches and sweltering heat in the Philippines, trying to ease Francis's distress over the film while discovering that he runs new cuts for another woman first. She is driven to poignant resorts: the documentary that Coppola gave her to make, the *I Ching*, and the Tarot pack. The book is weighed down by the unhappiness of a woman who waits for her husband to decide her future; but it has a richer feeling for human dilemma than his films have yet revealed:

> *Francis is a master of creating illusion. He is one of the most skilled professionals in the field around the world. Over and over again he creates the most convincing illusions that he sincerely wants to have a marriage and family life without a triangle. A little time passes and it becomes clear that it was an illusion.*

It is the consequence of a medium that promotes fantasy above experience, the rainbow and apocalypse over life and death in all their daily forms. Coppola's future is still very open. He borrowed heavily for *Apocalypse* (still a cheaper film than *Moonraker*): over $15 million. But he owns the film and probably needs to gross "only" $50 million to put himself in profit.

The crest of his wave may have broken. Yet he talks of Zoetrope being a base for future projects: as well as Carroll Ballard's *The Black Stallion*, there are schemes for American films by Wim Wenders, Hans-Jürgen Syberberg, Werner Herzog, Dusan Makavejev, and Akira Kurosawa. Coppola himself has considered the idea of a picture in Japan, the story of auto inventor Preston Tucker and Goethe's *Elective Affinities*. The trauma of failure could be wiped away by activity; the wounds will heal if the soul is superficial. But it is in the nature of American movies that self-regeneration speaks a trite language. As *Apocalypse Now* opened, *The New York Times* quoted this insight from Coppola. It is as perilously attached to panaceas and rainbows as Gatsby was to the green light:

> *I've been almost asking for a real shakedown. This is a period of strange turning points for me. I used to be sort of a goofy kid—oh boy, I have a new sportscar; gee, I'm directing a movie; wow, that girl likes me. Well, it's not like that after 40, I'd like to build a harmonious relationship between my personal life and my work—I'd like to be happy, to feel good.*[3]

23

The Lord of Overlook

The Overlook Hotel in *The Shining* never promises a relaxed vacation, it is so out of the ordinary. The lofty eminence of its name knows the mistake in looking down, for gods or authors. They risk the same dread and distraction in realizing that every moving dot is an anxious creature, humans as well as characters. So don't look down; shine into the dream.

The hotel is an incongruous structure amid the rugged upheaval of mountains. It has the sleek decadence of a movie palace in a hard-working neighborhood. Someone must have willed this ornate defiance of wilderness into being, laid all the stones together, and devised the riddle of the maze. It has a Lord. Movies, too, have the stamp of command. They may look cute or playful, but their majesty sings with obscure authority.

The Overlook has the hushed atmosphere of a place where the destiny of souls is decided. Its external gray and its inner emptiness are tense with spirituality. You can foresee reality being erased by its hallowed limelight. An Indian burial ground was desecrated so that it could be built, and a black is the apprehensive guardian of its insights. Say no more: These are less clues than omens. The mountain is magic, and the hotel is an enchantment waiting for us to enter.

For Jack Torrance it brings ice-statue immortality and a night of exultation as he sheds his own failure to be a lurching stage villain. See Jack drool, see Jack strike with the ax, see Jack run amok. He grins like a demon because he knows he's part of a story that will be told after his end. He has come to the Overlook like a pilgrim to make the great vow that gives up life for fiction. In return, he can have his wish: It is like buying a ticket to a movie, to be able to butcher one's wife and child. What are we doing at a horror film if we do not need to have such furtive impulses recognized?

The gullibly amiable would-be caretaker swallows the explanation that impassable roads ruled out the Overlook as a winter sports Xanadu. The film wants winter clear and desolate, a time of concentration. This "snow job" is the first nudge we get about Jack's madness and the film's contrivance. For *The Shining* can nudge us now and then without sacrificing its refinement. In the story not even the worst storm of the year (complete with TV weatherman coziness) prevents a Sno-Cat driven by the black cook from making the journey one way. And we must suppose that an exhausted mother and son will manage the return, chattering about what a very strange hubby and dad they had had. "Danny," you can hear the plaintive Shelley Duvall, jittery baby-sitter among mothers, "we were in a family with a *character*."

The hotel is not a possible place: Its striking presence only proves how far films occur in our minds. We see other guests and cars as the season ends—Jack Torrance takes one impure look at two departing young women and leaves us to wonder whether they were chambermaids or Overlook call girls. But they are toys, as if the place was already the little boy's playground or the director's storyboard. If you doubt that, remember the sequence of mother and son exploring the maze that gives way to the table-top model inside the hotel and the grinning malice of the Lord of Overlook already looming above with the power of authorship.

This glaringly metaphoric hotel is consumed with the significance of its name. It is not so much haunted as rigged and primed, a magician's coat full of concealed pockets, traditional surprises, and comic-horror diversions. "Splendid party, isn't it?" asks one toper, smiling through the bloody crack in his own brow. *The Shining* is not frightening because it is so tickled with its own fake aplomb, so entranced by its lifelike illusion, and so inclined to prefer the illusion to life. After all, to be a ghost or a magician is its own reward. What is there to fear if one is neither dead nor alive? The ghosts at the Overlook are harmless really: Theirs is a very long run, and actors so trapped must learn the sedation of eternity. Even Jack comes to kill, bubbling with jokes, lit up with his role.

The Overlook has an exterior photographed in the American Northwest, beyond the Denver that is the film's center of civilization. It may be a real building, but on film it is gray-stone Gothic, a fresh-scrubbed lie in the high-altitude sunlight. It is a folly (in the sense of a hollow facade) dipped in adrenalin, as perfect as the Poe-faced beginning: "Once upon a time, there was a hotel in a very remote and wild part of Colorado . . ." Just sitting there, waiting.

That's how *The Shining* starts, as a humble yellow Beetle—the epitome of toys—makes its way there by road, watched by an airborne eye as supreme as the one that initiates Leni Riefenstahl's *Triumph of the Will*. But it is a treacherous destiny that half-follows, half-induces Jack Nicholson to the Overlook: It is the look from above that leads him there.

The journey uncovers not beauty but an expressiveness that derides itself. The aspic stillness of the black lakes, the steepling crags made papier-mâché by helicopter shots, and the undergrowth of minatory music in which we imagine gloomy bird calls and the despair of imprisoned animals. This is not Oregon, but Erewhon. The panorama is as suspect as Eden on the first day. The creativity of the Lord makes him doubt the real. He can see nothing but decor, image, and metaphor. The imaginative power of *The Shining* is walleyed with solipsism. There is an enigmatic shot of Jack Torrance, head drooping, eyes up under his skull, looking out toward his author. As its baleful scrutiny is held, we feel like intruders caught in the mirror that joins Jack and Stanley.

The Overlook is also a collection of interior sets built at the EMI-Elstree studio in England, 5,000 miles from Colorado. The sets look out through large windows suffused with a creamy glare that gives the desert snowlight the force of silence, and suggests the crucible of expectation in which the tricky house rests. The conjuring that finds the ingredients of the Overlook in nature and in a studio presupposes a special threshold between the two. As the film progresses, any cut can cross it. The "interface" of sets and locations will be the ability and the longing of the characters in *The Shining* to see and live with the array of tricks in the magician's coat. Yet to shine is like going up out of the audience and into the screen, itself as brilliant as the roaring light outside the Overlook.

The Shining was released in the early summer of 1980 to all the anticipation that its large promotion budget and the reputation of Stanley Kubrick could inspire. It was meant to be a major summer entertainment, and it was regarded as the one harrowing experience that a season of cheerfulness would provide. The picture had cost $18 million, and Warners', its distributor, spent half as much again to convince audiences that they were in for a thorough scare. This was on the principle learned from the seventies that traumatic suspense had been profitable in picture-making.

The Christmas before *The Shining*'s opening, when the film was still being agonized over by the secretive Kubrick, a trailer ran in America. It was a single shot of the lobby of the hotel, looking toward the closed doors of the elevator. For several seconds nothing happened. Then a ponderous slippage of plum blood began to fall from the doorways of the elevators—as if the house were overripe or bleeding. This profuse flow surged toward the camera, lapping over its eye and bearing away heavy armchairs in the lobby. No person appeared in the shot. But this grim place was waiting for us.

That shot does occur in the finished film, but with no more explanation than the trailer offered. It is the first glimpse that young Danny has into the bloody underground river of the Overlook. But this is blood unlimited, and it could as easily be a reference to the entire movie heritage of horror as to the "red rum" of one mother and two little girls by an earlier incarnation of the caretaker. Whether by design or accident, the retention of that shot in the movie comments on the tenterhooks of all trailers and their wish to have you come back to see the enigma answered.

It is part of the humor of *The Shining* to be full of loose ends that invite knot-itchy fingers, and it is a cheeky feint that the lobby of blood is a horror that always remains offstage. This house has not been exhausted by the film, only raked over quickly. Those two homosexuals, Pig and Poke, have a tale to tell. Imagine a horror movie in a house with elevators that never exploits those cells of claustrophobia! What stronger encouragement could there be to our urge to shine; and what genre of movie is more aglow than the trailer? Kubrick may be the first artist to recognize that a trailer should never be fulfilled by the movie, just as the movie must never be resolved for its viewers.

On the other hand, he might be a vacillating director, harassed by Warners' pleas for a riveting Christmas trailer. In its rough-cut form of October, 1979, *The Shining* may have had a blood-polo match in the lobby and elevators as busy as the one in *Dressed to Kill*. As it is, between the picture's opening in New York and Los Angeles and a wider release, Kubrick cut out a brief epilogue in which Shelley Duvall is visited in the hospital by Barry Nelson, the manager of the Overlook who hired Nicholson to keep winter watch there.

Common sense tells us that pictures must come out of that

trial and error. The least experience with the process knows of compromise beneath every smooth surface, and understands that footage can be turned inside out by different editing policies. What looks like a performance or an event is really a fabrication so imbued with falsehood that we must redefine "truth." Yet even the worst movies of the year seem immune to error or uncertainty. Film has such ravishing authority. Our helplessness in front of the flow of motion grants it an elemental force beyond questions of right or wrong.

That certainty will appeal to perfectionists, a category that includes children, those who have failed to grow up, psychotics and fascists as well as capital G geniuses. Stanley Kubrick has never waited to be acclaimed: Like Orson Welles, he recognized that American fame relied on self-advertisement and stylistic bravura. But whereas Welles has been redeemed by hammy instincts—the love of food, show, company, talk—Kubrick is colder and less sociable. He has followed the line of austere retreat. In a culture of steady promotion, there is a resonance in reclusiveness that can seem religious.

So Kubrick gives no interviews. Rather than submit to the indignity of a press conference, like Coppola before *Apocalypse Now*, Kubrick understands that appearance has no substance. You shouldn't deal in apocalypse and be there in flesh and blood. Drab questions will make anyone seem commonplace, and Kubrick has as little taste for that as the Overlook apes Howard Johnson's. Legend will surround his pictures if he is the one director not available to engage in small talk about them.

What should an American artist do to escape that but exile himself to England and allege fear of flying? While Howard Hughes always seemed to be in the air, so that it was fitting for him to die in a plane, Kubrick has the pale face of someone buried in the dark. His characters are just as livid. I see him living in the Overlook maze, a haunt of bottle-green shadows and corners that move like knights on a chessboard.

Kubrick's solitude has made only a few films, on unexpected and enterprising subjects, all with a tone and style that take the breath away. I am writing as someone who had not liked any of his films since *The Killing* (1957), until *The Shining*. Now I am in the process of trying to reconcile or reappraise the uncontested impact of *Lolita*, *Dr. Strangelove*, *2001*, *Clockwork Orange*, and *Barry Lyndon*.

Six films in eighteen years, all shot in England but only two claiming to be set there. All the result of intense preparation and the kind of conspiratorial manufacture necessary for deadly weapons and the state of mind that need not worry over them. Britain may have been relief from an uncongenial Hollywood, or a third-world movie land where he could be emperor. But it was also another Overlook, proving the irrelevance of location compared with the expansiveness of imagination. Kubrick has a germ of von Sternberg in him, delighting to make Shanghai or Morocco in Los Angeles, upset on *Anatahan* that he had to use real water in his cellophane imitation of a desert island jungle.

The withdrawal was disastrous with *Lolita*. English suburbs were insipid when held up to Nabokov's aghast love letter to on-the-road Americana. Sue Lyon was all the more TV-like for not having the context of shabby-romantic motels, summer heat, poisoned snacks, and sticky magazines. But *The Shining*—which did risk America for its exteriors— has transcended the problem. Realities of place have become figments and shapes in the shining. Its action all takes place on the screen, that vacant white thing, like untrodden snow or Jack's unwritten book. Stupendous forests, geometrically exact mazes, and the spacious rooms of the Overlook are all patterns on celluloid, possessed of a uniform gloss, hugging themselves with the thought that in camera means in secret.

The scorn for people that was so ugly in some of Kubrick's films has turned into something more disconcerting. Intelligence and experience have been distilled in the macabre parable of seeing and being. The people are appreciated as tricks of the light, as elusive and pervasive as characters. *The Shining* has a tranquillity that is new in Kubrick: No wonder it is a financial failure when sold as a frightener. There is serenity in this concept of people as illusory or intermittent appearances.

Paths of Glory was leaden with righteous indignation. Nothing in the picture seemed conscious that the plot was as rigged as the court-martial. *Lolita* became a study in irony, grotesquery, and teasing because censorship forbade its silky fucking; choice had forsaken the lyrical highways of America, the medium was bereft of prose, and Kubrick could only mock people once enveloped by Nabokov's perplexed and rather dotty love.

It was Kubrick's worst choice of material, whatever Anthony Burgess claims for the interference done to *Clockwork Orange*. The book of *Lolita* is a homage to womanhood and words. Charlotte is treasured as much as Lo, the haze of affection is so widespread. But it is a love drawn off in words: Humbert talking to himself is more stimulating than talk with Lolita. The comic dilemma of the book is that the love songs are not uttered because Lo would not hear them. It is all in the head. That doesn't jeopardize Nabokov's tenderness or his nostalgia for reality. He is aroused by love as a verbal affliction, and he is touched by the willingness of the real to make itself available for fiction.

Maybe it took Kubrick eighteen years to read and understand *Lolita*, or maybe I have to grapple anew with his earlier films. But *The Shining* is Nabokovian, granted that its paranoia would bewilder that confident man. When anyone takes as long as Kubrick does, and seems so averse to society, he may read endlessly and repetitively, and he might be struck one day by *Lolita*'s assurance that the make-believe of art offsets the squalor of life. I see that as the refreshed spirit which has produced *The Shining* and chosen to make a film about a writer writing.

Jack Torrance dreams of writing a book. When he is away from home, he leaves *The New York Review of Books* out on the table for the camera to spy. He wants to escape ordinary hubbub so that he may at last become an author. He does not know that he is far more cramped by the family cliché he lives, or that he is too lazy, dreamy, and imaginative for the discipline of writing. But he has a naïve wife, so intent on *Catcher in the Rye* that she does not notice there is nothing in the sandwiches she and their son, Danny, are eating. This wife believes in Jack's noble ambition and will serve obediently as the burden that has prevented him from doing his life's work.

Some have complained that family life in *The Shining* is ridiculous. But the lack of interest the three parties have in each other is the most convincing human construction in the film. Look at the very poignant scenes in which Jack breakfasts in the mirror and cradles Danny without noticing him. The soulful self-pity of people who long to be alone but who are always crowded is the best study of domesticity Kubrick has done. That is no small point, for his films have catered to his own complacent mistrust of close company.

Jack sees the Overlook as a godsend. It is so like a book already, he will only have to fill his box with typed pages to acquit himself. The manager talks like a character in a ghost story: His good cheer is a suspicious warmth, as lacquered as the astute Barry Nelson can make it. The set-up scene in which Jack interviews is as owlishly cozy as the "Are-you-sitting-comfortably?" prelude to classical chillers. Jack alone is taken in, like the ideal reader he is. No matter the discreet warning, he has a pleasantry to turn it aside. His madness is implicit in his scheme to be a regular, obliging guy. When he smiles, we can believe that there are goblins behind his face, hauling the eyebrows up like drawbridges. The ability of the film to put us in the best position for seeing the fictional maneuver—the overlook—is enhanced by having Jack Nicholson play Jack, and by the consistent overplaying required of him. Reports say that Kubrick would not let Nicholson see the film, perhaps to protect the tottering largeness of this rendering of "Jack." This will never be the story of a decent, real man surrendering to ghosts because Jack is a phantom already—he has always been the caretaker —longing for spirits.

The child, Danny, is named after the actor, too. That may have been to help Danny Lloyd feel more comfortable; though, if one believed in shining, that could be regarded as an unkind trick. But when the two males in the family have this extra affinity with the core of the fiction, then the wife is that much more out in the cold. Wendy she is called —"Mrs. Torrance, are you a Winifred or a Winnie?" the lugubrious wordsmith, Halloran, asks her—as if her boys needed a Darling to look after them. And she does all the work at the Overlook, as sturdy as Buster Keaton in *The Navigator*. Just as Kubrick found for his Jack a very accessible actor, whose ease and intimacy make him feel like a buddy, so his wife is an actress who is the more enigmatic for having been sheltered in the work of one director.

Shelley Duvall in *3 Women* is either a superb actress or the thing itself. She was conventionally touching in Robert Altman's *Thieves Like Us*, conventionally kooky in his *Nashville*. It has always been intriguing to wonder what she was really like and whether she could be presentable or coherent away from the unique ensemble tolerance that Altman can conjure up.

The question remains open, as if Kubrick had that same uncertainty but was too tactful to probe it. What made *3 Women* so real was the notion that Shelley Duvall's Milly was actually programmed by a magazine dedicated to that kind of thoroughly modern Milly. She seemed to be operated from a distance. There is a moment in *The Shining*, on the staircase, where she dithers like a rag doll hung up to dry. We could be looking at a photographed figure, set on panic but animated by the urging of a far-away audience.

I don't think that impression is unintended. The Torrance marriage imprisons people who have no understanding of one another, despite a child and a home. The barriers begin in the marriage of opposite acting styles. For as soon as Nicholson behaves like someone who knows the script, so Duvall resembles a hapless amateur dumped down in a star part.

There is a moment when *The Shining* quotes from *3 Women*, and I take that as evidence for Kubrick's respect for Shelley Duvall as the spirit of America wanting hopelessly to be in movies, not touched by glamour but somehow actually in a picture. A terror waits behind her target eyes. No one has such casual humility, and it is unclear whether this is artless or affected. The style of *The Shining* being so streamlined, with Nicholson as wicked as the wolf who comes after the three little· pigs, it is all the more curious that his partner is apparently unqualified or unaware of the game going on.

Not that Kubrick dislikes her as he did earlier women: The rape in *Clockwork Orange* is one of the least comfortable sequences ever filmed, and Lady Lyndon in *Barry Lyndon* is a vacuous fashion plate, enervated by being looked at. No, Wendy wins support as a fighter and a doer. She does nurse inarticulate hurt when Jack turns on her with those well-rehearsed flourishes of unkindness. We can imagine beatings and disappointments she has endured, and we note her instinctive drive to get out of the Overlook. But Kubrick himself is as resigned to staying in the haunted house as Coppola was unable to give up the Corleones. He might echo Jack's hope that they never, ever, leave it. Jack's face may confront us, clenched stiff in the maze, lined with frost, but Kubrick's smile lurks there, like Mother's skull in Norman Bates's face.

That is the most speculative aspect of the "confession" in a film sold on the idea that if you look ardently enough you will see. It is more important that Jack is the hero despite threatening his family with slaughter. As a means of box-office suspense, he ought to be the hideous rogue trying to get in at the family, as unknowable as the killer in *Halloween*. But when Jack comes to the last door, his hands full of ax, his head full of nursery rhymes and the brainwashed bonhomie of "Here's Johnny!", Kubrick flits this way and that across the threshold. Because he shows us cowering Wendy and bloodthirsty Jack with equal favor, he dissolves the terror, emphasizes the black comedy, and introduces the theme of terrible frustration. Jack could stop this game at any time and tell Wendy it was all a joke. She would have to consent, her point of view is so dependent on him. But that would leave Jack stranded. If he kills her, he loses his greatest satisfaction: the thought of killing her. He would prefer the chase to go on forever.

We feel for Jack's failure from the first sequence: He so enjoys the oratory of small talk. We recognize him as the incipient killer before it dawns on him, and we read his deference to the servant, Grady, as proof of his beseeching inferiority. He kills Halloran, but it is like felling a waxwork—Kubrick tells us that murder is no finality, only a technical act requiring sachets of blood, sound effects, and nice timing. That's what leaves so little suspense in the picture. Jack is a poet of frustration whose appealing urge to create and murder will be confounded. He is the infant of the family, so much more innocent than wizened Danny and the harsh raven of experience, Tony, who lives in the child's mouth.

The Shining is the spectral fancy of a misfit who finds

beguiling fulfillment at the Overlook. Implicitly, Jack's dudgeon is aligned with Kubrick's ability to bring dragons out of the walls. Unable to write, regarded as a molester of his own child, Jack stalks off to a sumptuous but unstocked bar, beating the air in anger. He cries out for a merciful drink. Then he rubs his bleary eyes, and finds St. Lloyd of the Ice Bucket and an array of shining bottles in front of him. Lloyd's face is as yellow as Auschwitz lamps, yet this is the loveliest tableau in the film and its surest sign of sympathy for those who believe in magic. Every trace of family alienation is offset by the movie's conspiratorial glee at such fantastic treasure. Jack whiles away an hour at the bar; but when Wendy arrives with tears of woe, Lloyd, all the booze, and Jack's tainted breath vanish like understanding accomplices on a spree that wifey won't like.

A greater film might have been made, funnier and sadder, if Wendy had never seen spooks and never noticed Jack's banshee fits. "Oh thanks, hon, I needed that ax," she says and Jack's plan wilts away. Suppose that his every ecstatic plunge into evil went unregistered. Then you would have a movie full of the sunken calm of a family group murmuring, "Yes, dear . . . No, dear," while locomotive dreams hurtle behind eyes of zombie solicitude.

The events that fill the hotel are Jack's abortive novel, just as the manic invention with which he has typed "All work and no play makes Jack a dull boy" in so many different configurations is the equivalent of Kubrick's inane precision of style. What is shining but a metaphor for our willingness to believe in the screened image? Kubrick has transcended the adolescent sensationalism with which novelist Stephen King invests extrasensory perception, and which De Palma inherited for *Carrie*. That is a cute cult for nonbelievers who happen to have found a money-making trick. Instead, Kubrick has made a picture about the one thing he believes in: movies and the unreality that enables us to be moved by art. The Overlook is the house of fiction, and the predicament of artists who are cut off from being by being makers.

But it may be the defect of the film, the hangover from King, that it is still caught up in being sinister and horrific. The hotel should be a gallery for all visions. Ironically, the calmest ghosts are the most perturbing: Torrance and Grady, the fastidious waiter, preserved in a frozen pas de deux in a blood-red lavatory, discussing who they are. The surreal poise of that image is a sign of the instability of all character that imagination permits. So different, the two men are deployed like mirror images, and the film shivers with the intimation of collapsed, interchangeable identities. Instead of being the instrument that shows contempt for glamour, the mirror in *The Shining* is a way into the fictional world, as it was for Cocteau.

Kubrick was once a still photographer. Anyone who found his compositions fulsome or oppressive could echo the adage about movie directors becoming still photographers when they die. And *The Shining* is, very deliberately, a study of picturing. The mirrors mimic the closed nature of movies and the dilemma of the artist working in them, torn between skill and larger commitments. In *Barry Lyndon* Kubrick persistently zoomed away from very mannered compositions. The solemnity was not very exciting, but it was a mark of Kubrick's fascination with the illusionistic flatness of movies. The slow zoom teaches us the fraudulence of the picturesque, and it may have wanted to hint at the absurdity of that 1976 movie's "faultless" eighteenth century. There is also something melancholy about so many elegant but receding vistas, as if to say: If this is movie beauty, then a plague on it.

The movement is drastically reversed for *The Shining*. This is a film of compulsive forward motion, a suction that acts upon the wishful energy of shining. Is the screen flat, or is there a domain there as dense and spatial as the auditorium? As the picture ends with a tracking shot and a series of dissolves that guide us into the new mystery of a 1921 photograph containing Jack, so the film is built on awesomely smooth forward dolly shots. They are smooth because of the Steadicam equipment, and the absence of bumps and disturbances is both a proof of actuality and a demonstration of magic. The camera does fly, or move in the air, like another spirit in the house, urged on by will and imagination, never hindered by friction.

There are set pieces for the shot. Danny scoots along the empty corridors on his tricycle, the camera behind him like the Hound of Heaven, the sound track marking the intervals of floor and carpet. In the final pursuit in the maze, the rush is accentuated by the white of the snow and the wide-angle lens helps the tunnels swallow us. It is even a stroke of independence against the forward momentum that Danny thinks to save himself by reversing his steps, like a young philosopher defying the headlong rush to disaster.

Another forward movement takes Jack into room 237 and the arms of a Pent-up house nudie who will turn, with his kiss, into the most ulcerous hag Goya could conceive. Halloran's attempt at a rescue is in a Sno-Cat, penetrating snowy avenues not much wider than the pathways in the maze. As Jack sits at his typewriter, so the camera closes in behind him. There is a feeling of nightmarish slippage: We are falling into the movie through the suggestive force of all these sequences. The Overlook's gaze has seen and directed us.

It could be horrific, but instead it is exhilarating. We know that every now and then the forward drive will be arrested by the pop-up appearance of those prim porcelain girls at the end of a corridor, or even by the rising panic of the music being trumped by the black-out boo and "Tuesday," a pinch of Hitchcock and Buñuel instead of a bucket of blood. Though we are falling in, *The Shining* is a treatise on falling that lets us know how cool and premeditated this energy is. There is a parody of horror's chestnuts—eerie music, jump zooms, the tracking, cryptic fade-outs, unexpected close-ups, unsettling cuts, the fatality that waits in the ordinary, and the threat that anything imagined may materialize. *The Shining* is interested only in the experience of watching a film composed by a brilliant but distracted inventor.

Kubrick plays with his story like a director no longer satisfied with narrative but suspicious of any new form. When Jack hears about the mayhem of an earlier caretaker, he whistles and concedes that that is quite a story. Oh yes, everyone agrees proudly. The frightened Danny reminds himself of Halloran's advice—that the visions at the Overlook are just like pictures at an exhibition. Like his father, at one point he covers his eyes and then has to peep through them, a moviegoer too inquisitive to stay afraid. In the first month at the Overlook, Jack enjoys the déja vu of the hotel, coming around any corner and facing something you know already. Every step of the action is signaled—so often the actors sound as if they were on a stage. Their extra declamatoriness bespeaks a ritual more than an event. There are stock horrors—bodies marinated in blood and a salon so bored it turned into cobwebs and skeletons. But these are the memories of a man flipping through an anthology of horror movies, aware that a film is just a collection of old "gotchas."

Kubrick's *Shining* has given up the ghost of real experience, and it is on the threshold of a new reference: the fake. That is why the Torrance family life is null and void, while meetings with a barman and a waiter are exquisite. But the film does linger on its threshold because its great cost imposed stupid responsibilities, and because Kubrick is too misanthropic to enjoy his own fun. You cannot escape the feeling that Kubrick sees Jack's illness as an image of his own plight.

You can regard *The Shining* as an outrageous insolence:

$18 million and three years spent on a movie that is made like a whim or a private confession. It is a product of entropy and facetiousness, despite the shadow of significance it throws. It dabbles with the violence swelling in family situations and with murder as a domestic pastime. It is a compendium of film moments—at the very least, it nods to Lang's *M*; the overall precariousness of heroic stance in Hitchcock; *Citizen Kane*'s exaggerated interiors; Riefenstahl's *Triumph of the Will*; the gloating pursuit of innocence in Charles Laughton's *The Night of the Hunter*; Wellman's *Track of the Cat*; Clouzot's *Les Diaboliques*; Godard's *Les Carabiniers*, with the lady condescending to step out of her bath; Michael Snow's *Wavelength* and its dainty joke about looking at pictures; and the perpetual house of fiction in Rivette's *Céline and Julie Go Boating*.

Then again, it is a monument to cinema that only such rueful picturing can fashion. Like Nabokov's work, it realizes that art is an entire world, impossible, uninhabitable, and without currency in real life, but the only thing we know fit to be called beautiful or true.

It is also a little less than all those things. Kubrick, finally, is helpless with the problem of whether to be rich, secure, and commercial, or confined to the Overlook that trusts work and posterity. The family tragedy could have been greater if the director knew people better. The catalog of quotes is indulgent and recondite. As much as it is a parody of film, it is a cry of despair over the medium.

The Shining has the mystery of art. Whatever muddle may affect parts of it, it is graced by the absolute awareness that this is what film is. But it is weird folly as mass entertainment, and it is so nervous of its nihilism that it never grasps the full beauty of fiction. A puritan horror of imagination still lurks in the film, despite the vision of its new liberty. It is the story of America all over again.

References

Chapter 2

1. George Lucas, interview, *Rolling Stone*, 12 June 1980, p. 34.
2. Ibid.
3. Ibid., p. 31.
4. Ibid., p. 34.

Chapter 3

1. Ronald Reagan, *Los Angeles Daily News*, 3 July 1948.
2. Gore Vidal, interview, *American Film*, April 1977, p. 42.

Chapter 4

1. Richard Corliss, *The Hollywood Screenwriters* (New York, 1972), p. 227.
2. F. Scott Fitzgerald, *The Last Tycoon* (New York, 1941), chapter 4.
3. Andrew Sarris, *The American Cinema* (New York, 1968), p. 30.
4. Rex McGee, "The Life and Hard Times of *Fedora*," *American Film*, February 1979, p. 18.
5. Stephen Zito, "George Lucas Goes Far Out," *American Film*, April 1977, p. 12.
6. Ibid., p. 11.
7. Eleanor Coppola, *Notes* (New York, 1979), p. 266.

Chapter 5

1. Alexandre Astruc, "The Birth of a New Avant-Garde: La Caméra-Stylo," *Écran Français*, no. 144, 1948.
2. Gore Vidal, interview, *American Film*, April 1977, p. 36.
3. Pauline Kael, *The Citizen Kane Book* (London, 1971), p. 9.

4. Paul Schrader, interview, *Film Comment*, March–April 1980, p. 50.
5. "I write longhand, six pages a day . . . in the evening I do about an hour and a half. . . . If I can do six pages in an hour and a half, think of how much I could do writing all day, if I wasn't lazy. I could write a script in a week." John Milius, interview, *Film Comment*, July–August 1976, p. 17.
6. Schrader, *op. cit.*, pp. 50–51.
7. Steven Spielberg, interview, *American Film*, September 1978, pp. 49–50.
8. Hollis Alpert, "James Toback: For Love and Money," *American Film*, May 1980, p. 26.
9. Robert Towne, interview, *American Film*, December 1975, p. 42.
10. Joan Tewkesbury, *Nashville* (New York, 1976), introduction.
11. Harlan Kennedy, "The Illusions of Nicolas Roeg," *American Film*, January–February 1980, p. 22.

Chapter 6

1. Beverly Linet, *Ladd: The Life, The Legend, The Legacy of Alan Ladd* (New York, 1979), p. ix.
2. Joan Didion, "7000 Romaine, Los Angeles 38," *Slouching Towards Bethlehem* (New York, 1968), p. 71.
3. Ibid., p. 72.

Chapter 10

1. Manny Farber, "The Gimp," *Movies* (New York, 1971), pp. 72–73.
2. Paul Schrader, interview, *Film Comment*, March–April 1980, p. 51.
3. Susan Sontag, *On Photography* (New York, 1977), p. 167.
4. Walker Percy, *The Moviegoer* (New York, 1961), p. 16.
5. Schrader, *op. cit.*, p. 51.

Chapter 11

1. Paul Schrader, "Guilty Pleasures," *Film Comment*, January–February 1979, p. 62.

Chapter 12

1. François Truffaut, *The Films in My Life* (New York, 1978), p. 171.
2. François Truffaut, *Hitchcock* (London, 1969), p. 265.
3. Ibid.
4. Ibid., p. 266.
5. Ibid., pp. 276–77.
6. Truffaut, *The Films in My Life*, p. 79.
7. Truffaut, *Hitchcock*, p. 399.
8. Ibid., p. 349.

Chapter 13

1. François Truffaut, *Hitchcock* (London, 1969), p. 353.
2. Manny Farber, "Clutter," *Movies* (New York, 1971), p. 209.

Chapter 16

1. Rex Reed, *Baltimore Sun*, 22 November, 1970.
2. Ibid.

Chapter 17

1. Robert Towne, interview, *American Film*, December 1975, p. 44.
2. Ibid., p. 43.
3. Arthur Penn, *Take One*, vol. 1, no. 6, 1967.
4. Joan Mellen, *Big Bad Wolves* (New York, 1977), p. 329.

Chapter 19

1. Pauline Kael, *I Lost It at the Movies* (Boston, 1965), p. 114.
2. Kael, *When the Lights Go Down* (New York, 1979), p. 420.
3. Kael, *Deeper into Movies* (Boston, 1973), p. 500.
4. Ibid., p. xviii.
5. Ibid., p. 355.
6. Bruce Cook, *American Film*, December–January 1978, p. 6.
7. Kael, *Deeper into Movies*. p. xvii.
8. Kael, *I Lost It at the Movies*, pp. 228–29.
9. Kael, *Going Steady* (Boston, 1969), p. vi.

10. Kael, *I Lost It at the Movies*, p. 325.
11. Kael, *Deeper into Movies*, p. 370.
12. Kael, *I Lost It at the Movies*, p. 292.
13. Andrew Sarris, *The Village Voice*, 2–8 July 1980.
14. Renata Adler, *The New York Review of Books*, 14 August 1980.

Chapter 20

1. "Let's Talk About *Pierrot*," *Godard on Godard*, ed. Tom Milne (London, 1972), p. 217.
2. Alfred Hitchcock, interview, *Movie*, January 1963, p. 5.
3. Francis Ford Coppola, interview, *Film Comment*, July–August 1974, p. 49.
4. Jean Renoir, *My Life and My Films* (New York, 1974), p. 141.
5. Coppola, *op. cit.*, p. 45.
6. Ibid., p. 48.

Chapter 22

1. Eleanor Coppola, *Notes* (New York, 1979) , p. 254.
2. Michael Pye and Lynda Myles, *The Movie Brats* (New York, 1979), p. 83.
3. *The New York Times*, 12 August 1979.

Index